Charles Richards

Songs of praise and prayer

For the Sunday-school and social meeting

Charles Richards

Songs of praise and prayer
For the Sunday-school and social meeting

ISBN/EAN: 9783337265205

Printed in Europe, USA, Canada, Australia, Japan

Cover: Foto ©Lupo / pixelio.de

More available books at **www.hansebooks.com**

OF

PRAISE AND PRAYER;

FOR THE

SUNDAY-SCHOOL AND SOCIAL MEETING.

COMPILED AND EDITED BY
CHARLES H. RICHARDS, D.D.

TAINTOR BROTHERS, MERRILL & CO.,
18 & 20 ASTOR PLACE, NEW YORK.

PREFACE.

THIS little book has been prepared for use both in Sunday School and Prayer Meeting. There is a growing feeling that, while the desire of children for bright and sparkling melodies should be gratified, they should also be made familiar with the grand old hymns and tunes of the Church. There is also a feeling that, while the Social Meeting for devotion may well use the stately and tender hymns commonly used in the more formal Sabbath Service, it needs besides many of the more sprightly and popular songs that assist the devotional life of the Sunday School. The two services may thus greatly enrich and aid each other. An endeavor is here made to mingle the old and the new, the staid and the stirring, in such a way as to meet the needs of both these departments of Christian culture. A higher standard of quality than usual, both in words and music, has also been aimed at. It is also hoped that those who use it will find it of special service in Revival meetings, Temperance meetings, Missionary meetings, and Anniversary occasions.

Special acknowledgments are due to the Rev. Drs. J. E. RANKIN, E. P. PARKER, J. H. VINCENT, RAY PALMER, G. L. PRENTISS, S. WOLCOTT, S. D. PHELPS, S. F. SMITH, and D. MARCH; to Bishop A. C. COXE and Rev. C. L. HUTCHINS; also to Professors H. R. PALMER, F. A. PARKER, W. F. SHERWIN, G. F. ROOT, W. O. PERKINS, J. W. BISCHOFF, and J. M.

STILLMAN; to Mrs. J. F. KNAPP, and Messrs. C. C. CONVERSE and W. G. FISCHER; to Dr. U. C. BURNAP, and others, for favors received in the preparation of this book; also to A. S. BARNES & Co., for the use of Dr. BURNAP's tunes from "Hymns of the Church." Other acknowledgments are given in connection with tunes in the body of the book.

INDEX OF TOPICS.

	NUMBERS
PRAISE	1— 58
Assembling for Worship	1— 8
Praise to God the Father	9— 24
Praise to Christ	25— 44
God in Nature	45— 58
PRAYER	59—108
The Prayer Meeting	59— 94
Morning and Evening	95—108
THE HOLY SPIRIT	109—119
JESUS CHRIST	120—165
Christmas	120—135
His Life	136—145
His Sufferings and Death	146—151
Easter	152—158
His Ascension	159—160
THE CHURCH	161—166

	NUMBERS
THE CHRISTIAN LIFE	167—258
Invitation and Acceptance	167—188
Consecration	184—197
Trust	198—222
Christlikeness	223—229
Temptation and Victory	230—235
Soldiers of the Cross	236—247
Missions	248—258
CHILDREN'S SONGS	259—283
THE HOME	284—286
THE CHRISTIAN PILGRIMAGE	287—301
FOREGLEAMS OF HEAVEN	302—307
HEAVEN	308—315
THE BIBLE	316—319
THANKSGIVING	320—324
THE YEAR	325—327
OUR COUNTRY	328—333

SONGS OF PRAISE AND PRAYER.

1 ADORATION. 8s & 6s.
G. A. Macfarren.

1. Come, let us all with one ac-cord
A-dore and mag-ni-fy the Lord
And fes-tal ser-vice pay;
On this the day that God hath blest,
The day of peace and heaven-ly rest,
The Lord's own ho-ly day;

2 That saw primeval darkness break,
  And that more glorious life awake
    That lasteth evermore;
  That saw hell's legion's prostrate fall,
  And Christ triumphant over all
    His own to heaven restore.

3 This day the peace that flows from heaven
  Was unto the Apostles given,
    When doors were closed at night;
  This day the Holy Spirit's flame
  Upon the Church's teachers came,
    And filled their souls with light.

4 Then on this day let us adore
  Our God, and supplication pour,
    That when worlds pass away,
  Thro' Christ's dear grace our souls may rest
  In peace and joy forever blest,
    In His Eternal Day.
      H. M. C. in English Hymnary.

2 HAIL THE DAY OF PRAISE.

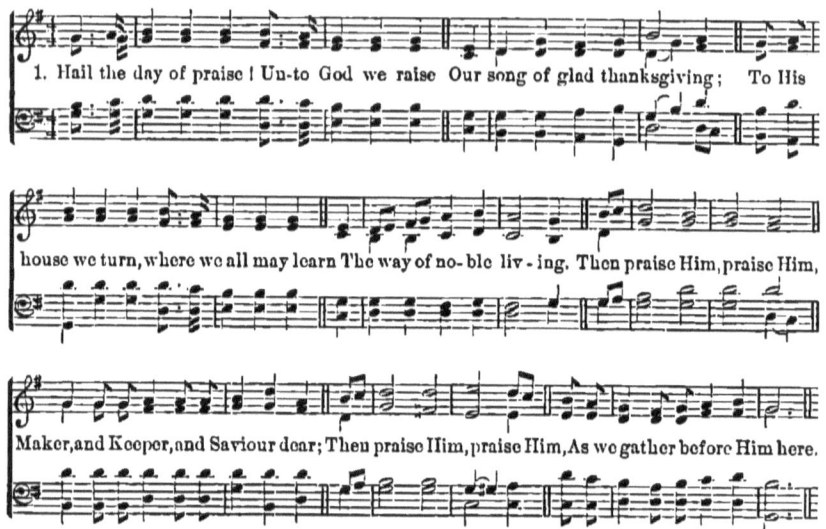

1. Hail the day of praise! Unto God we raise Our song of glad thanksgiving; To His house we turn, where we all may learn The way of noble living. Then praise Him, praise Him, Maker, and Keeper, and Saviour dear; Then praise Him, praise Him, As we gather before Him here.

2 Hail the day of Praise! Unto Christ we raise
 Our joyful salutation;
 For a light divine from His life doth shine,
 And He hath brought salvation.
 Then praise Him, praise Him,
  Lover, and Leader, and Saviour dear;
 Then praise Him, praise Him,
  As we gather before Him here.

3 Hail the day of Praise! Into heavenly ways
 May the Holy Spirit lead us;
 May no evil stain in our hearts remain,
 For He from sin hath freed us.
 Then praise Him, praise Him,
  Helper Almighty, and Saviour dear;
 Then praise Him, praise Him,
  As we gather before Him here.

3 ON OUR WAY REJOICING.

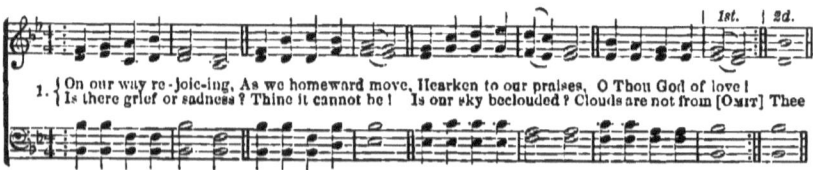

1. { On our way rejoicing, As we homeward move, Hearken to our praises, O Thou God of love!
     Is there grief or sadness? Thine it cannot be! Is our sky beclouded? Clouds are not from [OMIT] Thee

PRAISE.

{ March we with singing, Glad homage bringing; Hear, Lord, the praises Thy Church on earth upraises;
Ev-er con-fess-ing Christ and His blessing, Lift we the glad word, Ho-sanna to the [OMIT..] Lord!

2 If with honest-hearted love for God and man,
Day by day Thou find us doing what we can,
Thou who giv'st the seed-time wilt give large increase,
Crown the head with blessings, fill the heart with peace.—*Chorus.*

3 On our way rejoicing gladly let us go;
Conquered hath our Leader, vanquished is our foe!
Christ without, our safety; Christ within, our joy;
Who, if we be faithful, can our hope destroy?—*Chorus.*

4 Unto God the Father joyful songs we sing;
Unto God the Saviour thankful hearts we bring;
Unto God the Spirit bow we and adore,
On our way rejoicing now and evermore!—*Chorus.*

J. S. B. Monsell.

4   GREENVILLE.   8s, 7s & 4s.   *Jean Jacques Rousseau.* 1750.

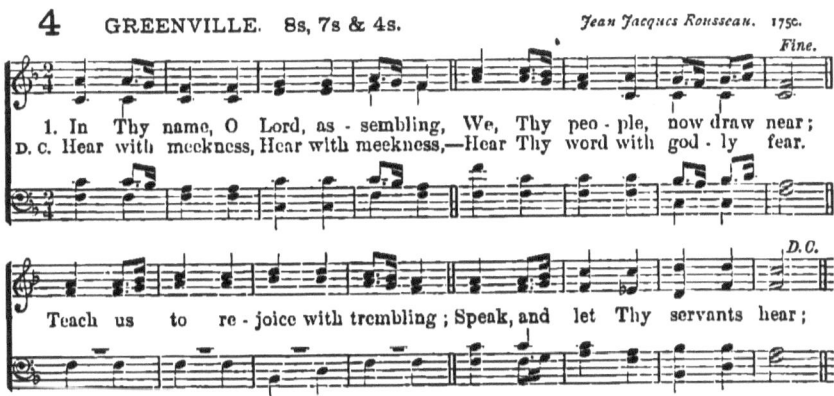

1. In Thy name, O Lord, as-sembling, We, Thy peo-ple, now draw near;
D.C. Hear with meekness, Hear with meekness,—Hear Thy word with god-ly fear.

Teach us to re-joice with trembling; Speak, and let Thy servants hear;

2 While our days on earth are lengthened,
   May we give them, Lord, to Thee;
Cheered by hope, and daily strengthened,
   May we run, nor weary be,
      Till Thy glory
Without clouds in heaven we see.

3 There, in worship purer, sweeter,
   Thee Thy people shall adore;
Tasting of enjoyment greater
   Far than thought conceived before:
      Full enjoyment,
Full, unmixed, and evermore.

Thomas Kelley. 1815.

PRAISE.

5 AUTUMN. 8s & 7s. *Spanish Melody.*

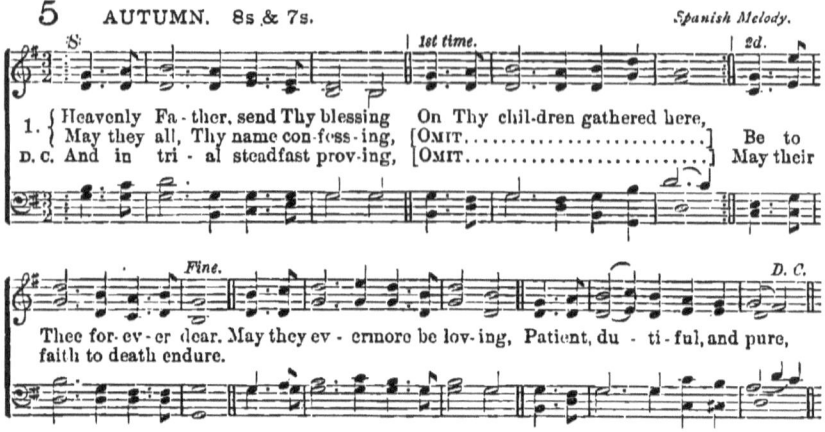

1. Heavenly Father, send Thy blessing On Thy children gathered here,
   May they all, Thy name confessing, [OMIT....] Be to Thee forever dear. May they evermore be loving, Patient, dutiful, and pure,
   D.C. And in trial steadfast proving, [OMIT....] May their faith to death endure.

2 Holy Saviour, who in meekness
   Didst vouchsafe a child to be,
  Guide their steps and help their weakness,
   Bless and make them like to Thee;
  Bear Thy lambs when they are weary
   In Thine arms and on Thy breast,
  Through life's desert dry and dreary,
   Bring them to Thy heavenly rest.

3 Spread Thy golden pinions o'er them,
   Holy Spirit from above,
  Guide them, lead them, go before them,
   Give them peace, and joy, and love :
  Thy true temples, Holy Spirit,
   May they with Thy glory shine,
  And immortal bliss inherit,
   And for evermore be Thine.
   Hymns Ancient and Modern.

6 RICHARDS. C. M. *Edwin Pond Parker.* 1882.

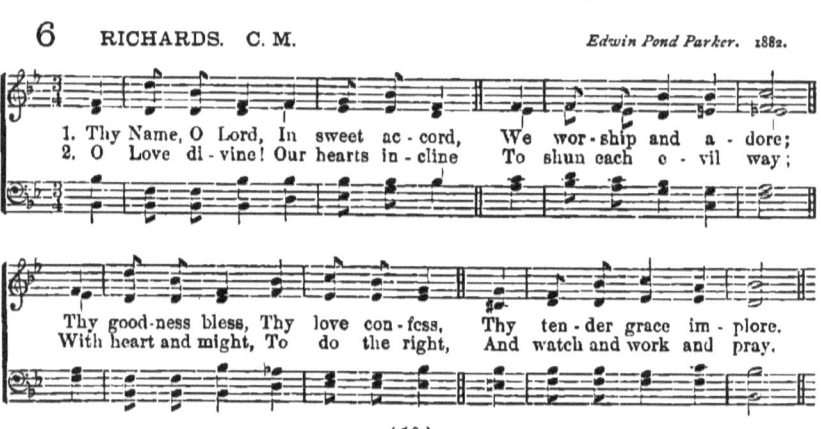

1. Thy Name, O Lord, In sweet accord, We worship and adore;
   Thy goodness bless, Thy love confess, Thy tender grace implore.
2. O Love divine! Our hearts incline To shun each evil way;
   With heart and might, To do the right, And watch and work and pray.

(10)

PRAISE.

3 O Light Divine!
 Within us shine,
Bid doubts and darkness cease;
 Our sins forgive,
 And help us live
In purity and peace.

4 Through all our days,
 In all our ways,
O, guide us from above;
 Till hopes and fears,
 And joys and tears
Shall bloom in heavenly love.
Edwin Pond Parker. 1882.

7 MESSIAH. 7s. D. *Arr. by George Kingsley.* 1838.

1. Pleasant are Thy courts above, In the land of light and love; Pleasant are Thy courts below, In this land of sin and woe. O my spirit longs and faints For the converse of Thy saints, In the brightness of Thy face, King of glory, God of grace.

2 Happy birds that sing and fly
Round Thy altars, O Most High
Happier souls that find a rest
In our heavenly Father's breast!
Like the wandering dove, that found
No repose on earth around.
They can to their ark repair,
And enjoy it ever there.

3 Happy souls! their praises flow
Even in this vale of woe;
Waters in the desert rise,
Manna feeds them from the skies:
On they go from strength to strength,
Till they reach Thy throne at length,
At Thy feet adoring fall,
Who hast led them safe through all.

4 Lord, be mine this prize to win!
Guide me through this world of sin:
Keep me by Thy saving grace;
Give me at Thy side a place;
Sun and shield alike Thou art;
Guide and guard my erring heart!
Grace and glory flow from Thee;
Shower, O shower them, Lord, on me.
Henry Francis Lyte. 1834.

8. KEGONSA. 11s & 8s.

1. Be joyful in God, all ye lands of the earth, O serve Him with gladness and fear; Exult in His presence with music and mirth, With love and devotion draw near.

2 Jehovah is God, and Jehovah alone,
  Creator and Ruler o'er all; [own;
  And we are His people, His sceptre we
  His sheep, and we follow His call.

3 O enter His gates with thanksgiving and
    song,
  Your vows in His temple proclaim;
  His praise with melodious accordance
    prolong,
  And bless His adorable name.

4 For good is the Lord, inexpressibly good,
  And we are the work of His hand;
  His mercy and truth from eternity stood,
  And shall to eternity stand.

James Montgomery. 1822.

9. ITALIAN HYMN. 6s & 4s.

Felice Giardini. 1760.

1. Come, Thou Almighty King, Help us Thy name to sing, Help us to praise; Father all-glorious, O'er all victorious, Come, and reign over us, Ancient of days.

2 Come, Thou incarnate Word,
  Gird on Thy mighty sword,
    Our prayer attend:
  Come, and Thy people bless,
  And give Thy word success:
    Spirit of holiness,
      On us descend.

3 Come, holy Comforter,
  Thy sacred witness bear,
    In this glad hour:
  Thou who Almighty art,
  Now rule in every heart;
  And ne'er from us depart,
    Spirit of power.

Charles Wesley. 1757.

PRAISE.

10 TO THEE, MY GOD AND SAVIOUR. 7s & 6s. D.

1. To Thee, my God and Saviour, My heart exulting sings, Rejoicing in Thy favor, Almighty King of kings! I'll celebrate Thy glory, With all Thy saints above, And tell the joyful story Of Thy redeeming love.

2 Soon as the morn with roses
  Bedecks the dewy east,
And when the sun reposes
  Upon the ocean's breast,
My voice, in supplication,
  Well-pleasèd, Thou shalt hear:
O grant me Thy salvation,
  And to my soul draw near.

3 By Thee through life supported,
  I'll pass the dangerous road,
With heavenly hosts escorted,
  Up to Thy bright abode;
There cast my crown before Thee,
  And, all my conflicts o'er,
Unceasingly adore thee:—
  What could an angel more?
        Thomas Haweis. 1792.

11 GLORIA PATRI.   *Richard Farrant.* 1570.

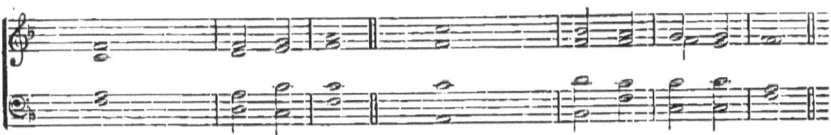

Glory be to the *Father*, and | to the | Son, ‖ *and* | to the | Ho-ly | Ghost;
As it was in the beginning, is *now*, and | ev-er | shall be, ‖ *world* | with-out | end.
    A- | men.

12 GLORIA IN EXCELSIS.

1 Glory *be* to | God on | high, ‖ and on *earth* | peace, good | will towards | men.
2 We praise Thee, we bless *Thee*, we | worship | Thee, ‖ we glorify Thee, we give *thanks* to | Thee for | Thy great | glory.

(Chant 2.)

3 O Lord *God*, | Heavenly | King, ‖ God the | Father | Al- — | mighty.
4 O Lord, the only-begotten *Son*, | Jesus | Christ, ‖ O Lord God, *Lamb* of | God, Son | of the | Father,

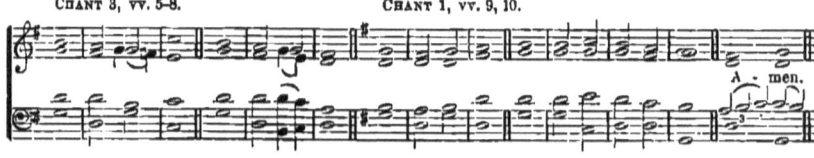

(Chant 3.)

5 That takest *away* the | sins · of the | world, ‖ have *mercy* | upon | us.
6 Thou that takest *away* the | sins · of the | world, ‖ have *mercy* | upon | us.
7 Thou that takest *away* the | sins · of the | world, ‖ re- | ceive our | prayer.
8 Thou that sittest at the right *hand* of | God · the | Father, ‖ have *mercy* | upon | us.

(Chant 1.)

9 For Thou on*ly* | art — | holy, ‖ *Thou* | only | art the | Lord.
10 Thou only, O *Christ*, with the | Holy | Ghost, ‖ art most *high* in the | glory of | God the | Father. ‖ Amen.

Ascribed to Telesphorus, Bishop of Rome, A.D. 139.

13 THE LORD'S PRAYER.

Thomas Tallis.

Our Father, who art in heaven, hallo*wed* | be Thy | name; ‖ Thy kingdom come; Thy will be *done* on | earth · as it | is in | heaven.

(14)

PRAISE.

Give us this *day* our | daily | bread, ‖ and forgive us our trespasses, as we for*give* | them that | trespass · a- | gainst us.
And lead us not into temptation, but de*liver* | us from | evil, ‖ for Thine is the kingdom, and the power, and the *glory*, for | ever · and | ever. ‖ A- | men.

14 WE ARE COMING TO OUR KING.   *Arr. from Verdi.*

1. We are com-ing to our King, And our joy-ful praise we bring; We will join with those a-bove In a song of grate-ful love. Men and angels, heaven and earth, Sing His glo-ry, tell His worth; Let it ring from shore to shore, "Glo-ry to Him ev-er-more!" Then your hap-py voi-ces raise, And ex-alt Him with your praise, Un-to God we ev-er sing Al-le-lu-ia!

2 We will all His mercies trace,
   And adore His loving grace;
   We will pledge to Him the heart,
   In His service do our part.

Let His banner, now unfurled,
Wave in triumph o'er the world,
Till they sing on every shore,
"Glory to Him evermore!"—*Chorus.*

PRAISE.

15 GOD'S LOVE TO ME.
Wm. F. Sherwin.

1. Grander than ocean's story, Or songs of forest trees; Purer than breath of morning, Or evening's gentle breeze; Clearer than mountain echoes Ring out from peaks above, Rolls on the glorious anthem Of God's eternal love.

2 Dearer than any lovings
 The truest friends bestow;
Stronger than all the yearning
 A mother's heart can know;
Deeper than earth's foundations,
 And far above all thought;
Broader than heaven's high arches,
 The love that Christ has brought!

3 Richer than all earth's treasure
 The wealth my soul receives;
Brighter than royal jewels
 The crown that Jesus gives;
Wondrous the condescension,
 And grace beyond degree!
I would be ever singing
 The love of Christ to me!
  William F. Sherwin.

16 SANCTUARY. 8s & 7s. D
John B. Dykes. 1867.

1. Round the Lord in glory seated, Cherubim and Seraphim Filled His temple, and repeated, Each to each, th' alternate hymn: "Lord, Thy glory fills the heaven, Earth is with its

(16)

PRAISE.

ful-ness stored, Un-to Thee be glo-ry giv-en, Ho-ly, ho-ly, ho-ly, Lord!

2 Heaven is still with glory ringing,
  Earth takes up the angels' cry,
  "Holy, holy, holy," singing,
  "Lord of hosts, the Lord most high."
  With His seraph train before Him,
  With His holy church below,
  Thus unite we to adore Him,
  Bid we thus our anthem flow.

3 Lord, Thy glory fills the heaven;
  Earth is with its fulness stored;
  Unto Thee be glory given,
  Holy, holy, holy Lord!
  Thus Thy glorious name confessing,
  We adopt the angels' cry,
  "Holy, holy, holy," blessing
  Thee, the Lord our God most high!

  Richard Mant. 1837.

17 ANGEL VOICES. *Arthur S. Sullivan.*

1. An-gel voi-ces ev-er singing Round Thy throne of light, Angel harps for-ev-er ringing
Rest not day nor night: Thousands only live to bless Thee, And confess Thee, Lord of might.

2 Thou, who art beyond the farthest
  Mortal eye can scan,
  Can it be that thou regardest
  Songs of sinful man?
  Can we know that thou art near us,
  And wilt hear us?
  Yea, we can.

3 Yea, we know that thou rejoicest
  O'er each work of Thine:
  Thou didst hearts, and hands, and voices,
  For Thy praise combine;
  Craftsman's art and music's measure
  For Thy pleasure
  Didst design.

4 In Thy house, great God, we offer
  Of Thine own to Thee,
  And for Thine acceptance proffer
  All unworthily
  Hearts and minds, and hands and voices,
  In our choicest
  Melody.   *F. Pott.*

18 GOD IS LOVE.

C. C. Converse.

1. God is Love! ye nations, hear Him, God is Love! a-dore, revere Him; God is Love! ye need not fear Him; His is tend'rest love. God is Love! and He is ho-ly, Nev-er false, He lov-eth tru-ly, Lov-eth all, the high and low-ly. With His yearning love.

2. God is Love! the breezes bring it;
God is Love! the bell-tones ring it;
God is Love! the song-birds sing it;
   God is perfect Love.
And the ocean as it foameth,
And the wild wind as it moaneth,
And each season, when it cometh,
   Tells us, God is Love.

3. Every passing breath of even,
Every object under heaven,
All the story he hath given,
   Whispers, "God is Love!"
Though the aching heart is sighing,
Though life's dearest hopes are dying,
There's an undertone replying,
   "God is lasting Love."

F. L. Keeler.

19 PRAISE, MY SOUL, THE KING OF HEAVEN.

Michael Haydn.

1. Praise, my soul, the King of heav-en, To His feet thy trib-ute bring; Ransomed, healed, re-stored, for-giv-en, Ev-er-more His prais-es sing;

PRAISE.

2 Praise Him for His grace and favor
   To our fathers in distress ;
Praise Him still the same as ever,
   Slow to chide, and swift to bless ;
Alleluia! Alleluia!
   Glorious in His faithfulness.

3 Father-like, He tends and spares us,
   Well our feeble frame He knows ;
In His hands He gently bears us,
   Rescues us from all our foes ;
Alleluia! Alleluia!
   Widely yet his mercy flows.

4 Angels in the height adore Him !
   Ye behold Him face to face ;
Saints triumphant bow before Him !
   Gathered in from every race :
Alleluia! Alleluia!
   Praise with us the God of grace.
         Henry Francis Lyte. 1834.

20 DAY BY DAY. 8s & 7s.   *Edmund S. Carter.*

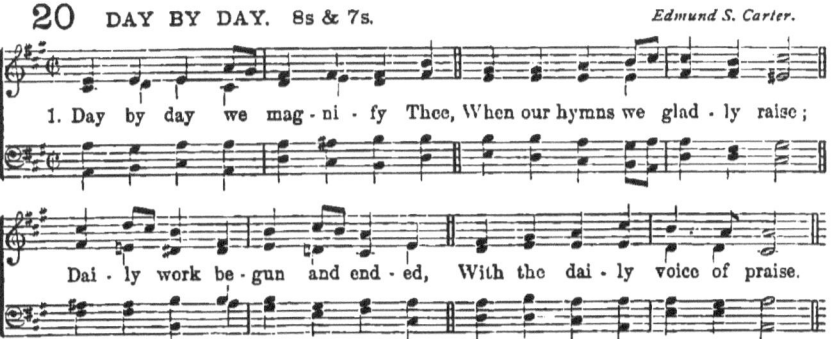

2 Day by day we magnify Thee—
   When as each new day is born,
On our knees at home we bless Thee
   For the mercies of the morn.

3 Day by day we magnify Thee—
   In our hymns before we sleep ;
Angels hear them, watching by us,
   Christ's dear lambs all night to keep.

4 Day by day we magnify Thee—
   Not in words of praise alone ;
Truthful lips and meek obedience
   Show Thy glory in Thine own.

5 Day by day we magnify Thee—
   When, for Jesus' sake, we try
Every wrong to bear with patience,
   Every sin to mortify.

6 Day by day we magnify Thee—
   Till our days on earth shall cease,
Till we rest from these our labors,
   Waiting for Thy Day in peace !

7 Then, on that eternal morning,
   With Thy great redeeméd host,
May we fully magnify Thee—
   Father, Son and Holy Ghost !
         Anon.

21 UPWARD WHERE THE STARS.

J. Baptiste Calkin.

1. Upward where the stars are burning, Silent, silent in their turning, Round the nev-er-changing pole; Upward where the sky is brightest, Upward where the blue is lightest,— Lift I now my longing soul.

2 Far beyond that arch of gladness,
Far beyond these clouds of sadness,
  Are the many mansions fair.
Far from pain and sin and folly,
In that palace of the holy,
  I would find my mansion there.

3 Where the Lamb on high is seated,
By ten thousand voices greeted:
  Lord of lords, and King of kings.
Son of man, they crown, they crown Him,
Son of God, they own, they own Him,
  With His name the palace rings.

4 Blessing, honor, without measure,
Heavenly riches, earthly treasure,
  Lay we at His blessèd feet.
Poor the praise that now we render,
Loud shall be our voices yonder,
  When before His throne we meet.

Horatius Bonar.

PRAISE.

22 CHILDREN'S VOICES.   *Edward J. Hopkins.*

1. A-bove the clear blue sky,...... In heav-en's bright a-bode,.... The An-gel host on high Sing prais-es to.... their God,... Al - le-lu-ia! They love to sing to God their King. Al-le-lu - ia!...

2 But God from infant tongues
   On earth receiveth praise;
   We then our cheerful songs
   In sweet accord will raise :
     Alleluia!
     We too will sing
     To God our King
     Alleluia!

3 O Blessed Lord, Thy Truth
   To us Thy babes impart,
   And teach us in our youth
   To know Thee as Thou art.
     Alleluia!
     Then shall we sing
     To God our King
     Alleluia!

4 O may Thy holy Word
   Spread all the world around;
   And all with one accord
   Uplift the joyful sound,
     Alleluia!
     All then shall sing
     To God their King
     Alleluia!
          John Chandler. 1841.

PRAISE.

23 GOD OF HEAVEN! HEAR OUR SINGING.

1. God of heaven! hear our singing; On-ly lit-tle ones are we, Yet a great pe-ti-tion bringing, Fa-ther, now we come to Thee. Let Thy kingdom come, we pray Thee, Let the world in Thee find rest; Let all know Thee and obey Thee, Loving, praising, blessing, blest.

2 Let the sweet and joyful story
   Of the Saviour's wondrous love,
   Wake on earth a song of glory
   Like the angels' song above.

Father, send the glorious hour,
   Every heart be Thine alone;
   For the kingdom, and the power,
   And the glory are Thine own.
         Frances Ridley Havergal.

24 DUKE STREET. L. M.   *John Hatton.* 1790.

1. Be - fore Je - ho - vah's aw - ful throne, Ye na - tions, bow with sa - cred joy; Know that the Lord is God a - lone; He can cre - ate, and He de - stroy.

PRAISE TO CHRIST.

2 His sovereign power, without our aid,
Made us of clay, and formed us men;
And when, like wandering sheep, we strayed,
He brought us to his fold again.

3 We are His people, we His care,
Our souls, and all our mortal frame:
What lasting honors shall we rear,
Almighty Maker, to Thy name?

4 We'll crowd Thy gates with thankful songs,
High as the heaven our voices raise;
And earth, with her ten thousand tongues,
Shall fill Thy courts with sounding praise.

5 Wide as the world is Thy command,
Vast as eternity Thy love;
Firm as a rock Thy truth shall stand,
When rolling years shall cease to move.
Isaac Watts. 1719.

25 LIGHT OF THE WORLD, WE HAIL THEE. 7s & 6s. D.

1. Light of the world, we hail Thee, Flushing the eastern skies; Never shall darkness veil Thee, Again from human eyes. Too long, alas! withholden, Now spread from shore to shore; Thy light, so glad and golden, Shall set on earth no more.

2 Light of the world, Thy beauty
Steals into every heart,
And glorifies with duty
Life's poorest, humblest part;
Thou robest in Thy splendor
The simple ways of men,
And helpest them to render
Light back to Thee again.

3 Light of the world, before Thee
We would in homage fall;
We worship, we adore Thee,
Thou Light, the life of all;
With Thee is no forgetting
Of all Thine hand hath made;
Thy rising hath no setting,
Thy sunshine hath no shade.

4 Light of the world, illumine
This darkened world of Thine,
Till everything that's human
Be filled with what's divine;
Till every tongue and nation,
From sin's dominion free,
Rise in the new creation
Which springs from Love and Thee.
John S. B. Monsell.

PRAISE TO CHRIST.

26 CROWN HIM. S. M. D.   *Joseph Barnby.* 1872.

1. Crown Him with many crowns, The Lamb up-on His throne; Hark, how the heavenly anthem drowns All mu-sic but its own: With His most precious blood From sin He set us free: We hail Him as our matchless King Thro' all e-ter-ni-ty.

2 Crown Him, the Lord of love:
 Behold His hands and side,
 Rich wounds, yet visible above
 In beauty glorified:
 No angel in the sky
 Can fully bear that sight,
 But downward bends His burning eye
 At mysteries so bright.

3 Crown Him the Lord of peace:
 Whose power a sceptre sways
 From pole to pole, that wars may cease,
 And all be prayer and praise:
 His reign shall know no end,
 And round His pierced feet
 Fair flowers of Paradise extend
 Their fragrance ever sweet.

4 Crown Him the Lord of heaven,
 One with the Father known,
 One with the Spirit through Him given
 From yonder glorious throne!
 To Thee be endless praise,
 For Thou for us hast died;
 Be Thou, O Lord, through endless days
 Adored and magnified.
     Matthew Bridges. 1847.

DIADEMATA. S. M. D. [SECOND TUNE.]   *G. J. Elvey.*

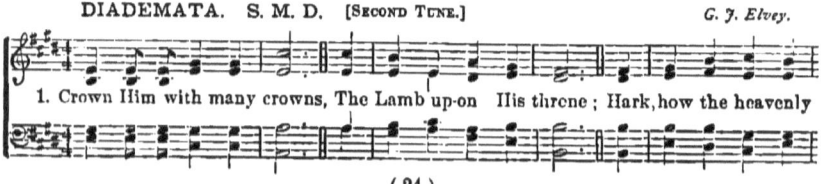

1. Crown Him with many crowns, The Lamb up-on His throne; Hark, how the heavenly

PRAISE TO CHRIST.

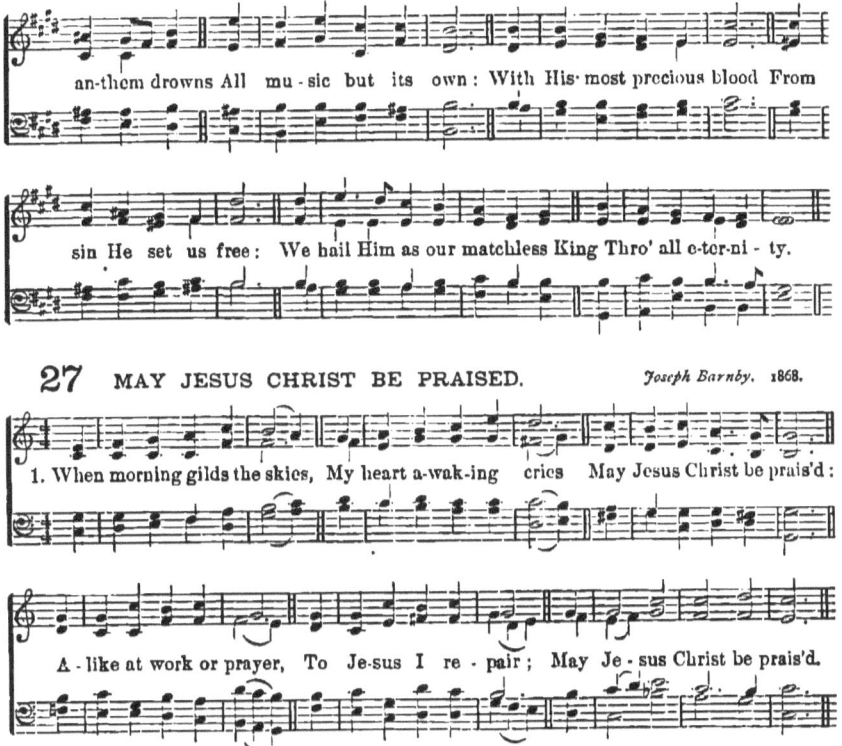

27 MAY JESUS CHRIST BE PRAISED.   *Joseph Barnby.* 1868.

1. When morning gilds the skies, My heart a-wak-ing cries May Jesus Christ be prais'd: A-like at work or prayer, To Jesus I re-pair; May Jesus Christ be prais'd.

2 Whene'er the sweet church-bell
Peals over hill and dell,
　May Jesus Christ be prais'd:
O hark to what it sings,
As joyously it rings,
　May Jesus Christ be prais'd.

3 Does sadness fill my mind?
A solace here I find,
　May Jesus Christ be prais'd:
Or fades my earthly bliss?
My comfort still is this,
　May Jesus Christ be prais'd.

4 The night becomes as day,
When from the heart we say
　May Jesus Christ be prais'd:
The powers of darkness fear,
When this sweet chant they hear,
　May Jesus Christ be prais'd.

5 In heaven's eternal bliss
The loveliest strain is this,
　Let Jesus Christ be prais'd:
Let earth, and sea, and sky
From depth to height reply,
　May Jesus Christ be prais'd.
　　　　　　E. Caswall. 1849.

PRAISE TO CHRIST.

28 SINGING FOR JESUS.

1. Singing for Jesus, our Saviour and King, Singing for Jesus, the Lord whom we love; All adoration we joyfully bring, Longing to praise as they praise Him above.

Chorus.
Singing for Jesus, singing with joy, Thus will we praise Him and tell out his love, Till He shall call us to brighter employ; Singing for Jesus, forever and ever above.

2 Singing for Jesus, and trying to win
   Many to love Him, and join in the song;
   Calling the weary and wandering in,
   Rolling the chorus of gladness along.
   Cho.—Singing for Jesus, etc.

3 Singing for Jesus, our Life and our Light,
   Singing for Him, as we press to the mark; [bright,
   Singing for Him when the morning is
   Singing, still singing for Him in the dark.
   Cho.—Singing for Jesus, etc.
   Frances Ridley Havergal.

29 CHRISTUS REX. 6s. *From Gioacchimo Rossini.*

1. Come, let us gladly sing Praises to Christ our King! The Prince of life and love Is

PRAISE TO CHRIST.

throned in light a-bove. Praise Christ our King! Praise Christ our King! Wake, wake the anthem sweet! Praise to our Lord is meet: Christ is our heavenly king, Before His throne we'll sing.

2 Thorn-crowned, in splendor now,
　Angels before Him bow;
　Hear their cherubic call!
　"Immanuel, Lord of all!"
　　Praise Christ our King!—*Chorus.*

3 Into that kingdom fair
　He'll bring each ransomed heir;
　Sing, sinner saved by grace,
　For you shall see His face.
　　Praise Christ our King!—*Chorus.*

30　DELIGHT. C. M.　　　*A. R. Reinagle.* 1840.

1. O Jesus! thou the beauty art
　Of angel worlds above;
　Thy name is music to the heart,
　Enchanting it with love.

2 O Jesus, Saviour! hear the sighs
　Which unto Thee I send;
　To Thee my inmost spirit cries,
　My being's hope and end.

3 Stay with us, Lord! and with Thy light
　Illume the soul's abyss;
　Scatter the darkness of our night,
　And fill the world with bliss.

4 O Jesus, King of earth and heaven,
　Our life and joy! to Thee
　Be honor, thanks and blessing given
　Through all eternity!

Bernard of Clairvaux. 1140.　*Tr. Edward Caswall.* 1849.

PRAISE TO CHRIST.

31 O SAVIOUR, PRECIOUS SAVIOUR. *T. R. Matthews.*

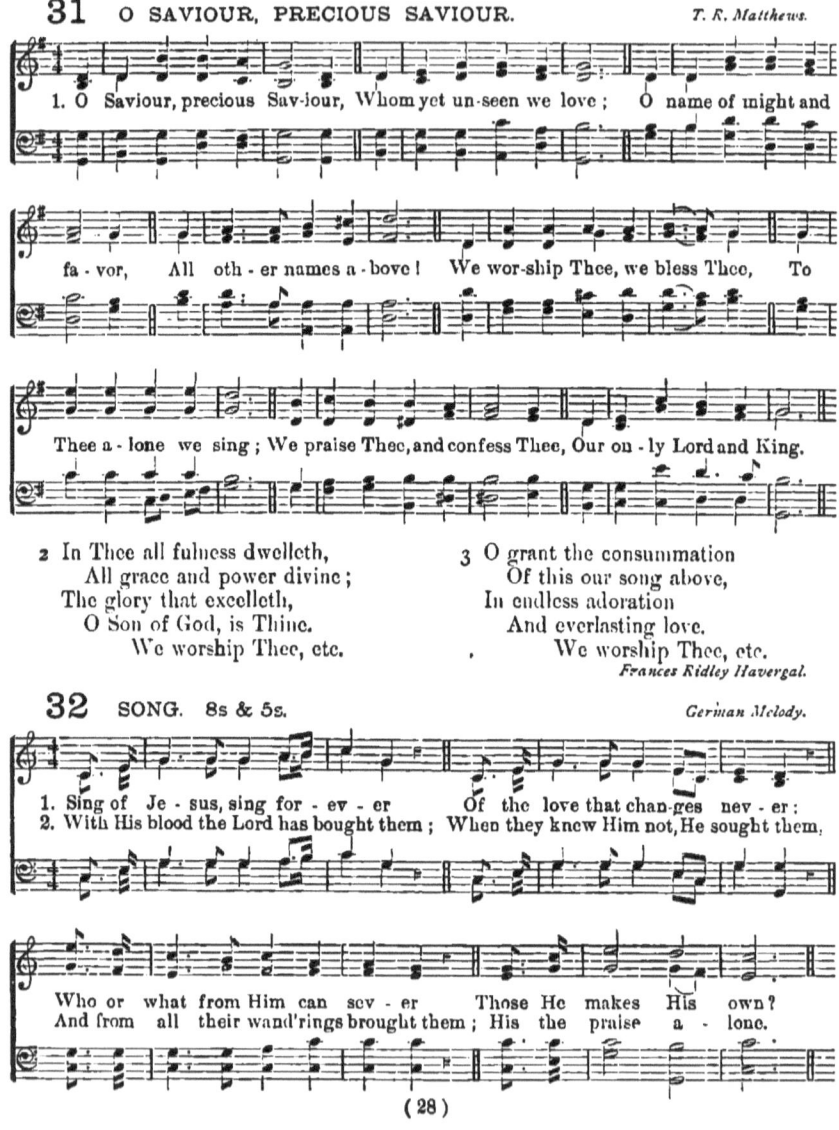

1. O Saviour, precious Saviour, Whom yet unseen we love; O name of might and favor, All other names above! We worship Thee, we bless Thee, To Thee alone we sing; We praise Thee, and confess Thee, Our only Lord and King.

2 In Thee all fulness dwelleth,
All grace and power divine;
The glory that excelleth,
O Son of God, is Thine.
We worship Thee, etc.

3 O grant the consummation
Of this our song above,
In endless adoration
And everlasting love.
We worship Thee, etc.

Frances Ridley Havergal.

32 SONG. 8s & 5s. *German Melody.*

1. Sing of Jesus, sing forever Of the love that changes never: Who or what from Him can sever Those He makes His own?
2. With His blood the Lord has bought them; When they knew Him not, He sought them, And from all their wand'rings brought them; His the praise alone.

PRAISE TO CHRIST.

3 Through the desert Jesus leads them,
  With the bread of heaven He feeds them,
  And through all the way He speeds them
    To their home above.

4 There they see the Lord who bought them,
  Him who came from heaven, and sought them,
  Him who by His Spirit taught them,
    Him they serve and love.

5 Let His people sing with gladness,
  Other mirth than this is madness,
  Mirth it is that ends in sadness,
    Be it far away.

6 'Tis the saints have solid treasure,
  They can sing with holy pleasure,
  And their joy will know no measure,
    In the final day.
                                Thomas Kelly. 1815.

33 COME. PRAISE YOUR LORD AND SAVIOUR. 7s & 6s. D.

1. Come, praise your Lord and Saviour In strains of holy mirth, Give thanks to Him, O children, Who lived a child on earth. He loved the little children, And called them to His side, His loving arms embraced them, And for their sake He died.

2 O Jesus, we would praise Thee
    With songs of holy joy,
  For Thou on earth didst sojourn
    A pure and spotless boy.
  Make us like Thee obedient,
    Like Thee, from sin-stains free,
  Like Thee in God's own temple,
    In lowly home like Thee.

3 O Jesus, we too praise Thee,
    The lowly maiden's son;
  In Thee all gentlest graces
    Are gathered into one;
  O give that best adornment
    That Christian maid can wear,
  The meek and quiet spirit
    That shone in Thee so fair.

4 O Lord, with voices blended
    We sing our songs of praise,
  Be Thou the light and pattern
    Of all our childhood's days;
  And lead us ever onward,
    That while we stay below,
  We may like Thee, O Jesus,
    In grace and wisdom grow.
                          William Walsham How.

PRAISE TO CHRIST.

34 ANTIOCH. C. M. *Lowell Mason. (From Handel.)* 1836.

1. Joy to the world, the Lord is come! Let earth receive her King; Let every heart prepare Him room, And heav'n and nature sing, And heav'n and nature sing, And heav'n, And heav'n and nature sing.

2 Joy to the world, the Saviour reigns;
Let men their songs employ;
While fields and floods, rocks, hills and plains
Repeat the sounding joy.

3 No more let sin and sorrow grow,
Nor thorns infest the ground;
He comes to make His blessings flow
Far as the curse is found.

4 He rules the world with truth and grace,
And makes the nations prove
The glories of His righteousness,
And wonders of His love.
Isaac Watts. 1709.

35 CORONATION. C. M. *Oliver Holden.* 1793.

1. All hail the pow'r of Jesus' name! Let angels prostrate fall! Bring forth the royal diadem, And crown Him Lord of all; Bring forth the royal di-a-dem, And crown Him Lord of all.

2 Ye chosen seed of Israel's race,
Ye ransomed from the fall;
Hail Him who saves you by His grace,
And crown Him Lord of all.

3 Sinners, whose love can ne'er forget
The wormwood and the gall;
Go, speed your trophies at His feet,
And crown Him Lord of all.

4 Let every kindred, every tribe,
On this terrestial ball,
To Him all majesty ascribe,
And crown Him Lord of all.

5 O that with yonder sacred throng,
We at His feet may fall;
We'll join the everlasting song,
And crown Him Lord of all.
Edward Perronet. 1780.

PRAISE TO CHRIST.

36 DEDHAM. C. M. — *William Gardiner.* 1830.

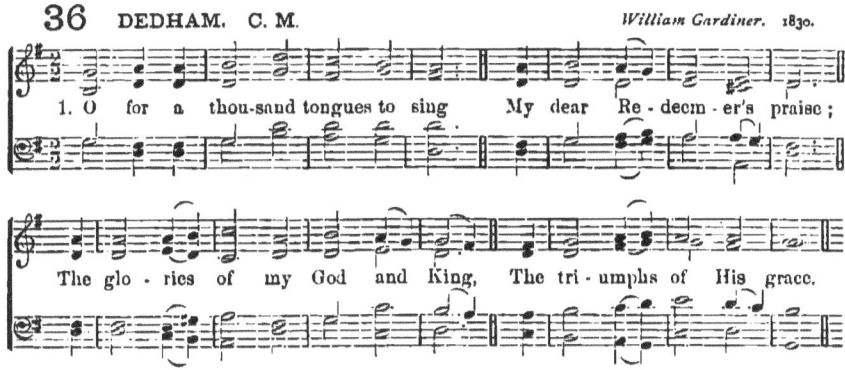

1. O for a thousand tongues to sing My dear Redeemer's praise; The glories of my God and King, The triumphs of His grace.

2 My gracious Master and my God,
Assist me to proclaim,
To spread through all the earth abroad,
The honors of Thy name.

3 Jesus, the name that charms our fears,
That bids our sorrows cease;
'Tis music in the sinner's ears,
'Tis life, and health, and peace.

4 He breaks the power of reigning sin,
He sets the prisoner free;
His blood can make the foulest clean,
His blood availed for me.
Charles Wesley. 1740.

37 HARK! HOW THE ANGELS SWEETLY SING. — *Henry Lahee.*

1. Hark, how the angels sweetly sing! Their voices fill the sky; They hail their great, victorious King, And welcome Him on high.

2 We'll catch the note of lofty praise;
Their joys in part we feel;
With them our thankful songs we'll raise,
And emulate their zeal.

3 Lift up the voice, and grateful sing
Of Christ, our risen Lord,
Of Christ, the everlasting King,
Of Christ, th' incarnate Word.

4 Hail! mighty Saviour, Thee we hail,
Who fillest the throne above!
Till heart and flesh together fail,
We'll sing Thy matchless love.
Thomas Kelley. 1809.

38. AT THE NAME OF JESUS. 6s & 5s. D.

Henry Smart. 1874.

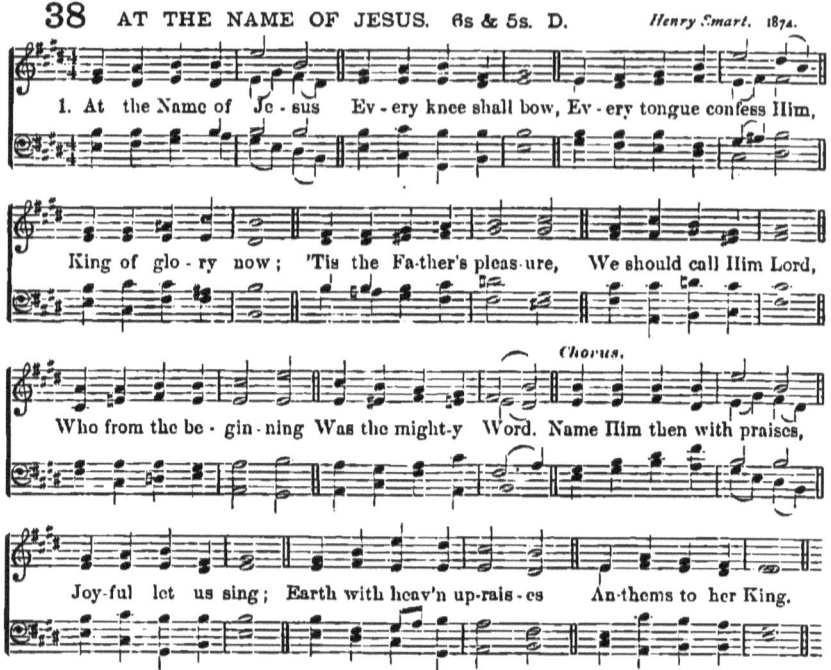

1. At the Name of Je-sus Ev-ery knee shall bow, Ev-ery tongue confess Him, King of glo-ry now; 'Tis the Father's pleas-ure, We should call Him Lord, Who from the be-gin-ning Was the might-y Word. Name Him then with praises, Joy-ful let us sing; Earth with heav'n up-rais-es An-thems to her King.

2 Humbled for a season,
  To receive a Name
From the lips of sinners
  Unto whom He came:
Faithfully He bore it,
  Spotless to the last;
Brought it back victorious
  When from death He passed.—*Cho.*

3 Name Him, brothers, name Him
  With love strong as death,
But with awe and wonder,
  And with bated breath;
He is Christ the Saviour,
  He is Christ the Lord,
Ever to be worshiped,
  Trusted and adored.—*Cho.*

4 In your hearts enthrone Him,
  Then let Him subdue
All that is not holy,
  All that is not true:
Crown Him as your captain
  In temptation's hour;
Let His will enfold you
  In its light and power.—*Cho.*

5 Brothers, this Lord Jesus
  Shall return again,
With His Father's glory,
  With His angel train;
For all wreaths of empire
  Meet upon His brow,
And our hearts confess Him
  King of glory now.—*Cho.*

Caroline M. Noel.

39 O GRACIOUS REDEEMER.

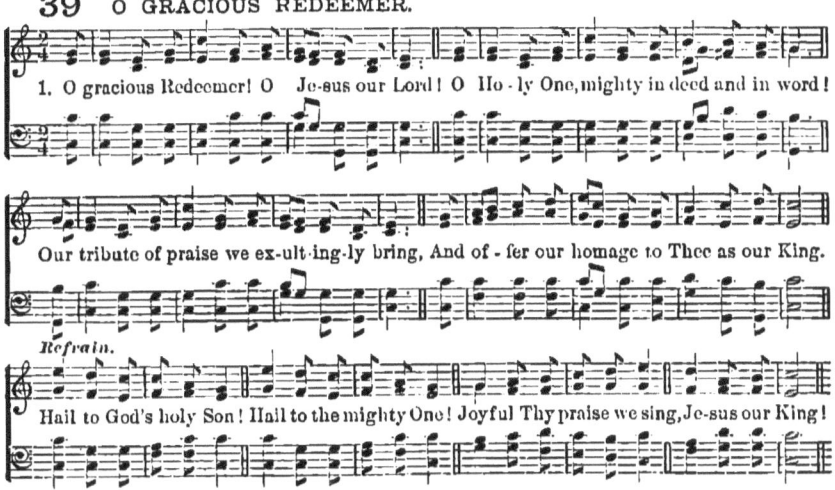

1. O gracious Redeemer! O Jesus our Lord! O Holy One, mighty in deed and in word!
Our tribute of praise we exultingly bring, And offer our homage to Thee as our King.

Refrain.
Hail to God's holy Son! Hail to the mighty One! Joyful Thy praise we sing, Jesus our King!

2 O Saviour of sinners! O Lamb that was slain!
Our souls by Thy cleansing are freed from their stain;
The grace of Thy pardon is sealed on our hearts,
And peace like a river Thy bounty imparts.—*Refrain.*

3 O Prince of salvation! O conquering King!
Thine arm to the righteous shall victory bring;
Outstretched o'er the waiting creation Thy rod
Shall wake on its bosom the smile of its God.—*Refrain.*

4 O Fullness of Godhead! O Ancient of days!
Thy saints on Thy glory with rapture shall gaze,
And changed to Thine image, O Presence divine,
From glory to glory resplendent shall shine.—*Refrain.*   Samuel Wolcott.

40 MANOAH. C. M.

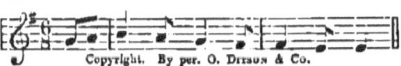
Copyright. By per. O. Ditson & Co.

1 Come, let us join our cheerful songs,
  With angels round the throne;
  Ten thousand thousand are their tongues,
  But all their joys are one.

2 "Worthy the Lamb that died," they cry,
  "To be exalted thus!"
  "Worthy the Lamb," our lips reply,
  "For He was slain for us!"

3 Jesus is worthy to receive
  Honor and power divine;
  And blessings, more than we can give,
  Be, Lord, for ever Thine.

4 Let all who dwell above the sky,
  And air, and earth, and seas,
  Conspire to lift Thy glories high,
  And speak Thine endless praise.
                    Isaac Watts. 1709.

PRAISE TO CHRIST.

41 WARE. L. M.

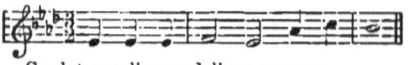

So let our lips and lives express
The holy gospel we profess;
So let our works and virtues shine
To prove the doctrine all divine.

2 Thus shall we best proclaim abroad
The honors of our Saviour God,
When His salvation reigns within,
And grace subdues the power of sin.
Isaac Watts. 1709.

42 ORTONVILLE. C. M.

1 MAJESTIC sweetness sits enthroned
Upon the Saviour's brow;
His head with radiant glories crowned,
His lips with grace o'erflow.

2 He saw me plunged in deep distress,
And flew to my relief;
For me He bore the shameful cross,
And carried all my grief.

3 To Him I owe my life and breath,
And all the joys I have;
He makes me triumph over death,
And saves me from the grave.

4 Since from His bounty I receive
Such proofs of love divine,
Had I a thousand hearts to give,
Lord, they should all be thine.
Samuel Stennett. 1787.

43 ST. THOMAS. S. M.

1 COME, we that love the Lord!
And let our joys be known:
Join in a song with sweet accord,
And thus surround the throne.

2 Let those refuse to sing,
That never knew our God;
But children of the heavenly King
May speak their joys abroad.

3 The hill of Zion yields
A thousand sacred sweets,
Before we reach the heavenly fields,
Or walk the golden streets.

4 Then let our songs abound,
And every tear be dry;
We're marching through Immanuel's
To fairer worlds on high. [ground,
Isaac Watts. 1709.

44 WE PRAISE THEE, O GOD.

1 WE praise Thee O God! for the Son of Thy love,
For Jesus who died, and is now gone above.

Cho.—Hallelujah! Thine the glory, Hallelujah! Amen.
Hallelujah! Thine the glory, revive us again.

2 We praise Thee, O God! for Thy Spirit of light,
Who has shown us our Saviour, and scattered our night.—*Cho.*

3 All glory and praise to the God of all grace,
Who has bought us, and sought us, and guided our ways.—*Cho.*

4 Revive us again; fill each heart with Thy love;
May each soul be rekindled with fire from above.—*Cho.*
Rev. Wm. Paton Mackey. 1866.

GOD IN NATURE.

45 THE VALLEYS AND THE MOUNTAINS. *Joseph Barnby.*

1. The valleys and the mountains, The woodland and the plain, The rivers and the fountains, The sunshine and the rain, The stars that shine above me, The flowers that deck the sod, Proclaim aloud the glory of our God. Praises, holy adoration, Praises to our God above; Praises thro' the wide creation, Sound aloud His greatness and His love.

2 And shall the voice of nature
   Thus glorify its King,
And man, the noblest creature,
   No grateful tribute bring?
Shall mercy strew his pathway,
   And all his senses please,
And man withhold the sacrifice of praise?

Cho.—Praise Him, ye that live forever;
   Praise Him, every heart and voice;
Praise Him, He's the glorious Giver;
   Praise Him, in your sorrows and
      your joys.

3 Then train your youthful voices
   To hymn His praise above;
For he who here rejoices
   In Jesus' dying love,
Around His throne of glory
   Shall all His love proclaim,
And sing the song of Moses and the Lamb.

Cho.—Praise Him, praise the eternal Father;
   Praise Him, praise the eternal Son;
Praise Him, let us praise together,
   Father, Son, and Spirit, Three in
      One.

GOD IN NATURE.

46 ALL GOOD GIFTS AROUND US.

Hymns Ancient and Modern.

1. We plough the fields, and scatter The good seed on the land, But it is fed and wa-tered By God's al-migh-ty hand; He sends the snow in win-ter, The warmth to swell the grain, The breezes, and the sun-shine, A soft, re-fresh-ing rain. All good gifts around us Are sent from heaven above, Then thank the Lord, O thank the Lord, For all His love.

2 He only is the Maker
  Of all things near and far;
 He paints the wayside flower,
  He lights the evening star;
 The winds and waves obey Him,
  By Him the birds are fed;
 Much more to us, His children,
  He gives our daily bread.—*Ref.*

2 We thank Thee, then, O Father,
  For all things bright and good,
 The seed-time and the harvest,
  Our life, our health, our food;
 Accept the gifts we offer
  For all Thy love imparts,
 And, what Thou most desirest,
  Our humble, thankful hearts.—*Ref.*

Matthias Claudius. (1740–1815.) *Tr. Wm. J. M. Campbell.* 1861.

GOD IN NATURE.

47 THE SPRINGTIDE HOUR.

1. The spring-tide hour brings leaf and flower, With songs of life and love; And many a lay wears out the day In every leafy grove. Bird, flower and tree seem to agree Their choicest gifts to bring; Shall this poor heart not bear its part, In it is there no spring? *Chorus.* Praises praises to our Lord, Lift we up with glad accord; Let us hallelujah sing In the joyous spring.

2 Dews fall apace, the dews of grace,
   Upon this soul of sin:
And Love Divine delights to shine
   Upon the waste within.
Yet year by year, fruits, flowers appear,
   And birds their praises sing;
Shall this poor heart not bear its part?
   Its winter have no spring?—*Cho.*

3 Lord, let Thy love, fresh from above,
   Soft as the south wind blow;
Call forth its bloom, wake its perfume,
   And bid its spices flow:
And when Thy voice makes earth rejoice,
   The hillsides laugh and sing,
Lord! make my heart to bear its part,
   And join the praise of spring.—*Cho.*
                 J. S. B. Monsell.

GOD IN NATURE.

48 CREATION. L. M. D.
Francis Joseph Haydn. 1798.

1. The spacious fir-ma-ment on high, With all the blue e-the-real sky,
And spangled heav'ns, a shining frame, Their great O-rig-i-nal [OMIT....] proclaim:
Th' unwearied sun, from day to day, Does his Cre-a-tor's pow'r dis-play;
And pub-lish-es to ev-ery land The work of an Al-might-y hand.

2 Soon as the evening shades prevail,
The moon takes up the wondrous tale
And nightly, to the listening earth,
Repeats the story of her birth;
While all the stars that round her burn,
And all the planets in their turn,
Confirm the tidings as they roll,
And spread the truth from pole to pole.

3 What though in solemn silence, all
Move round the dark terrestial ball,—
What though no real voice nor sound
Amid their radiant orbs be found,—
In reason's ear they all rejoice,
And utter forth a glorious voice,
For ever singing as they shine,
"The hand that made us is divine."
Joseph Addison. 1712.

49 OUR SONG OF PRAISE.

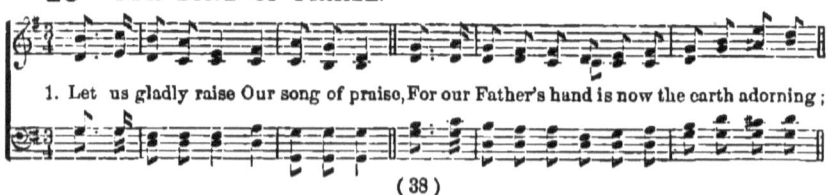

1. Let us gladly raise Our song of praise, For our Father's hand is now the earth adorning;

GOD IN NATURE.

And the love-ly flowers In woodland bowers With fragrance fill the summer morning.
All the world is grate-ful trib-ute bring-ing, Hap-py birds their notes are sing-ing,
Field and for-est, sparkling lake and riv - er, Join to praise the bounteous Giver.

Chorus.
Then we gladly raise Our song of praise. Un-to God we lift our hymn in joy-ful cho-rus;
Then praise Him, praise Him, Lift we our joy-ful cho-rus,
And our trib-ute pay To Him to-day, Who bends in lov-ing mer-cy o'er us.

2 While the angels sing To God their King,
    And the heavenly courts resound with happy voices,
We will lift a song Full sweet and strong,
    In token that the earth rejoices.
For His children here the Lord is leading,
    Safely guiding, gently feeding,
And the notes of men and angels blending,
    Should lift up the song unending.—*Chorus.*

GOD IN NATURE.

50. SONG OF MERCY.

1. God has made the birds that sing, In the heavens car-ol-ing, And He formed each ti-ny wing That sails the sky a-bove. Then for them car-ing, God's mer-cies shar-ing, We will kind-ly treat these creatures of His love.

Cho. Mer-cy we will show to all, For we hear our Fa-ther's call; He who notes the sparrow's fall Bids us, "Be mer-ci-ful."

2 God with bounteous hand doth feed
Hungry creatures that have need;
Every being He will heed
   In lake, and field, and wood.
   Then for them caring,
   God's mercies sharing,
Let us gentle be, and ever show them good.
   Cho.—Mercy we will, etc.

3 God to us doth pity show,
In our weakness here below;
Pity from our hearts must flow
   To humbler creatures still.
   Then for them caring,
   God's mercies sharing,
Kindness we will give, as 'tis our Father's [will.
   Cho.—Mercy we will, etc.

51. SUMMER SUNSHINE.

Samuel Smith. 1871.

Joyous.

1. Summer suns are glowing Over land and sea, Happy light is flow-ing Bounti-ful and free. Everything rejoices In the mellow rays, All earth's thousand voices Swell the psalm of praise.

(40)

GOD IN NATURE.

2 God's free mercy streameth
  Over all the world,
And His banner gleameth
  Everywhere unfurled.
Broad and deep and glorious
  As the heaven above,
Shines in might victorious
  His eternal Love.

3 Lord, upon our blindness
  Thy pure radiance pour;
For Thy loving-kindness
  Make us love Thee more.
And when clouds are drifting
  Dark across our sky,
Then, the veil uplifting,
  Father, be Thou nigh.

4 We will never doubt Thee,
  Though Thou veil Thy light;
Life is dark without Thee;
  Death with Thee is bright.
Light of light shine o'er us
  On our pilgrim way,
Go Thou still before us
  To the endless day.
    William Walsham How. 1871.

52 PSALM OF PRAISE. *Edwin Pond Parker.*

1. For the beau-ty of the earth, For the glo-ry of the skies,
For the love which from our birth O-ver and a-round us lies;
Christ, our Lord, to Thee we raise This our hymn of grate-ful praise.

From the "Christian Hymnal," by per.

2 For the wonder of each hour
  Of the day and of the night;
Hill and vale, and tree and flower,
  Sun and moon, and stars of light;
Christ, our Lord, to Thee we raise
This our hymn of grateful praise.

3 For the joy of human love,
  Brother, sister, parent, child;
Friends on earth, and friends above,
  Pleasures pure and undefiled;
Christ, our Lord, to Thee we raise
This our hymn of grateful praise.

4 For Thy Church that evermore
  Lifts her holy hands above,
Offering up on every shore
  Her pure sacrifice of love;
Chsist, our Lord, to Thee we raise
This our hymn of grateful praise.
    F. S. Pierpoint. 1864.

GOD IN NATURE.

53. ANGELS HOLY, HIGH AND LOWLY.
Fred. A. Gore Ouseley.

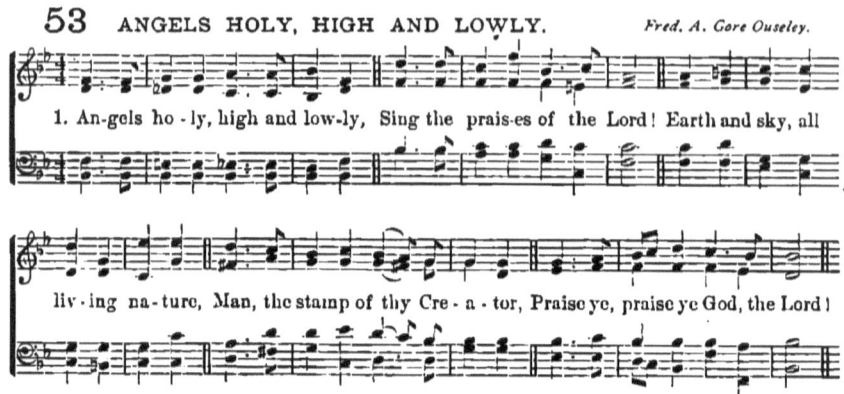

1. An-gels ho-ly, high and low-ly, Sing the prais-es of the Lord! Earth and sky, all liv-ing na-ture, Man, the stamp of thy Cre-a-tor, Praise ye, praise ye God, the Lord!

2. Sun and moon, bright night and moon-light;
Starry temples, azure-floored;
Cloud and rain, and wild wind's madness
Sons of God that shout for gladness,
Praise ye, praise ye God, the Lord!

3. Ocean hoary, tell His glory;
Cliffs, where trembling seas have roared
Pulse of waters, blithely beating,
Wave advancing, wave retreating,
Praise ye, praise ye God, the Lord!

4. Rolling river, praise Him ever,
From the mountains' deep vein poured;
Silver fountain, clearly gushing,
Troubled torrent, wildly rushing,
Praise ye, praise ye God, the Lord:

5. Praise Him ever, bounteous Giver;
Praise Him, Father, Friend, and Lord!
Each glad soul its free course winging,
Each glad voice its free song singing,
Praise the great and mighty Lord!
John Stuart Blackie.

54. ALL THINGS BEAUTIFUL.
German.

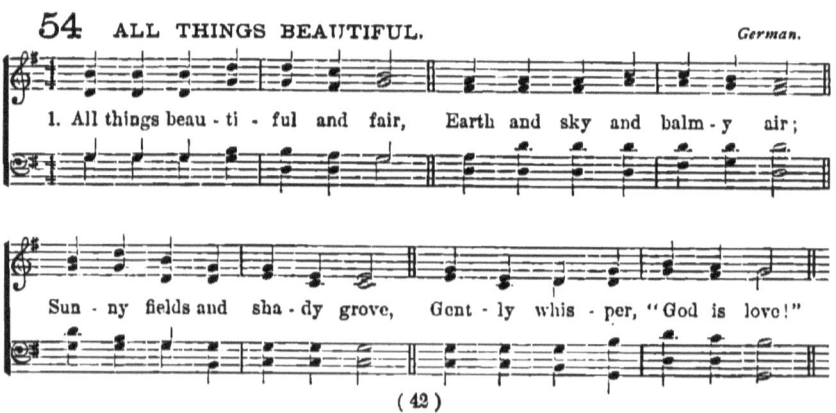

1. All things beau-ti-ful and fair, Earth and sky and balm-y air; Sun-ny fields and sha-dy grove, Gent-ly whis-per, "God is love!"

GOD IN NATURE.

2 Every tree and flower we pass,
Every tuft of waving grass;
Every leaf and opening bud,
Seem to tell us "God is good."

3 Little streams that glide along,
Verdant, mossy banks among,
Shadowing forth the clouds above,
Softly murmur, "God is love!"

4 He who dwelleth high in heaven,
Unto us has all things given;
Let us, as through life we move,
Ever feel that "God is love!"
Mrs. Follen.

55 EVERY MORNING, THE RED SUN.
John B. Dykes. 1868.

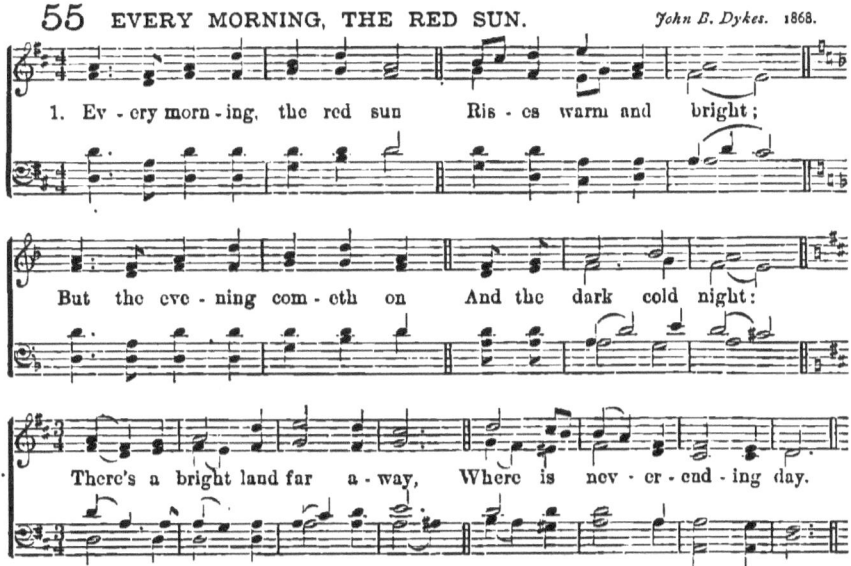

1. Ev-ery morn-ing, the red sun Ris-es warm and bright;
But the eve-ning com-eth on And the dark cold night:
There's a bright land far a-way, Where is nev-er-end-ing day.

2 Every spring the sweet young flowers
Open fresh and gay;
Till the chilly autumn hours
Wither them away:
There's a land we have not seen,
Where the trees are always green!

3 Little birds sing songs of praise
All the summer long;
But in colder, shorter days
They forget their song;
There's a place where angels sing
Ceaseless praises to their King.

4 Christ our Lord is ever near
Those who follow Him!
But we cannot see Him here,
For our eyes are dim:
There's a blissful, happy place
Where men always see His face.

5 Who shall go to that bright land?
All who do the right:
Holy children there shall stand
In their robes of white.
For that heaven so bright and blest,
Is our everlasting rest.
Mrs. Cecil F. Alexander. 1848.

GOD IN NATURE.

56 VANHALL'S HYMN. L. M.
Vanhall.

1. All praise to Him who built the hills; All praise to Him the streams who fills; All praise to Him who lights each star That sparkles in the blue afar, That sparkles in the blue afar.

2 All praise to Him who makes the morn,
And bids it glow with beams new-born;
Who draws the shadows of the night,
Like curtains, o'er our wearied sight.

3 All praise to Him whose love hath given,
In Christ His Son, the Life of heaven;
Who gives us for our darkness light,
And turns to day our deepest night.

4 All praise to Him the chain who broke,
The prison opened, burst the yoke,
Led forth its captives, glad and free,
The heirs of endless liberty.
Horatius Bonar.

57 PARK STREET. L. M.
Venua.

1. Yes, God is good; in earth and sky, From ocean-depths and spreading wood, Ten thousand voices seem to cry, "God made us all, and God is good! God made us all, and God is good!"

2 The sun that keeps his trackless way,
And downward pours his golden flood,
Night's sparkling hosts, all seem to say,
In accents clear, that God is good.

3 The merry birds prolong the strain,
Their song with every spring renewed;
And balmy air, and falling rain,
Each softly whisper, "God is good."

4 I hear it in the rushing breeze;
The hills that have for ages stood,
The echoing sky and roaring seas,
All swell the chorus, "God is good."

5 Yes, God is good, all Nature says,
By God's own hand with speech endued;
And man, in louder notes of praise,
Should sing for joy that God is good.
John H. Gurney.

GOD IN NATURE.

58 THE GIVER OF ALL.

Arr. from Donizetti.

2 In the beauty of nature His glory
   Is revealed, and our homage we render;
But His love shines in Calvary's story
   Till our hearts are o'ercome with the splendor.
For the gift of His Son we adore Him,
And we gratefully worship before Him.—*Chorus.*

PRAYER.

59 LONGWOOD. 11s. Copyright. By per. Biglow & Main. *William B. Bradbury.* 1847.

1. The Lord is my Shepherd, no want shall I know; I feed in green pastures, safe folded I rest;
He leadeth my soul where the still waters flow, Restores me when wand'ring, redeems when oppress'd.

2 Through the valley and shadow of death though I stray,
Since Thou art my Guardian, no evil I fear;
Thy rod shall defend me, Thy staff be my stay;
No harm can befall, with my Comforter near.

3 In the midst of affliction, my table is spread;
With blessings unmeasured my cup runneth o'er;
With perfume and oil thou anointest my head;
O what shall I ask of Thy providence more?

4 Let goodness and mercy, my bountiful God,
Still follow my steps till I meet Thee above;
I seek, by the path which my forefathers trod
Through the land of our sojourn, Thy kingdom of love.
James Montgomery. 1822.

60 NETTLETON. 8s & 7s. *A. Nettleton.* 1825.

1. Come, Thou Fount of ev-ery bless-ing, Tune my heart to sing Thy grace;
Streams of mer-cy nev-er ceas-ing, Call for songs of loud-est praise:
D. C. Fill my soul with sa-cred pleas-ure, While I sing re-deem-ing love.

Teach me some me-lo-dious meas-ure, Sung by rap-tured saints a-bove;

2 O, to grace how great a debtor,
Daily I'm constrained to be;
Let Thy goodness, as a fetter,
Bind my wandering heart to Thee.

Prone to wander, Lord, I feel it,
Prone to leave the God I love;
Here's my heart, O take and seal it,
Seal it for Thy courts above.
R. Robinson. 1758.

(46)

PRAYER.

61. THE MERCY-SEAT. C. M. D.

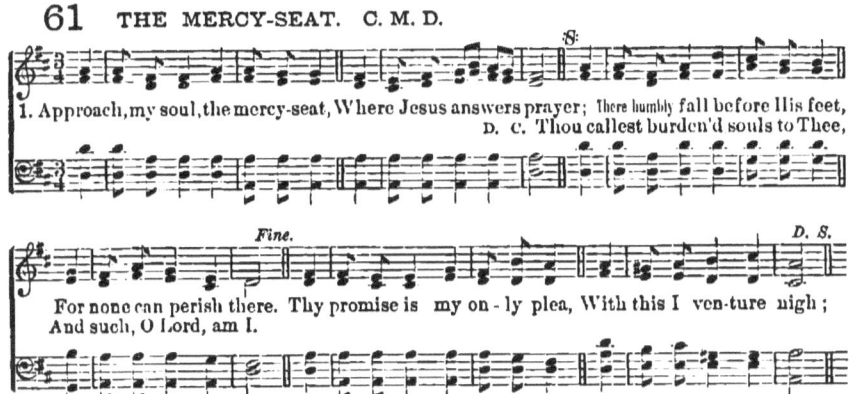

1. Approach, my soul, the mercy-seat, Where Jesus answers prayer; There humbly fall before His feet, For none can perish there. Thy promise is my on-ly plea, With this I ven-ture nigh; Thou callest burden'd souls to Thee, And such, O Lord, am I.

2 Bowed down beneath a load of sin,
　By Satan sorely pressed,
By war without, and fears within,
　I come to Thee for rest.

O wondrous love! to bleed and die,
　To bear the cross and shame,
That guilty sinners, such as I,
　Might plead Thy gracious name.
　　　　　　　John Newton. 1779.

62. MY GOD, HOW WONDERFUL! C. M. *From "Oratory Hymns."*

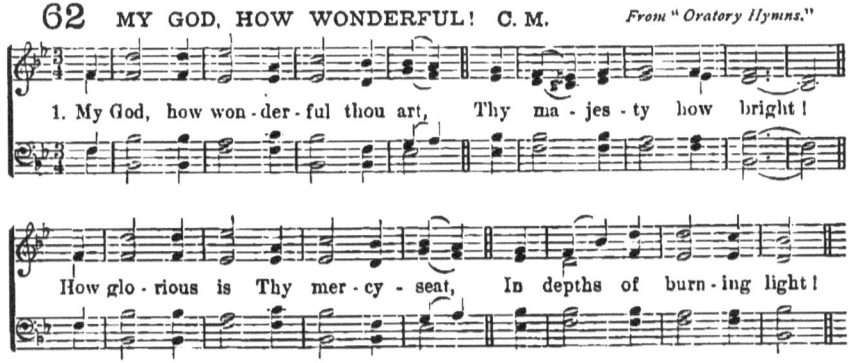

1. My God, how won-der-ful thou art, Thy ma-jes-ty how bright! How glo-rious is Thy mer-cy-seat, In depths of burn-ing light!

2 Yet I may love Thee too, O Lord,
　Almighty as Thou art;
For Thou hast stooped to ask of me
　The love of my poor heart.

3 No earthly father loves like Thee,
　No mother half so mild

Bears and forbears, as Thou hast done
　With me, Thy sinful child.

4 My God, how wonderful Thou art,
　Thou everlasting Friend!
On Thee I stay my trusting heart,
　Till faith in vision end.
　　　　　　　F. W. Faber. 1849.

PRAYER.

63 GO WHEN THE MORNING SHINETH. 7s & 6s. D.

1. Go when the morning shineth, Go when the noon is bright; Go when the day declineth, Go in the hush of night; Go with pure heart and feeling, Cast earthly thoughts away, And in thy chamber kneeling, Do thou in secret pray.

2 Remember all who love thee,
All who are loved by thee;
Pray, too, for those who hate thee,
If any such there be;
Then for thyself, in meekness,
A blessing humbly claim;
And blend with each petition
Thy great Redeemer's name.

3 Or, if 'tis e'er denied thee
In solitude to pray,
Should holy thoughts come o'er thee,
When friends are round thy way,
E'en then, the silent breathing
Thy spirit lifts above,
Will reach His throne of glory,
Where dwells eternal love.

Simpson.

64 LAMBETH. C. M.

English.

1. Prayer is the soul's sincere desire, Uttered or unexpressed; The motion of a hidden fire That trembles in the breast.

PRAYER.

2 Prayer is the burden of a sigh,
  The falling of a tear,
 The upward glancing of an eye,
  When none but God is near.

3 Prayer is the simplest form of speech
  That infant lips can try;
 Prayer, the sublimest strains that reach
  The Majesty on high.

4 Prayer is the Christian's vital breath,
  The Christian's native air,
 His watchword at the gates of death,
  He enters heaven with prayer.

5 Prayer is the contrite sinner's voice,
  Returning from his ways;
 While angels in their songs rejoice,
  And cry, "Behold, he prays."

6 O Thou, by whom we come to God,
  The Life, the Truth, the Way!
 The path of prayer thyself hast trod;
  Lord, teach us how to pray.
   James Montgomery. 1819.

65 I NEED THEE, PRECIOUS JESUS.

1. I need Thee, precious Jesus, For I am full of sin; My soul is dark and guilty, My heart is dead within.

Chorus.
I need Thee, blessed Saviour, With Thy redeeming power; I need Thee, blessed Saviour, To help me every hour.

2 I need the love of Jesus
   To cheer me on my way,
  To guide my doubting footsteps,
   To be my strength and stay.—*Cho.*

3 I need Thee, precious Jesus,
   I need a friend like Thee,
  A friend to soothe and pity,
   A friend to care for me.—*Cho.*

4 I need the heart of Jesus
   To feel each anxious care,
  To tell my every trouble,
   And all my sorrows share.—*Cho.*

5 I need Thee, precious Jesus,
   And hope to see Thee soon,
  Encircled with the rainbow,
   And seated on Thy throne.—*Cho.*
      F. Whitfield.

PRAYER.

66. WOODSTOCK. C. M.
Deodatus Dutton. 1829.

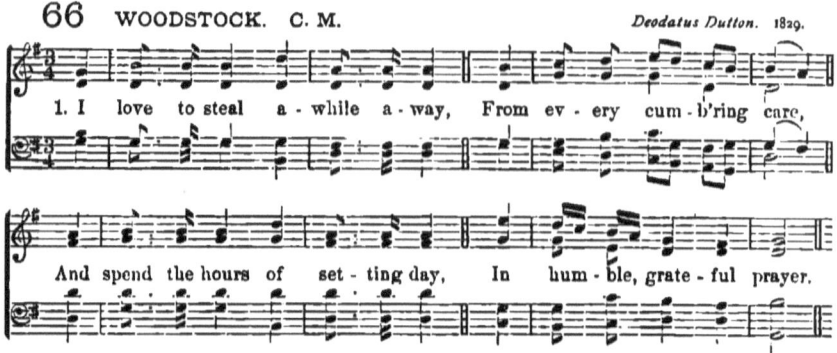

1. I love to steal a while away, From every cumb'ring care, And spend the hours of setting day, In humble, grateful prayer.

2 I love in solitude to shed
   The penitential tear,
And all His promises to plead,
   Where none but God can hear.

3 I love to think on mercies past,
   And future good implore,
And all my cares and sorrows cast
   On Him whom I adore.

4 I love by faith to take a view
   Of brighter scenes in heaven;
The prospect doth my strength renew,
   While here by tempests driven.

5 Thus, when life's toilsome day is o'er,
   May its departing ray
Be calm as this impressive hour,
   And lead to endless day.
Phœbe H. Brown. 1824.

67. VENICE. S. M.
English.

1. Come at the morning hour, Come, let us kneel and pray; Prayer is the Christian pilgrim's staff To walk with God all day.

2 At noon, beneath the Rock
   Of Ages, rest and pray;
Sweet is that shelter from the sun
   In weary heat of day.

3 At evening, in thy home,
   Around its altar, pray;
And finding there the house of God,
   With heaven then close the day.

4 When midnight veils our eyes,
   O, it is sweet to say,
I sleep, but my heart waketh, Lord!
   With Thee to watch and pray.
James Montgomery. 1853.

PRAYER.

68 KÜCKEN. 7s. *From Kucken.*

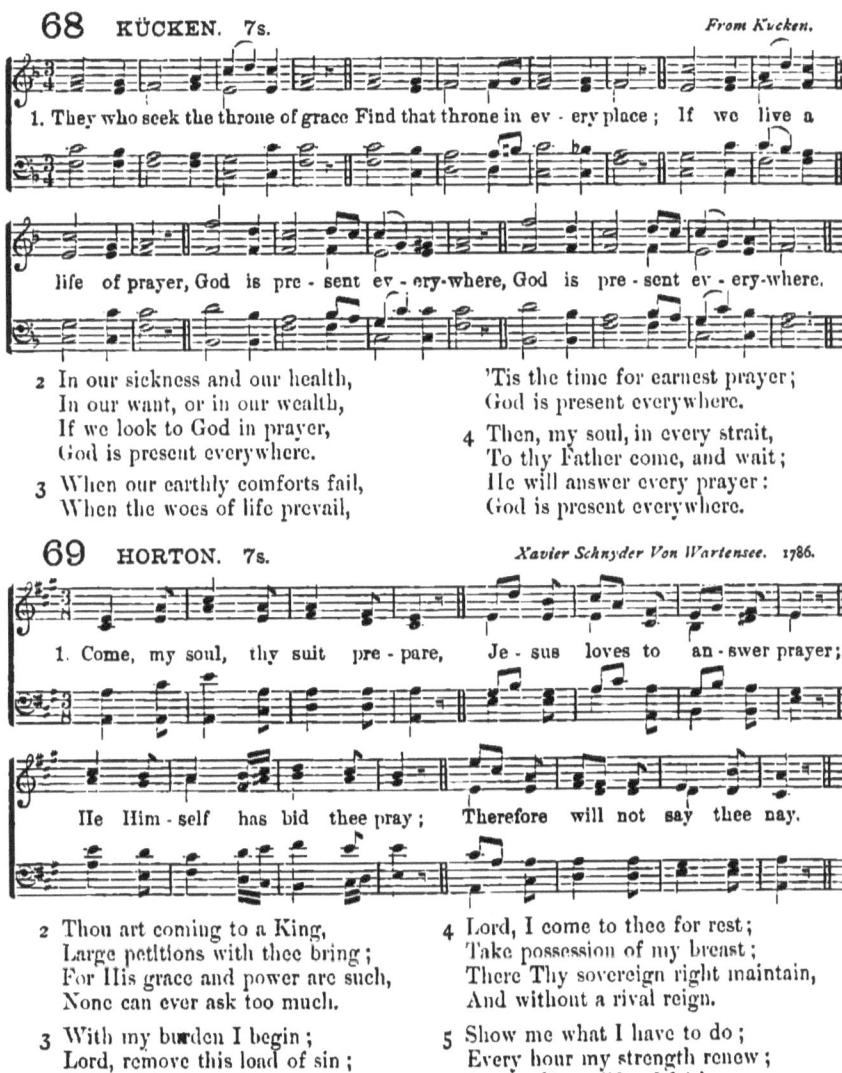

1. They who seek the throne of grace Find that throne in ev-ery place; If we live a life of prayer, God is pre-sent ev-ery-where, God is pre-sent ev-ery-where.

2 In our sickness and our health,
In our want, or in our wealth,
If we look to God in prayer,
God is present everywhere.

3 When our earthly comforts fail,
When the woes of life prevail,
'Tis the time for earnest prayer;
God is present everywhere.

4 Then, my soul, in every strait,
To thy Father come, and wait;
He will answer every prayer:
God is present everywhere.

69 HORTON. 7s. *Xavier Schnyder Von Wartensee.* 1786.

1. Come, my soul, thy suit pre-pare, Je-sus loves to an-swer prayer; He Him-self has bid thee pray; Therefore will not say thee nay.

2 Thou art coming to a King,
Large petitions with thee bring;
For His grace and power are such,
None can ever ask too much.

3 With my burden I begin;
Lord, remove this load of sin;
Let Thy blood, for sinners spilt,
Set my conscience free from guilt.

4 Lord, I come to thee for rest;
Take possession of my breast;
There Thy sovereign right maintain,
And without a rival reign.

5 Show me what I have to do;
Every hour my strength renew;
Let me live a life of faith;
Let me die Thy people's death.
John Newton. 1779.

PRAYER.

70 MARIE. 8s.

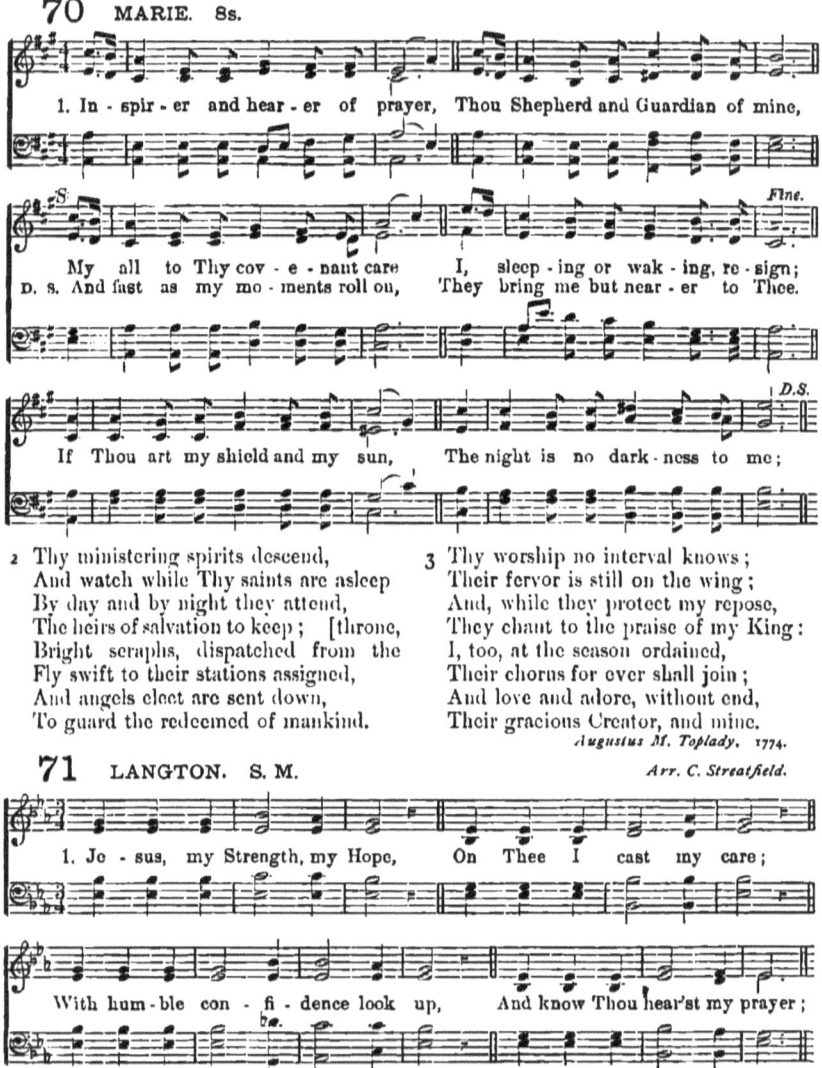

1. In-spir-er and hear-er of prayer, Thou Shepherd and Guardian of mine,
My all to Thy cov-e-nant care I, sleep-ing or wak-ing, re-sign;
D. S. And fast as my mo-ments roll on, They bring me but near-er to Thee.
If Thou art my shield and my sun, The night is no dark-ness to me;

2 Thy ministering spirits descend,
And watch while Thy saints are asleep
By day and by night they attend,
The heirs of salvation to keep; [throne,
Bright seraphs, dispatched from the
Fly swift to their stations assigned,
And angels elect are sent down,
To guard the redeemed of mankind.

3 Thy worship no interval knows;
Their fervor is still on the wing;
And, while they protect my repose,
They chant to the praise of my King:
I, too, at the season ordained,
Their chorus for ever shall join;
And love and adore, without end,
Their gracious Creator, and mine.

Augustus M. Toplady. 1774.

71 LANGTON. S. M.

Arr. C. Streatfield.

1. Je-sus, my Strength, my Hope, On Thee I cast my care;
With hum-ble con-fi-dence look up, And know Thou hear'st my prayer;

PRAYER.

2 Give me on Thee to wait,
   Till I can all things do;
   On Thee, Almighty to create,
   Almighty to renew.

3 I want a sober mind,
   A self-renouncing will,
   That tramples down, and casts behind,
   The baits of pleasing ill;

4 A soul inured to pain,
   To hardship, grief, and loss:

Bold to take up, firm to sustain,
   The consecrated cross.

5 I want a godly fear,
   A quick discerning eye,
   That looks to Thee when sin is near,
   And sees the tempter fly;

6 A spirit still prepared,
   And armed with jealous care;
   For ever standing on its guard,
   And watching unto prayer.

Charles Wesley. 1742.

72 LORD OF MY LIFE.

German Melody.

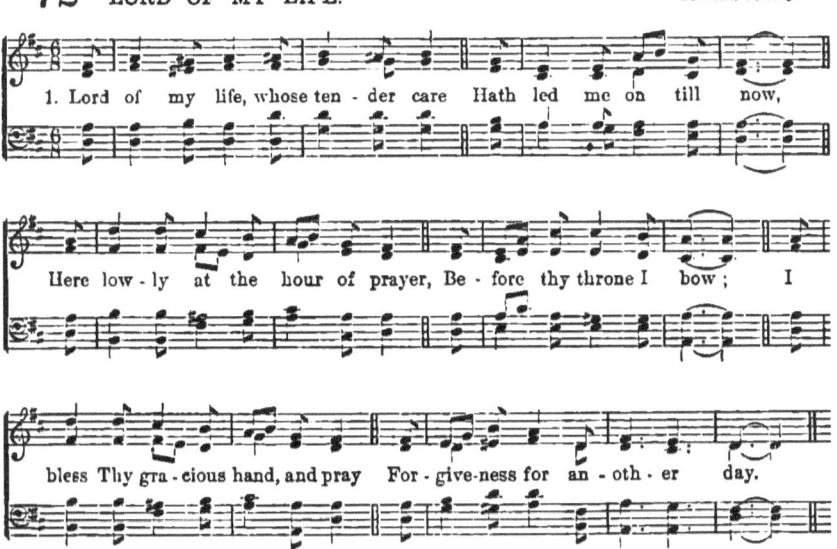

1. Lord of my life, whose tender care Hath led me on till now, Here lowly at the hour of prayer, Before thy throne I bow; I bless Thy gracious hand, and pray Forgiveness for another day.

2 O, may I daily, hourly strive
   In heavenly grace to grow;
   To Thee and to Thy glory live,
   Dead to all else below;
   Tread in the path my Saviour trod,
   Though thorny, yet the path of God.

3 With prayer, my humble praise I bring,
   For mercies day by day:
   Lord, teach my heart, Thy love to sing,
   Lord, teach me how to pray.
   All that I am and have, to Thee
   I offer through eternity.

"St Chelsea." 1838.

PRAYER.

73　SERENITY. C. M.　　*Arr. from William Vincent Wallace.* (1814-1865.)

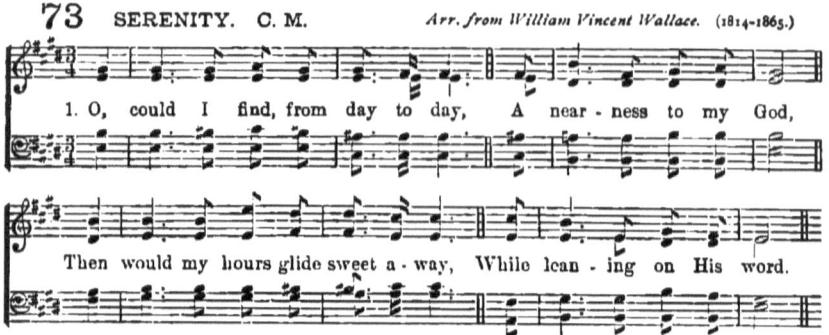

1. O, could I find, from day to day, A near-ness to my God,
Then would my hours glide sweet a-way, While lean-ing on His word.

2 Lord, I desire with Thee to live
　Anew from day to day,
　In joys the world can never give,
　Nor ever take away.

3 Blest Jesus, come and rule my heart,
　And make me wholly Thine,
　That I may never more depart,
　Nor grieve Thy love divine.

4 Thus, till my last, expiring breath,
　Thy goodness I'll adore;
　And when my frame dissolves in death,
　My soul shall love Thee more.

　　　　　　　Benjamin Cleveland. 1790.

74　ST. AGNES. C. M.　　*J. B. Dykes.* 1868.

1. Fa-ther of love, our Guide and Friend, O lead us gen-tly on,
Un-til life's tri-al time shall end, And heavenly peace be won.

2 We know not what the path may be,
　As yet by us untrod;
　But we can trust our all to Thee,
　Our Father and our God.

3 But if some darker lot be good,
　O teach us to endure
　The sorrow, pain, or solitude,
　That makes the heart be pure.

4 Christ by no flowery pathway came,
　And we, His servants here,
　Must do Thy will and praise Thy Name,
　In hope, and love, and fear.

5 And till in heaven we sinless bow,
　And faultless anthems raise,
　O Father, Son, and Spirit, now
　Accept our feeble praise.

　　　　　　　William J. Irons. 1853.

(54)

PRAYER.

75 SWEET IS THY MERCY, LORD. S. M.   *J. Barnby.* 1866.

1. Sweet is Thy mercy, Lord! Before Thy mercy-seat My soul, adoring, pleads Thy word, And owns Thy mercy sweet.

2 Where'er Thy name is blest,
Where'er Thy people meet,
There I delight in Thee to rest,
And find Thy mercy sweet.

3 Light Thou my weary way,
Lead Thou my wand'ring feet,
That while I stay on earth I may
Still find Thy mercy sweet.

4 Thus shall the heavenly host
Hear all my songs repeat,
To Father, Son, and Holy Ghost,
Thy joy, Thy mercy sweet.
J. S. B. Monsell. 1865.

76 ELLIOTT. 8s & 4s.   *J. B. Dykes.*

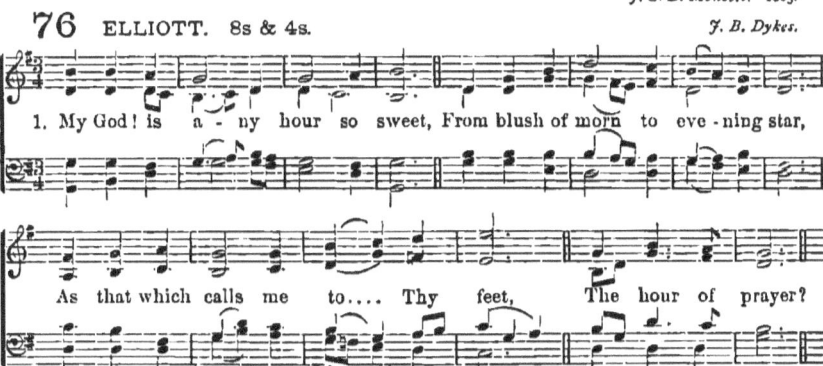

1. My God! is any hour so sweet, From blush of morn to evening star, As that which calls me to.... Thy feet, The hour of prayer?

2 Blest is the tranquil hour of morn,
And blest that solemn hour of eve
When, on the wings of prayer upborne,
The world I leave.

3 Then is my strength by Thee renewed;
Then are my sins by Thee forgiven;
Then dost Thou cheer my solitude
With hopes of heaven.

4 No words can tell what sweet relief
Here for my every want I find,
What strength for warfare, balm for grief,
What peace of mind.

5 Lord! till I reach that blissful shore,
No privilege so dear shall be,
As thus my inmost soul to pour
In prayer to Thee.
Charlotte Elliott. 1834.

PRAYER.

77 WHAT A FRIEND. 8s & 7s. D.
C. C. Converse.

1. What a friend we have in Jesus, All our sins and griefs to bear! What a privilege to carry
Every thing to God in prayer! O, what peace we often forfeit, O, what needless pain we bear,
D.S. All because we do not carry Every thing to God in prayer!

2 Have we trials and temptations?
  Is there trouble anywhere?
We should never be discouraged,—
  Take it to the Lord in prayer.

Can we find a friend so faithful,
  Who will all our sorrows share?
Jesus knows our every weakness—
  Take it to the Lord in prayer.
Horatius Bonar.

78 SHIRLAND. S. M.
Samuel Stanley. 1800.

1. Behold the throne of grace, The promise calls me near; There Jesus shows a smiling face, And waits to answer prayer.

2 My soul, ask what thou wilt,
  Thou canst not be too bold;
Since His own blood for thee He spilt,
  What else can He withhold?

3 Thine image, Lord, bestow,
  Thy presence and Thy love;

I ask to serve Thee here below,
  And reign with Thee above.

4 Teach me to live by faith,
  Conform my will to Thine,
Let me victorious be in death,
  And then in glory shine.
John Newton. 1779.

PRAYER.

79 THINE FOREVER, GOD OF LOVE.

1. Thine for-ev-er, God of love! Hear us from Thy throne above; Thine forever may we be,
D.S. Thou, the Life, the Truth, the Way,
Here and in e-ter-ni-ty. Thine forev-er, Lord of life! Shield us thro' the earthly strife;
Guide us to the realms of day.

2 Thine for ever, O how blest
They who find in Thee their rest;
Saviour, Guardian, heavenly Friend!
O defend us to the end.

Thine for ever, Saviour, keep
These Thy frail and trembling sheep;
Safe alone beneath Thy care,
Let us all Thy goodness share.
Mary F. Maude. 1848.

80 BLAKESLEY. C. M.
From "Geistliche Lieder."

1. The twi-light falls, the night is near, I fold my work a-way,
And kneel to One who bends to hear The sto-ry of the day.

2 The old, old story; yet I kneel
To tell it at Thy call,
And cares grow lighter as I feel
That Jesus knows them all.

3 Thou knowest all: I lean my head;
My weary eyelids close;
Content and glad awhile to tread
This path, since Jesus knows.

4 And He has loved me: All my heart
With answering love is stirred,
And every anguished pain and smart
Finds healing in the word.

5 So here I lay me down to rest,
As nightly shadows fall,
And lean confiding on His breast
Who knows and pities all.
Unknown Author.

PRAYER.

81 HURSLEY. L. M.
From F. J. Haydn. Arr. by William Henry Monk. 1861.

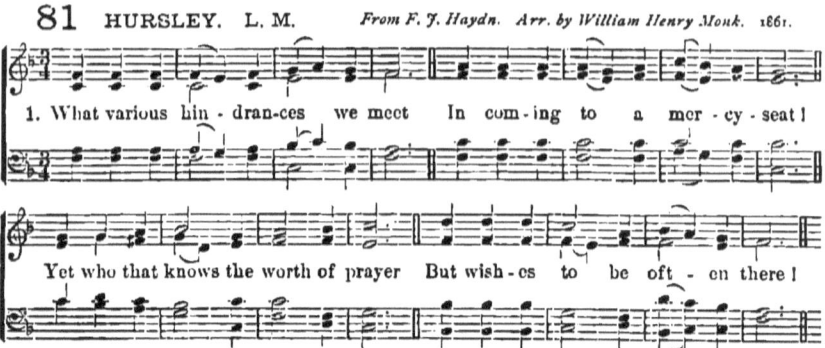

1. What various hin-dran-ces we meet In com-ing to a mer-cy-seat!
Yet who that knows the worth of prayer But wish-es to be oft-en there!

2 Prayer makes the darkened clouds withdraw,
Prayer climbs the ladder Jacob saw,
Gives exercise to faith and love,
Brings every blessing from above.

3 Restraining prayer, we cease to fight;
Prayer makes the Christian's armor bright;
And Satan trembles when he sees
The weakest saint upon his knees.

4 Have you no words! Ah, think again!
Words flow apace when you complain,
And fill a fellow-creature's ear
With the sad tale of all your care.

5 Were half the breath thus vainly spent
To heaven in supplication sent,
Our cheerful song would oftener be,
"Hear what the Lord hath done for me!"
William Cowper. 1779.

82 DAWN. S. M.
Edwin P. Parker. 1871.

1. If through un-ruf-fled seas Toward heaven we calm-ly sail,
With grate-ful hearts, O God, to Thee We'll own the fav-oring gale.

2 But should the surges rise,
And rest delay to come,
Blest be the sorrow—kind the storm,
Which drives us nearer home.

3 Soon shall our doubts and fears
All yield to Thy control:
Thy tender mercies shall illume
The midnight of the soul.

4 Teach us, in every state,
To make Thy will our own;
And when the joys of sense depart,
To live by faith alone.
Augustus M. Toplady. 1776.

PRAYER.

83 THE WHITE DOVE.

Joseph Barnby.

1. There sitteth a Dove, so white and fair, Upon a lily spray; And she listens when to our Saviour dear The little children pray. Lightly she spreads her friendly wings, And speeds to heaven her way, And to the heavenly Father bears The prayers which the children say, The prayers which the children say.

2 And downward she comes from heaven's gate,
  And brings—that Dove so mild—
From the Father in heaven, who hears her speak,
  A grace for every child.
Children, lift up your pious prayers,
  It hears whate'er you say,
That holy Dove, so white and fair,
  That sits on the lily spray.

PRAYER.

84 HOLY OFFERINGS. R. Redhead.

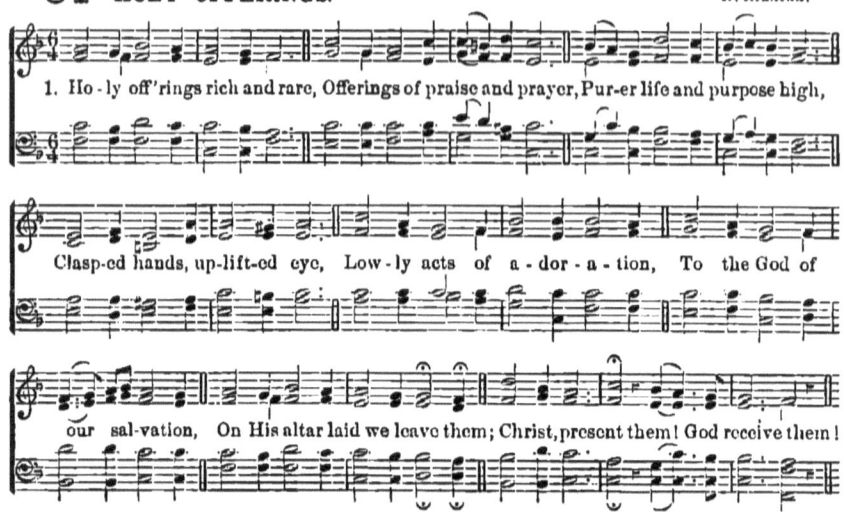

1. Ho-ly off'rings rich and rare, Offerings of praise and prayer, Pur-er life and purpose high, Clasp-ed hands, up-lift-ed eye, Low-ly acts of a-dor-a-tion, To the God of our sal-vation, On His altar laid we leave them; Christ, present them! God receive them!

2 Vows and longings, hopes and fears,
Broken-hearted sighs and tears,
Dreams of what we yet might be,
Could we cling more close to Thee,
Which, despite of faults and failings,
Help Thy grace in its prevailings—
On Thine altar laid we leave them ;
Christ, present them ! God receive them !

3 Homage of each humble heart,
Ere we from Thy house depart ;
Worship fervent, deep and high,
Adoration, ecstasy ;

All that childlike love can render
Of devotion true and tender—
On Thine altar laid we leave them ;
Christ, present them ! God receive them !

4 To the Father, and the Son,
And the Spirit, Three in One,
Though our mortal weakness raise
Off'rings of imperfect praise,
Yet with hearts bowed down most lowly,
Crying, Holy ! Holy ! Holy !
On Thine altar laid we leave them ;
Christ, present them ! God receive them !

85 BOYLSTON. S. M.

1 Blest be the tie that binds
   Our hearts in Christian love ;
The fellowship of kindred minds
   Is like to that above.

2 Before our Father's throne
   We pour our ardent prayers ;

Our fears, our hopes, our aims are
   one,—
Our comforts and our cares.

3 We share our mutual woes:
   Our mutual burdens bear ;
And often for each other flows
   The sympathizing tear.

John Fawcett. 1772.

PRAYER.

86 RETREAT. L. M.

1 From every stormy wind that blows,
From every swelling tide of woes,
There is a calm, a sure retreat;
'Tis found beneath the mercy-seat.

2 There is a place where Jesus sheds
The oil of gladness on our heads;
A place than all besides more sweet,—
It is the blood-bought mercy-seat.

3 There is a scene where spirits blend,
Where friend holds fellowship with friend;
Though sunder'd far, by faith we meet,
Around one common mercy-seat.
Hugh Stowell. 1832.

87 GREENVILLE. 8s, 7s & 4s.

1 Saviour! visit Thy plantation;
  Grant us, Lord! a gracious rain;
All will come to desolation
  Unless Thou return again.
    Lord! revive us,
All our help must come from Thee.

2 Break the tempter's fatal power;
  Turn the stony heart to flesh;
And begin from this good hour
  To revive Thy work afresh.
    Lord, revive us, etc. *J. Newton.* 1779.

88 SWEET HOUR OF PRAYER.

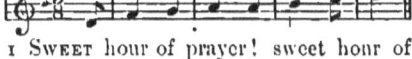

1 Sweet hour of prayer! sweet hour of prayer!
That calls me from a world of care,
And bids me at my Father's throne,
Make all my wants and wishes known.
In seasons of distress and grief,
My soul has often found relief,
And oft escaped the tempter's snare
By thy return, sweet hour of prayer.

2 Sweet hour of prayer! sweet hour of prayer!
Thy wings shall my petition bear
To Him whose truth and faithfulness,
Engage the waiting soul to bless;
And since He bids me seek His face,
Believe His word, and trust His grace,
I'll cast on Him my every care,
And wait for thee, sweet hour of prayer.

3 Sweet hour of prayer! sweet hour of prayer!
May I thy consolation share;
Till from Mount Pisgah's lofty height,
I view my home, and take my flight:
This robe of flesh I'll drop, and rise
To seize the everlasting prize;
And shout, while passing thro' the air,
Farewell, farewell, sweet hour of prayer.
W. W. Walford. 1846.

89 BETHANY. 6s & 4s.

Copyright. By per. of O. Ditson & Co.

1 Nearer, my God, to Thee,
    Nearer to Thee,
  E'en tho' it be a cross,
    That raiseth me,
  Still all my song shall be,
  Nearer, my God, to Thee,
    Nearer to Thee.

2 Tho' like a wanderer,
    The sun gone down,
  Darkness comes over me,
    My rest a stone,
  Yet in my dreams I'd be,
  Nearer, my God, to Thee,
    Nearer to Thee.

3 Or, if on joyful wing,
    Cleaving the sky,
  Sun, moon, and stars forgot,
    Upward I fly,
  Still all my song shall be,
  Nearer, my God, to Thee,
    Nearer to Thee.
Sarah F. Adams. 1840.

PRAYER.

90 BOYLSTON. S.M.

1 Jesus, who knows full well
   The heart of every saint,
Invites us all our grief to tell,
   To pray and never faint.

2 He bows His gracious ear,—
   We never plead in vain;
Then let us wait till He appear,
   And pray, and pray again.

3 Then let us earnest cry,
   And never faint in prayer;
He sees, He hears, and from on high
   Will make our cause His care.
                    John Newton. 1779.

91 NAOMI. C. M.

1 Father, whate'er of earthly bliss
   Thy sovereign will denies,
Accepted at Thy throne of grace,
   Let this petition rise :—

3 Give me a calm, a thankful heart,
   From every murmur free;
The blessings of Thy grace impart,
   And make me live to Thee.

4 Let the sweet hope that Thou art mine,
   My life and death attend;
Thy presence thro' my journey shine,
   And crown my journey's end.
                    Anne Steele. 1760.

92 GREENVILLE. 8s, 7s & 4s.

1 Lord, dismiss us with Thy blessing;
   Fill our hearts with joy and peace;
Let us each, Thy love possessing,
   Triumph in redeeming grace;
     O refresh us,
Traveling through this wilderness.

2 Thanks we give, and adoration,
   For Thy gospel's joyful sound;
May the fruits of Thy salvation
   In our hearts and lives abound;
     May Thy presence
With us evermore be found.

3 So, whene'er the signal's given,
   Us from earth to call away,
Borne on angels' wings to heaven,
   Glad the summons to obey,
     May we ever
Reign with Christ in endless day.
                    Walter Shirley. 1774.

93 RATHBUN. 8s & 7s.

Copyright. Used by per. of O. Ditson & Co.

1 In the cross of Christ I glory,
   Towering o'er the wrecks of time;
All the light of sacred story
   Gathers round its head sublime.

2 When the woes of life o'ertake me,
   Hopes deceive and fears annoy,
Never shall the cross forsake me;
   Lo! it glows with peace and joy.

3 Bane and blessing, pain and pleasure,
   By the cross are sanctified;
Peace is there that knows no measure,
   Joys that through all time abide.
                    J. Bowring. 1825.

94 HAMBURG. L. M.

1 O, the sweet wonders of that cross
   Where my Redeemer loved and died!
Her noblest life my spirit draws [side.
   From His dear wounds, and bleeding

2 I would forever speak His name
   In sounds to mortal ears unknown;
With angels join to praise the Lamb,
   And worship at His Father's throne.
                    Isaac Watts. 1707.

95 MORNING HYMN. L. M.

F. H. Barthelemon. 1768.

1. A-wake, my soul, and with the sun Thy dai-ly stage of du-ty run; Shake off dull sloth, and joy-ful rise, To pay thy morn-ing sac-ri-fice.

2 Wake and lift up thyself, my heart,
And with the angels bear thy part,
Who, all night long, unwearied sing
High praise to the eternal King.

3 All praise to Thee who safe hast kept,
And hast refreshed me while I slept;
Grant, Lord! when I from death shall wake,
I may of endless life partake.

4 Lord! I my vows to Thee renew;
Scatter my sins as morning dew;
Guard my first springs of thought and will,
And with Thyself my spirit fill.

Thomas Ken. 1697.

96 EVENING HYMN. L. M.

Thomas Tallis. 1567.

1. All praise to Thee, my God, this night, For all the bless-ings of the light: Keep me, O keep me, King of kings, Be-neath Thine own Al-might-y wings.

2 Forgive me, Lord, for Thy dear Son,
The ill that I this day have done;
That with the world, myself, and Thee,
I, ere I sleep, at peace may be.

3 Teach me to live, that I may dread
The grave as little as my bed;
Teach me to die, that so I may
Rise glorious at the awful day.

4 O may my soul on Thee repose,
And may sweet sleep my eyelids close:
Sleep, that may me more vigorous make
To serve my God, when I awake.

5 Praise God from whom all blessings flow;
Praise Him, all creatures here below;
Praise Him above, ye heavenly host;
Praise Father, Son, and Holy Ghost.

Thomas Ken. 1697.

MORNING AND EVENING.

97 MORNING PRAISE. 11s & 10s.   *John Stainer.*

1. Now, when the dusk-y shades of night re-treat-ing Be-fore the sun's red ban-ner swift-ly flee; Now, when the ter-rors of the dark are fleet-ing, O Lord, we lift our thank-ful hearts to Thee;

2 To Thee, whose word the fount of life unsealing,
  When hill and dale in thickest darkness lay,
Awoke bright rays across the dim earth stealing,
  And bade the eve and morn complete the day.

3 Look from the height of heaven, and send to cheer us
  Thy light and truth, and guide us onward still;
Still let Thy mercy, as of old, be near us,
  And lead us safely to Thy Holy Hill.

4 So, when that morn of endless light is waking,
  And shades of evil from its splendors flee,
Safe may we rise, this earth's dark vale forsaking,
  Through all the long bright day to dwell with Thee.

5 Be this by Thee, O God Thrice Holy, granted,
  O Father, Son, and Spirit, ever blest;
Whose glory by the heaven and earth is chanted,
  Whose Name by men and angels is confest.

From "Hymnologia Christiana."

98 ROSEFIELD. 7s. 6 lines.   *Cæsar H. A. Malan.* 1830.

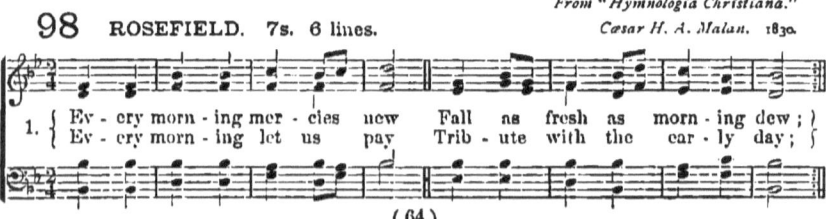

1. { Ev-ery morn-ing mer-cies new   Fall as fresh as morn-ing dew; }
   { Ev-ery morn-ing let us pay   Trib-ute with the ear-ly day; }

MORNING AND EVENING.

For thy mer-cies, Lord, are sure; Thy com-pas-sion doth en-dure.

2 Still the greatness of Thy love
Daily doth our sins remove;
Daily, far as east from west,
Lifts the burden from the breast;
Gives unbought to those who pray
Strength to stand in evil day.

3 Let our prayers each morn prevail,
That these gifts may never fail;
And, as we confess the sin

And the tempter's power within,
Feed us with the Bread of Life;
Fit us for our daily strife.

4 As the morning light returns,
As the sun with splendor burns,
Teach us still to turn to Thee,
Ever blessed Trinity,
With our hands our hearts to raise,
In unfailing prayer and praise.
Horatius Bonar. 1868.

99 NIGHTFALL. 8s & 7s. *J. Barnby.* 1870.

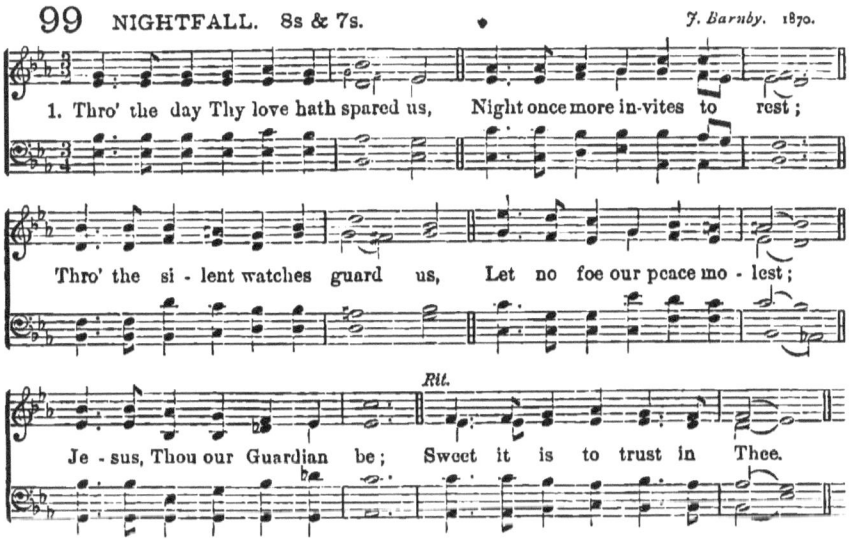

1. Thro' the day Thy love hath spared us, Night once more in-vites to rest;
Thro' the si-lent watches guard us, Let no foe our peace mo-lest;
Je-sus, Thou our Guardian be; Sweet it is to trust in Thee.

2 Pilgrims here on earth, and strangers,
Dwelling in the midst of foes,
Us and ours preserve from dangers;
In Thy love may we repose,
And, when life's short day is past,
Rest with Thee in heaven at last.

3 Blessèd God, let all adore Thee,
Saints on earth, and saints in heaven;
Every creature bow before Thee,
Who hast all their being given;
Who dost seek and save the lost;
Father, Son, and Holy Ghost.
Thomas Kelly. 1820.

EVENING.

100 SEPARATION. 8s & 7s.
U. C. Burnap. 1872.

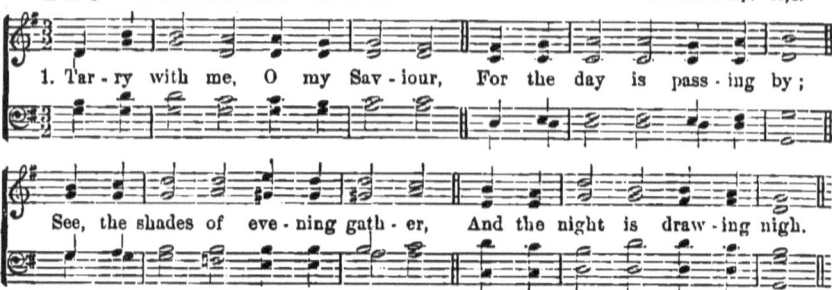

1. Tar-ry with me, O my Sav-iour, For the day is pass-ing by;
See, the shades of eve-ning gath-er, And the night is draw-ing nigh.

2 Deeper, deeper grow the shadows,
Paler now the glowing west;
Swift the night of death advances;
Shall it be the night of rest?

3 Feeble, trembling, fainting, dying,
Lord, I cast myself on Thee·

Tarry with me through the darkness;
While I sleep, still watch by me.

4 Tarry with me, O my Saviour;
Lay my head upon Thy breast
Till the morning, then awake me,—
Morning of eternal rest.
Caroline S. Smith. 1855.

101 EVENING. S. M.
Aaron Chapin. 1813.

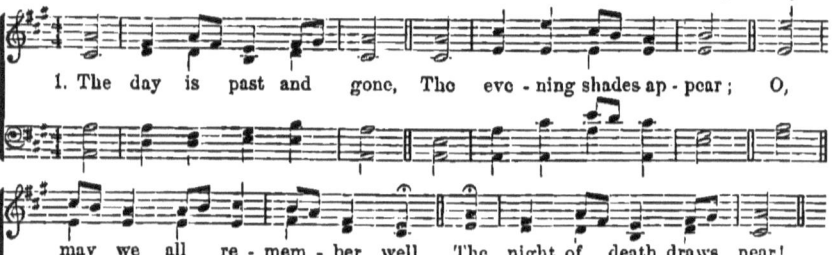

1. The day is past and gone, The eve-ning shades ap-pear; O,
may we all re-mem-ber well The night of death draws near!

2 We lay our garments by,
Upon our beds to rest;
So death will soon disrobe us all
Of what we here possessed.

3 Lord, keep us safe this night,
Secure from all our fears;
May angels guard us while we sleep,
Till morning light appears.

4 And when we early rise,
And view the unwearied sun,
May we set out to win the prize,
And after glory run.

5 And when our days are past,
And we from time remove,
O may we in Thy bosom rest,
The bosom of Thy love!
John Leland. 1799.

EVENING.

102 TEMPLE. 8s & 4s. *Edward J. Hopkins. 1869.*

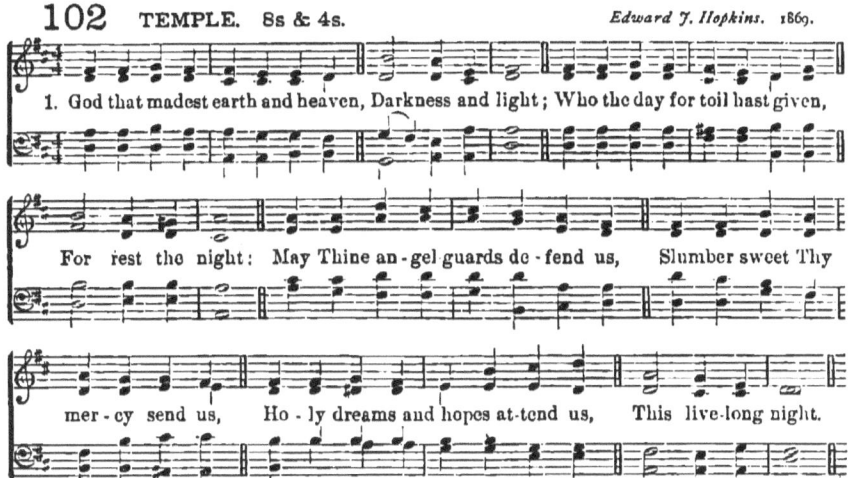

1. God that madest earth and heaven, Darkness and light; Who the day for toil hast given, For rest the night: May Thine an-gel guards de-fend us, Slumber sweet Thy mer-cy send us, Ho-ly dreams and hopes at-tend us, This live-long night.

2 And when morn again shall call us
  To run life's way,
 May we still, whate'er befall us,
  Thy will obey;
 From the power of evil hide us,
 In the narrow pathway guide us,
 Nor Thy smile be e'er denied us,
  The livelong day.

3 Guard us waking, guard us sleeping,
  And when we die,
 May we in Thy mighty keeping
  All peaceful lie;
 When the last dread call shall wake us,
 Do not Thou, our God, forsake us,
 But to reign in glory take us
  With Thee on high.

Reginald Heber. 1827. v. 1, 2. Richard Whately. v. 3.

103 EVENING SACRIFICE. *H. S. Irons.*

1. The sun is sinking fast, The daylight dies; Let love awake, and pay Her evening sacrifice.

2 As Christ upon the cross
   His Head inclined,
  And to His Father's hands
   His parting soul resigned:

3 So now herself my soul
   Would wholly give
  Into His sacred charge,
   In whom all spirits live.

4 Thus would I live; yet now
   Not I, but He
  In all His power and love
   Henceforth alive in me.

5 One sacred Trinity!
   One Lord Divine!
  May I be ever His,
   And He forever mine.

From the Latin. Tr. E. Caswall.

EVENING.

104 OLD HUNDRED L. M.
Guillaume Franc. 1543.

DOX. Praise God, from whom all blessings flow! Praise Him, all creatures here below!
Praise Him above, ye heavenly host! Praise Father, Son, and Holy Ghost.

1 From all that dwell below the skies,
Let the Creator's praise arise:
Let the Redeemer's name be sung,
Through every land, by every tongue.

2 Eternal are Thy mercies, Lord!
Eternal truth attends Thy word: [shore,
Thy praise shall sound from shore to
Till sun shall rise and set no more.
Isaac Watts. 1719.

105 HURSLEY. L. M.
Peter Ritter (1760-1846). *Arr. by W. H. Monk.* 1861.

1. Sun of my soul, Thou Saviour dear, It is not night if Thou be near;
O, may no earth-born cloud arise To hide Thee from Thy servant's eyes.

2 When the soft dews of kindly sleep
My wearied eyelids gently steep,
Be my last thought how sweet to rest
Forever on my Saviour's breast.

3 Abide with me from morn till eve,
For without Thee I cannot live;
Abide with me when night is nigh,
For without Thee I dare not die.

4 If some poor wandering child of Thine
Have spurned to-day the voice divine—
Now, Lord, the gracious work begin;
Let him no more lie down in sin.

5 Watch by the sick; enrich the poor
With blessings from Thy boundless store;
Be every mourner's sleep to-night,
Like infant's slumbers, pure and light.

6 Come near and bless us when we wake,
Ere through the world our way we take;
Till in the ocean of Thy love
We lose ourselves in heaven above.
John Keble. 1827.

EVENING.

106 HOLLEY. 7s.
George Hews. 1835.

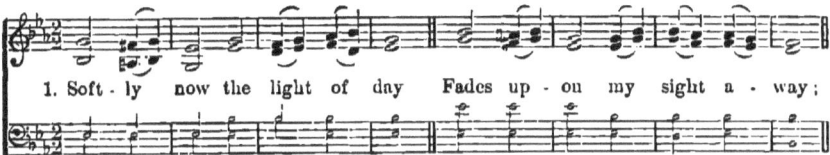

1. Soft-ly now the light of day Fades up-on my sight a-way;
Free from care, from la-bor free, Lord, I would commune with Thee.

2 Thou, whose all-pervading eye
　Naught escapes without, within,
　Pardon each infirmity,
　Open fault, and secret sin.

3 Soon, for me, the light of day
　Shall for ever pass away;

Then, from sin and sorrow free,
Take me, Lord, to dwell with Thee.

4 Thou who, sinless, yet hast known
　All of man's infirmity;
　Then from Thine eternal throne,
　Jesus, look with pitying eye.
　　　　　　George W. Doane. 1824.

107 ST. SYLVESTER. 8s & 7s.
John B. Dykes. 1861.

1. Je-sus, ten-der Shepherd, hear me, Bless Thy lit-tle lamb to-night;
Through the dark-ness be Thou near me, Keep me safe till morn-ing light.

2 All this day Thy hand hast led me,
　And I thank Thee for Thy care;
　Thou hast clothed me, warmed and fed
　Listen to my evening prayer. [me,

3 Let my sins be all forgiven,
　Bless the friends I love so well;
　Take me when I die to heaven,
　Happy there with Thee to dwell.
　　　　　Mary Lundie Duncan. 1839.

EVENING.

108 EVENTIDE. 10s.   *William H. Monk.* 1861.

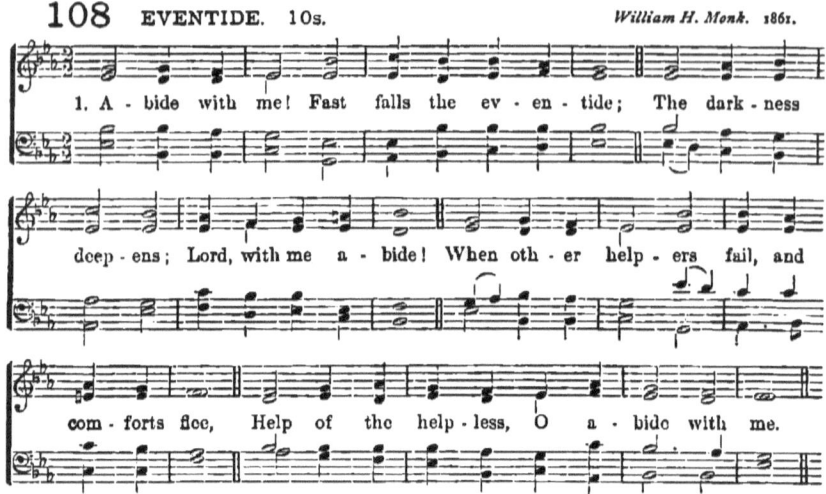

1. Abide with me! Fast falls the eventide; The darkness deepens; Lord, with me abide! When other helpers fail, and comforts flee, Help of the helpless, O abide with me.

2 Swift to its close ebbs out life's little day;
Earth's joys grow dim; its glories pass away;
Change and decay in all around I see:
O Thou who changest not, abide with me!

3 I need Thy presence every passing hour,
What but Thy grace can foil the tempter's power?
Who like Thyself my guide and stay can be?
Through cloud and sunshine, O abide with me!

4 I fear no foe, with Thee at hand to bless;
Ills have no weight, and tears no bitterness:
Where is death's sting? where, grave, thy victory?
I triumph still, if Thou abide with me.

5 Hold Thou Thy cross before my closing eyes,
Shine through the gloom, and point me to the skies;
Heaven's morning breaks, and earth's vain shadows flee:
In life, in death, O Lord, abide with me!

                                        Henry Francis Lyte. 1847.

TROYTE. [SECOND TUNE.]   *Arthur H. D. Troyte.* d. 1859.

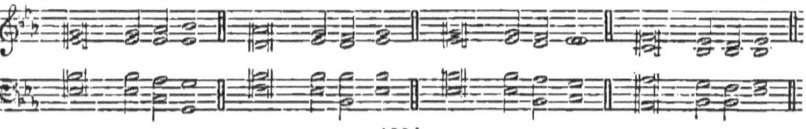

THE HOLY SPIRIT.

109 ST. AGNES. C. M. — John B. Dykes. 1868.

1. Come, Holy Spirit, heavenly Dove, With all thy quickening powers, Kindle a flame of sacred love In these cold hearts of ours.

2 Look! how we grovel here below,
Fond of these trifling toys!
Our souls can neither fly nor go,
To reach eternal joys.

3 In vain we tune our formal songs;
In vain we strive to rise;
Hosannas languish on our tongues,
And our devotion dies.

4 Dear Lord, and shall we ever live
At this poor, dying rate,—
Our love so faint, so cold to Thee,
And Thine to us so great?

5 Come, Holy Spirit, heavenly Dove,
With all Thy quickening powers,
Come, shed abroad a Saviour's love,
And that shall kindle ours.
Isaac Watts. 1709.

110 ARLINGTON. C. M. — Thomas A. Arne. 1744.

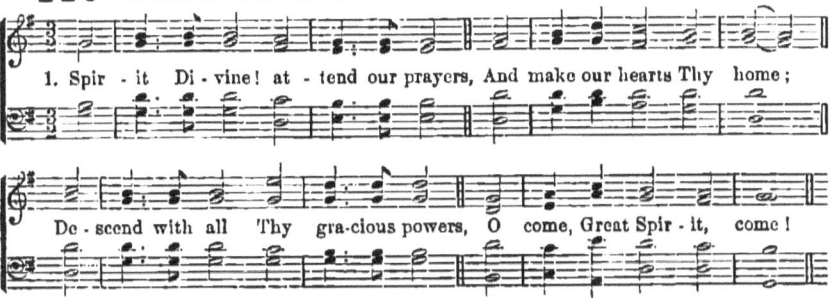

1. Spirit Divine! attend our prayers, And make our hearts Thy home; Descend with all Thy gracious powers, O come, Great Spirit, come!

2 Come as the light; to us reveal
Our emptiness and woe;
And lead us in those paths of life
Where all the righteous go.

3 Come as the fire; and purge our hearts,
Like sacrificial flame;
Let our whole soul an offering be
To our Redeemer's name.

4 Come as the dove; and spread Thy wings,
The wings of peaceful love;
And let Thy church on earth become
Blessed as the church above.
Andrew Reed. 1843.

THE HOLY SPIRIT.

111　INVOCATION.　6s & 4s.　　　　*Edwin Pond Parker.*

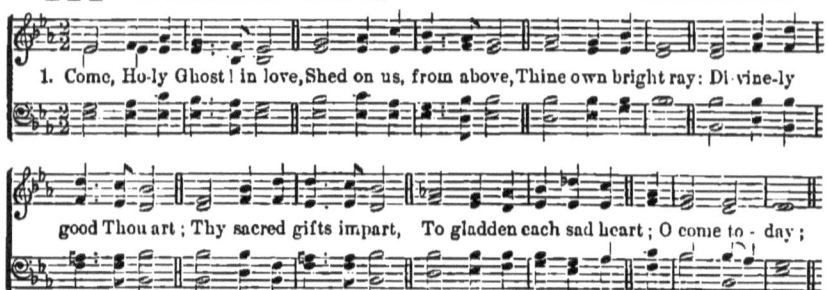

1. Come, Ho-ly Ghost! in love, Shed on us, from above, Thine own bright ray: Di-vine-ly good Thou art; Thy sacred gifts impart, To gladden each sad heart; O come to-day;

2 Come, tenderest Friend, and best,
　Our most delightful Guest!
　　With soothing power;
　Rest, which the weary know;
　Shade, 'mid the noontide glow;
　Peace, when deep griefs o'erflow;
　　Cheer us this hour!

3 Come, Light serene! and still
　Our inmost bosoms fill;
　　Dwell in each breast:
　We know no dawn but Thine;
　Send forth Thy beams divine,
　On our dark souls to shine,
　　And make us blest.

4 Exalt our low desires;
　Extinguish passion's fires;
　　Heal every wound;
　Our stubborn spirits bend;
　Our icy coldness end;
　Our devious steps attend,
　　While heavenward bound.

5 Come, all the faithful bless;
　Let all who Christ confess,
　　His praise employ:
　Give virtue's rich reward;
　Victorious death accord,
　And, with our glorious Lord,
　　Eternal joy!

Tr. Ray Palmer.

112　OUR BLEST REDEEMER.　　　　*John B. Dykes.*

1. Our blest Redeemer, ere He breathed His last farewell, A Guide, a Comforter, bequeathed With us to dwell.

2 He comes, His graces to impart,
　　A willing guest,
　While He can find one humble heart
　　Wherein to rest.

3 He breathes that gentle voice we hear
　　As breeze of even;

That checks each fault, that calms each
　And speaks of heaven.　　[fear,

4 Spirit of purity and grace!
　　Our weakness see;
　O, make our hearts Thy dwelling-place,
　　And worthier Thee!

Harriet Auber. 1829.

THE HOLY SPIRIT.

113 ELYRIA. 7s. *Maria Luigi Cherubini.* (1760-1842).

1. Gracious Spirit, Love divine! Let Thy light within me shine; All my guilty fears remove, Fill me with Thy heavenly love.

2 Speak Thy pardoning grace to me
Set the burdened sinner free;
Lead me to the Lamb of God,
Wash me in His precious blood.

3 Life and peace to me impart,
Seal salvation on my heart;

Breathe Thyself into my breast,
Earnest of immortal rest.

4 Let me never from Thee stray,
Keep me in the narrow way;
Fill my soul with joy divine,
Keep me, Lord, forever Thine.
John Stocker. 1776.

114 HOPKINS. 10s. *Edward J. Hopkins.* 1866.

1. Spirit of God! descend upon my heart; Wean it from earth, thro' all its pulses move; Stoop to my weakness, mighty as Thou art, And make me love Thee as I ought to love.

2 I ask no dream, no prophet ecstasies;
No sudden rending of the veil of clay;
No angel visitant, no opening skies;
But take the dimness of my soul away.

3 Teach me to feel that Thou art always nigh;
Teach me the struggles of the soul to bear;
To check the rising doubt, the rebel sigh;
Teach me the patience of unanswered prayer.

4 Teach me to love Thee as Thine angels love,
One holy passion filling all my frame;
The baptism of the heaven-descended Dove,
My heart an altar, and Thy love the [flame!
George Croly. 1830.

(73)

THE HOLY SPIRIT.

115 DENNIS. S. M.

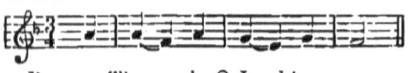

1 Revive Thy work, O Lord!
  Thy mighty arm make bare;
  Speak with the voice that wakes the [dead,
  And make Thy people hear.

2 Revive Thy work, O Lord!
  Exalt Thy precious name;
  And, by the Holy Ghost, our love
  For Thee and Thine inflame.

3 Revive Thy work, O Lord!
  And give refreshing showers;
  The glory shall be all Thine own,
  The blessing, Lord! be ours.
  Albert Midlane.

116 STATE STREET. S. M.

1 O cease, my wandering soul,
  On restless wing to roam;
  All this wide world, to either pole,
  Hath not for thee a home.

2 Behold the ark of God!
  Behold the open door!
  O, haste to gain that dear abode,
  And rove, my soul, no more.

3 There safe thou shalt abide,
  There sweet shall be thy rest;
  And every longing satisfied,
  With full salvation blest.
  W. A. Muhlenberg. 1826.

117 BOYLSTON. S. M

1 Now is the accepted time,
  Now is the day of grace;
  O sinners! come, without delay,
  And seek the Saviour's face.

2 Now is the accepted time,
  The gospel bids you come;
  And every promise in His word
  Declares there yet is room.

3 Lord, draw reluctant souls,
  And feast them with Thy love;
  Then will the angels spread their [wings,
  And bear the news above.
  Dobell.

118 OLMUTZ. S. M.

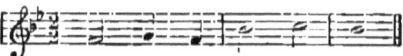

1 Come, Holy Spirit, come!
  Let Thy bright beams arise;
  Dispel the sorrow from our minds,
  The darkness from our eyes.

2 Revive our drooping faith,
  Our doubts and fears remove,
  And kindle in our breasts the flame
  Of never-dying love.

3 'Tis Thine to cleanse the heart,
  To sanctify the soul,
  To pour fresh love in every part,
  And new-create the whole.
  Joseph Hart. 1759.

119 STOCKWELL. 8s & 7s.

1 Jesus calls us, o'er the tumult
  Of our life's wild, reckless sea;
  Day by day His sweet voice soundeth,
  Saying, Christian, follow me!

2 Jesus calls us from the worship
  Of the vain world's golden store;
  From each idol that would keep us,
  Saying, Christian, love me more!

3 Jesus calls us! by Thy mercies,
  Saviour, may we hear Thy call;
  Give our hearts to Thy obedience,
  Serve and love Thee best of all!
  Cecil Frances Alexander. 1853.

CHRISTMAS.

120 RING OUT THE MERRY, MERRY BELLS.

1. Ring out the mer-ry, mer-ry bells, The mer-ry Christmas bells, Their mu-sic bears the an-gel-song, And joy-ful news it tells; "Fear not: the Saviour of the world In Beth-le-hem is born!" Then let our hearts sing out their joy, And fill with praise the morn. Ring out the mer-ry, mer-ry bells, The mer-ry Christmas bells; Good news of God's great love to men Their joyful music tells.

2 Ring out the merry, merry bells
In pealing tones of praise;
We'll echo back the angel-song
As hymns of joy we raise:
"All glory be to God most high,"
Who reigns in light above;
"Peace on the earth, good-will to men,"
Shall mark His reign of love.—*Cho.*

3 Ring out the merry, merry bells:
For in the Saviour's birth
Our Father in His mercy gave
His choicest gift to earth.
And we will give our gifts of love
To those around us here, [world,
Till Christ's "good-will" shall rule the
And life is full of cheer.—*Cho.*

CHRISTMAS.

2 Lo, within a manger lies
He who built the starry skies;
He, who throned in height sublime,
Sits amid the Cherubim!—*Cho.*

3 Say, ye holy shepherds, say,
What your joyful news to-day?
Wherefore have ye left your sheep
On the lonely mountain steep?—*Cho.*

4 "As we watched at dead of night,
Lo, we saw a wondrous light;
Angels singing peace on earth,
Told us of the Saviour's birth."—*Cho.*

5 Sacred Infant, all Divine,
What a tender love was Thine;
Thus to come from highest bliss
Down to such a world as this.—*Cho.*

6 "Teach, O teach us, Holy Child,
By Thy face so meek and mild,
Teach us to resemble Thee,
In Thy sweet humility!—*Cho.*
Edward Caswall. 1849.

122 JUBILEE. 8s & 7s. D.

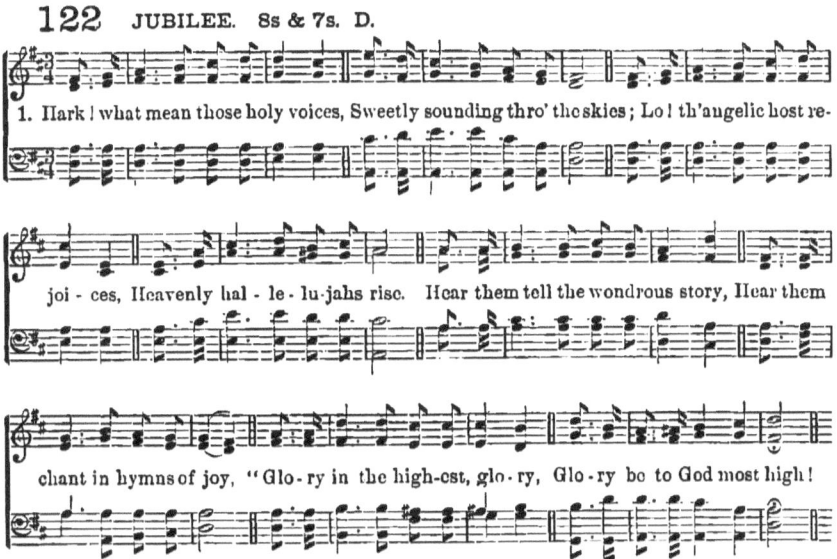

1. Hark! what mean those holy voices, Sweetly sounding thro' the skies; Lo! th' angelic host rejoices, Heavenly hal-le-lu-jahs rise. Hear them tell the wondrous story, Hear them chant in hymns of joy, "Glo-ry in the high-est, glo-ry, Glo-ry be to God most high!

2 "Peace on earth, good-will from heaven,
Reaching far as man is found;
Souls redeemed, and sins forgiven!
Loud our golden harps shall sound.
Christ is born, the great Anointed;
Heaven and earth His praises sing!
Glad receive whom God appointed
For your Prophet, Priest, and King!"

3 Let us learn the wondrous story
Of our great Redeemer's birth,
Spread the brightness of His glory
Till it cover all the earth.
Haste, ye mortals, to adore Him;
Learn His name, and taste His joy:
Till in heaven ye sing before Him,
"Glory be to God most high!"
John Cawood. 1819.

CHRISTMAS.

123 ONCE AGAIN, O BLESSED TIME. *John B. Dykes.*

1. Once a-gain, O bless-ed time, Thankful hearts em-brace thee; If we lost thy fes-tal chime, What could e'er re-place thee? What could e'er re-place thee? Change will darken many a day, Many a bond dis-sev-er; Many a joy shall pass a-way, But the "Great Joy" nev-er! But the "Great Joy" nev-er! But the "Great Joy" nev-er!

2 Once again the Holy Night
  Breathes its blessing tender;
Once again the Manger Light
  Sheds its gentle splendor;
O could tongues by angels taught
  Speak our exultation
In the Virgin's Child that brought
  All mankind salvation!

3 Welcome Thou to souls athirst,
  Fount of endless pleasure;
Gates of hell may do their worst,
  While we clasp our Treasure:
Welcome, though an age like this
  Puts Thy Name on trial,
And the truth that makes our bliss
  Pleads against denial!

CHRISTMAS.

4 Yea, if others stand apart,
    We will press the nearer;
  Yea, O best fraternal heart,
    We will hold Thee dearer;
  Faithful lips shall answer thus
    To all faithless scorning,
  "Jesus Christ is God with us,
    Born on Christmas morning."

5 While Thy birth-day morn we greet
    With our best devotion,
  Bathe us, O most true and sweet!
    In Thy mercy's ocean.
  Thou whose love bestows a worth
    On each poor endeavor,
  Have Thou joy in this Thy birth
    In our praise forever.
            William Bright.

124 GLORY TO GOD.

1. { "Glo-ry to God," hear the an-gels sing, Loud thro' the sky doth the mes-sage ring;
   { Nev-er has dawn'd such a glorious morn, [OMIT..................................]

For now the Sav-iour of the world is born. { "Glo-ry to God in the highest," then,
{ "Peace on the earth, good-will to men."

Joy-ful the tid-ings that an-gel's voice, Let all in heav-en and on earth re-joice.

2 Now He has come, the Prince of Light,
  Conquering sin, and enthroning Right;
  Banished from earth shall be hate and wrong,
  And all its weeping shall be turned to song.—*Cho.*

3 Kings with their gifts, coming from afar,
  Followed the light of His guiding star;
  Star of our life, we will follow Thee,
  Till in Thy glory we at last shall be.—*Cho.*

CHRISTMAS.

125 HERALD-ANGELS. *Mendelssohn.*

1. Hark! the herald-angels sing Glory to the new-born King: Peace on earth, and mercy mild, God and sinners reconciled. Joyful, all ye nations, rise, Join the triumph of the skies; With th' angelic host proclaim Christ is born in Bethlehem. Hark! the herald-angels sing Glory to the new-born King.

2 Christ, by highest heaven adored,
Christ, the everlasting Lord,
Come to show His saving power,
Ruined nature to restore.
Veiled in flesh the Godhead see!
Hail, the Incarnate Deity!
Pleased as Man with man to dwell
Jesus, our Immanuel.
    Hark! the herald-angels sing
    Glory to the new-born King.

3 Hail, the heaven-born Prince of Peace!
Hail, the Sun of Righteousness!
Light and life to all He brings,
Risen with healing in His wings.
Mild He lays His glory by,
Born that man no more may die,
Born to raise the sons of earth,
Born to give them second birth.
    Hark! the herald-angels sing
    Glory to the new-born King.
C. Wesley. 1739.

CHRISTMAS.

126 CHRISTMAS CAROL. *Edwin Pond Parker.*

1. Wake, O wake, ye weary! once more th' angel-ic strain, Floating down from Heaven o'er all the earth again, Sheds its benediction on human want and pain; For Christ the Lord is born. Glory in the highest! Glory in the highest, For Christ the Lord is born.

From the "Christian Hymnal."

2 Fear not, O ye sinful, who shed the contrite tear;
Fear not, ye who sorrow for those who were most dear;
Fear not, O ye trembling, the grave that seems so drear;
    For Christ the Lord is born!

3 Fear not, O ye troubled, whose pathway clouds surround;
Fear not, O ye faithful, though foes may rage around;
Fear not, O ye peoples in bitter bondage bound·
    For Christ the Lord is born!

4 Wake, and sing, ye weary! for yours is all the light,—
All the heavenly music of angels in the height;
All the joy and glory of that first Christmas night
    When Christ the Lord was born. *Edwin Pond Parker.*

CHRISTMAS.

127 CAROL. C. M. D. *Richard Storrs Willis.*

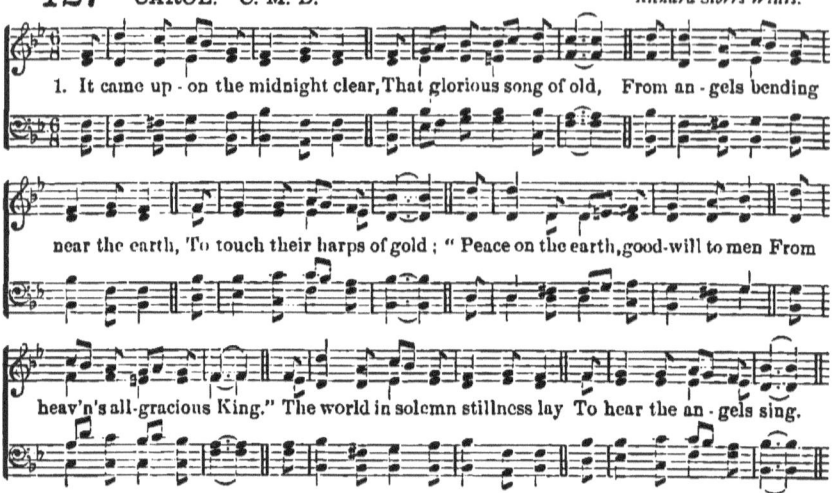

1. It came up-on the midnight clear, That glorious song of old, From an-gels bending near the earth, To touch their harps of gold; "Peace on the earth, good-will to men From heav'n's all-gracious King." The world in solemn stillness lay To hear the an-gels sing.

2 Still through the cloven skies they come,
  With peaceful wings unfurled;
And still their heavenly music floats
  O'er all the weary world:
Above its sad and lowly plains
  They bend on hovering wing,
And ever o'er its Babel sounds
  The blessèd angels sing.

3 But with the woes of sin and strife
  The world has suffered long;
Beneath the angel-strain have rolled
  Two thousand years of wrong;
And man, at war with man, hears not
  The love-song which they bring:
O hush the noise, ye men of strife,
  And hear the angels sing.

4 And ye, beneath life's crushing load
  Whose forms are bending low,
Who toil along the climbing way,
  With painful steps and slow,—
Look now; for glad and golden hours
  Come swiftly on the wing:
O rest beside the weary road,
  And hear the angels sing.

5 For lo, the days are hastening on
  By prophet bards foretold,
When with the ever-circling years
  Comes round the age of gold:
When Peace shall over all the earth
  Its ancient splendors fling,
And the whole world give back the song
  Which now the angels sing.
      Edmund H. Sears. 1850.

128 CHRISTMAS HYMN. *Edwin Pond Parker.*

1. With an-gel voic-es blending, Our joy-ful songs we raise To sing Mes-si-ah's praise,

CHRISTMAS.

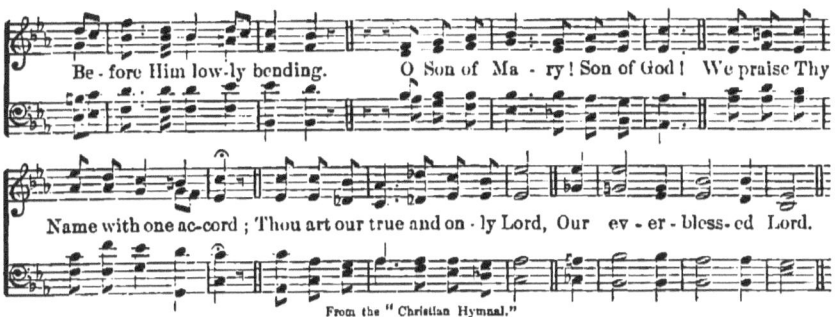

Be-fore Him low-ly bending. O Son of Ma-ry! Son of God! We praise Thy Name with one ac-cord; Thou art our true and on-ly Lord, Our ev-er-bless-ed Lord.

From the "Christian Hymnal."

2 The shepherds tell His story;
The sages see His star
And hail it from afar,
And haste to give Him glory.
Sweet incense, gold, and myrrh they [bring,
And worship Mary's child as King!
Dear Lord, accept our offering—
Our humble offering.

3 Now ends the night of sadness,
Behold the Day-star gleams!
With healing in His beams
Upsprings the Sun of gladness!
O Sun of righteousness, we pray,
Chase all the night of sin away,
Pour forth the noontide light of day—
The light of perfect day.
Edwin Pond Parker.

129 DIX. 7s. 6 lines. *Conrad Kocher.* 1838.

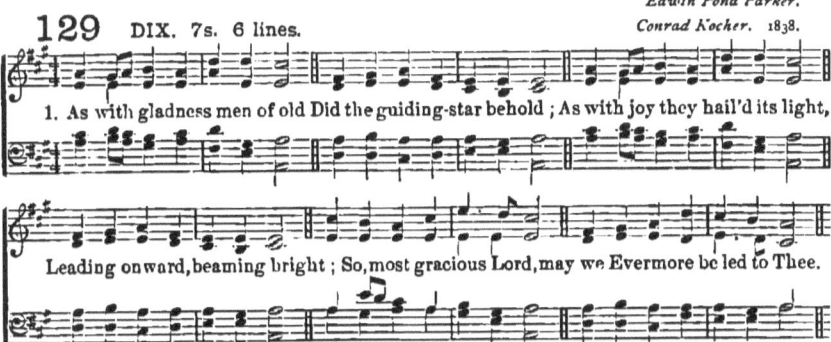

1. As with gladness men of old Did the guiding-star behold; As with joy they hail'd its light, Leading onward, beaming bright; So, most gracious Lord, may we Evermore be led to Thee.

2 As with joyful steps they sped,
Saviour, to Thy manger-bed,
There to bend the knee before
Thee whom heaven and earth adore;
So may we with willing feet
Ever seek the mercy-seat.

3 As they offered gifts most rare
At Thy cradle rude and bare,
So may we with holy joy,
Pure and free from sin's alloy,
All our costliest treasures bring,
Christ, to Thee our heavenly King.

4 Holy Jesus, every day
Keep us in the narrow way;
And, when earthly things are past,
Bring our ransomed souls at last
Where they need no star to guide,
Where no clouds Thy glory hide.
W. C. Dix. 1859.

130. GOD REST YE, MERRY GENTLEMEN.

1. God rest ye, mer-ry gen-tle-men, Let nothing you dismay; For Jesus Christ, your Saviour, Was born on Christmas-day. The dawn was red on Bethlehem, The stars shone thro' the gray, When Jesus Christ, your Saviour, Was born on Christmas-day. *Chorus.* Ring out the song, the strain prolong, And cheerful homage pay; For Je-sus Christ, your Saviour, Was born on Christmas-day.

2 God rest ye, little children,
   Let nothing you affright,
For Jesus Christ, your Saviour,
   Was born this happy night.
Along the hills of Galilee
   The white flocks sleeping lay,
When Jesus Christ, your Saviour,
   Was born on Christmas-day.

3 God rest ye, all good Christians,
   For on this blessed morn
The Lord of all good Christians
   Was of a woman born.
Now all your sorrows He doth heal,
   Your sins He takes away;
For Jesus Christ, your Saviour,
   Was born on Christmas-day.

Dinah Maria Mulock-Craik.

THE GUIDING STAR.

131 HOLY NIGHT! PEACEFUL NIGHT! J. Barnby. 1868.

1. Holy night! peaceful night! Thro' the darkness beams a light; Holy night! peaceful night! Thro' the darkness beams a light, Thro' the darkness beams a light; Yonder, where they sweet vigils keep O'er the Babe, who in silent sleep, Rests in heavenly peace, Rests in heavenly peace

2 Silent night! holiest night!
Darkness flies and all is light!
Shepherds hear the angels sing—
" Hallelujah! hail the King!
Jesus Christ is here!"

3 Silent night! holiest night!
Guiding Star, O lend thy light!
See the eastern wise men bring
Gifts and homage to our King!
Jesus Christ is here!

4 Silent night! holiest night!
Wondrous Star! O lend thy light!
With the angels let us sing
Hallelujah to our King!
Jesus Christ is here!

CHRISTMAS.

132 APPROACH, ALL YE FAITHFUL. *J. Barnby.*

1. Approach, all ye faithful, Joyful and triumphant; O come ye, O come ye to Beth-le-hem; See in a man-ger The Monarch of an-gels: O come let us a-dore Him, O come, let us a-dore Him, O come, let us a-dore Him, Christ the Lord.

2 O sing Allelulia,
  Ye bright Choirs of Angels,
O fill ye the courts of heaven with song;
  Sing ye "All glory
  To God in the Highest;"
  O come, let us adore Him,
  O come, let us adore Him,
O come, let us adore Him, Christ the [Lord.

3 O hail, Lord Incarnate,
  Son of the Father, [Flesh;
Born of the Virgin, the Word made
  Glory and honor
  Give we Thee, O Jesus;
  O come, let us adore Him,
  O come, let us adore Him,
O come, let us adore Him, Christ the [Lord.

133 THE JOYFUL MORN IS BREAKING. *E. J. Hopkins.*

1. The joy-ful morn is break-ing, The brightest morn of earth, Through all cre-a-tion wak-ing The joy of Je-sus' birth. His star a-bove is glistening, Where

(86)

CHRISTMAS.

Je-sus cra-dled lies, And all the earth is listening The car-ol of the skies.

2 High strains of praise are swelling
From angel hosts on high,
And one soft voice is telling
Glad tidings from the sky;
Tidings of free salvation,
Of peace on earth below;
Through every land and nation
The blessed Word shall go!

3 His children's songs shall name Him
In many a tongue to-day;
His Church shall yet proclaim Him
To people far away;
Till idols fall before Him,
Till strife and wrong shall cease,
Till all the earth adore Him,
The eternal Prince of Peace!

134   COME TO THE MANGER.   *Samuel Smith.*

1. Come to the man-ger in Beth-le-hem, A sweet Child lies there-in,....
A Ho-ly Child come down to earth To save the world from sin;
A lit-tle Child with a Heart so large, It takes the whole world in!....

2 But the heart of the world is far too small
To take in that little Child:
It sends Him away; there is no room
For His face so sweet and mild;
They would turn Him out, if they could,
To the storm so rude and wild.

3 Come to the manger in Bethlehem,
Never mind the frost and snow,
We will think of the Child, and the
thought of Him
Shall warm us as we go;
We will kiss His holy hands and feet,
And tell Him we love Him so!

4 And the more the cold world turns Him out,
The more we will take Him in;
When our hearts are full of the holy Child
They will have no room for sin;
Come to the manger of Bethlehem,
For a sweet Child lies therein!

135 MERRY CHRISTMAS.

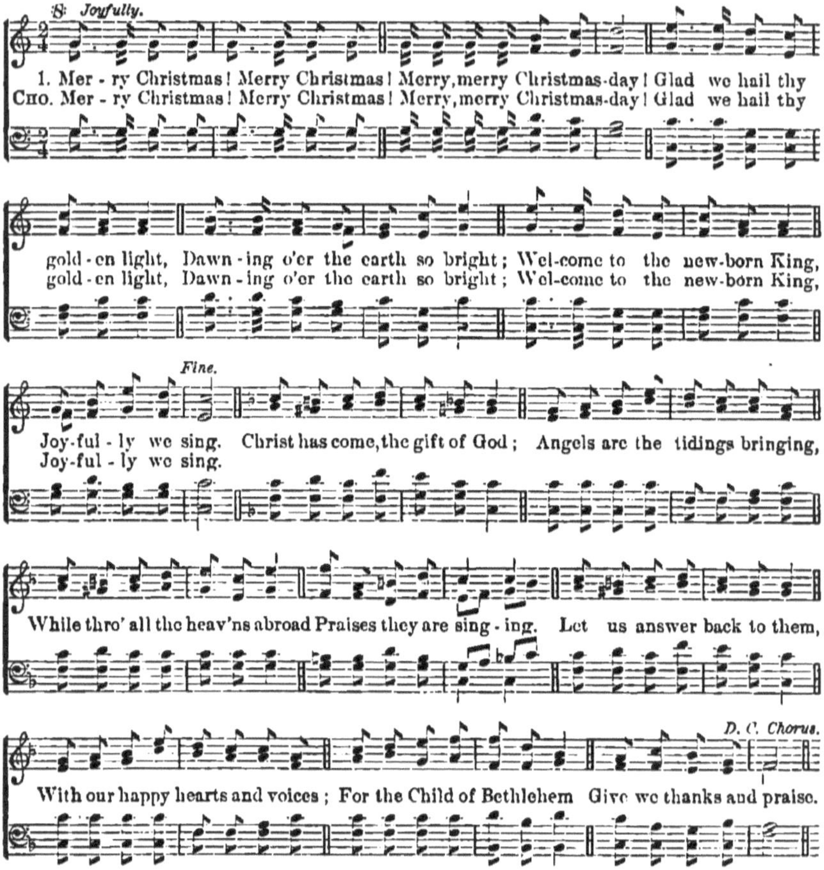
Joyfully.
1. Mer - ry Christmas! Merry Christmas! Merry, merry Christmas-day! Glad we hail thy
Cho. Mer - ry Christmas! Merry Christmas! Merry, merry Christmas-day! Glad we hail thy
gold - en light, Dawn - ing o'er the earth so bright; Wel-come to the new-born King,
gold - en light, Dawn - ing o'er the earth so bright; Wel-come to the new-born King,
Fine.
Joy-ful - ly we sing. Christ has come, the gift of God; Angels are the tidings bringing,
Joy-ful - ly we sing.
While thro' all the heav'ns abroad Praises they are sing - ing. Let us answer back to them,
D. C. Chorus.
With our happy hearts and voices; For the Child of Bethlehem Give we thanks and praise.

2 Merry Christmas! Merry Christmas!
Merry, merry Christmas-day!
Happy greetings, cheerful mirth,
Well may sound through all the earth,
For to-day the joy of heaven
Unto us is given.
Christ has come to put to flight
All the gloom of sin and sorrow,
Come to lead us out of night
To a fairer morrow.
Gladly let us follow Him,
Love Him, trust Him, serve Him ever,
Till He, from earth's twilight dim,
Leads to perfect day.—*Chorus.*

CHRIST'S CHILDHOOD.

136   THE CHILD JESUS.   *Henry J. Gauntlett.* 1856.

1. Once in royal David's city
Stood a lowly cattle-shed,
Where a mother laid her Baby
In a manger for His bed:
Mary was that mother mild,
Jesus Christ that little Child.

2 He came down to earth from heaven
  Who is God and Lord of all,
And His shelter was a stable,
  And His cradle was a stall;
With the poor, and mean, and lowly,
Lived on earth our Saviour holy.

3 And, thro' all His wondrous childhood,
  He would honor and obey,
Love and watch the lowly maiden
  In whose gentle arms He lay;
Christian children all must be
Mild, obedient, good as He.

4 For He is our childhood's Pattern,
  Day by day like us He grew,
He was little, weak and helpless,
  Tears and smiles like us He knew;
And He feeleth for our sadness,
And He shareth in our gladness.

5 And our eyes at last shall see Him,
  Through His own redeeming love,
For that Child so dear and gentle
  Is our Lord in heaven above;
And He leads His children on
To the place where He is gone.

6 Not in that poor lowly stable,
  With the oxen standing by,
We shall see Him; but in heaven,
  Set at God's right hand on high;
When like stars His children crowned
All in white shall wait around.
      Cecil Frances Alexander. 1848.

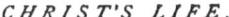

CHRIST'S LIFE.

ship where lies The Master of ocean, and earth, and skies; They all shall sweetly obey Thy will, Peace, be still! Peace, be still! They all shall sweetly obey Thy will, Peace, peace, be still!

2 Master, with anguish of spirit
   I bow in my grief to-day;
The depths of my sad heart are troubled,
   O waken, and save, I pray!
Torrents of sin and of anguish
   Sweep o'er my sinking soul;
And I perish! I perish! dear Master,
   O hasten, and take control.

3 Master, the terror is over,
   The elements sweetly rest:
Earth's sun in the calm lake is mirrored,
   And heaven's within my breast.
Linger, O blessed Redeemer,
   Leave me alone no more!
And with joy I shall make the blest harbor,
   And rest on the blissful shore.
M. A. Baker.

138   ST. AELRED.   8s & 3s. *John B. Dykes.*

1. Fierce raged the tempest o'er the deep, Watch did Thine anxious servants keep, But Thou wast wrapped in guileless sleep, Calm and still.

2 "Save, Lord, we perish," was their cry,
   "O save us in our agony!"
Thy word above the storm rose high,
   "Peace, be still."

3 The wild winds hushed; the angry deep
Sank, like a little child, to sleep;
The sullen billows cease to leap,
   At Thy will.

4 So, when our life is clouded o'er,
And storm-winds drift us from the shore,
Say, lest we sink to rise no more,
   "Peace, be still."
Godfrey Thring. 1858.

CHRIST'S LIFE.

139 CHILDREN'S HOSANNA. 7s & 6s. D.

1. When His salvation bringing, To Zion Jesus came, The children all stood singing Hosanna to His Name. Nor did their zeal offend Him, But as He rode along, He let them still attend Him, And smiled to hear their song.

Cho. Fling out, fling out the banner Of Christ, our heavenly King; Ring out, ring out Hosanna, And Hallelujah sing.

2 And since the Lord retaineth
  His love to children still,
Though now as King He reigneth
  On Zion's heavenly hill;
We'll flock around His banner,
  We'll bow before His throne,
And cry aloud, Hosanna
  To David's royal Son.—*Chorus.*

3 For should we fail proclaiming
  Our great Redeemer's praise,
The stones our silence shaming,
  Would their hosannas raise.
But shall we only render
  The tribute of our words?
No; while our hearts are tender,
  They too shall be the Lord's.—*Cho.*

Joshua King. 1819.

140 THE NINETY-AND-NINE. *Arr. from F. W. Cowen.*

1. There were ninety-and-nine that safely lay In the shelter of the fold;
But one was out on the hills away, Far off from the gates of gold.

CHRIST'S LIFE.

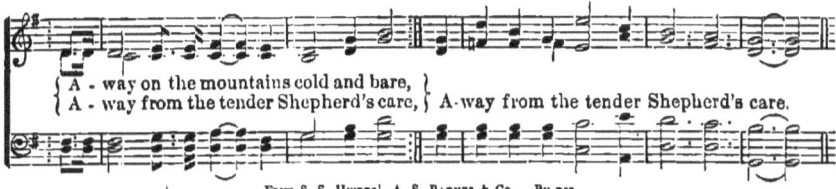

A-way on the mountains cold and bare,
A-way from the tender Shepherd's care, A-way from the tender Shepherd's care.

From S. S. Hymnal, A. S. Barnes & Co.   By per.

2 Lord, Thou hast here Thy ninety-and-
  Are they not enough for Thee? [nine,
But the Shepherd answered: "One of
  Has wandered away from me. [mine
And tho' the way be rough and steep,
I go to the desert to find my sheep."

3 But none of the ransomed ever knew
  How deep were the waters crossed;
Nor how dark the night which the Lord
  went thro',

Ere He found the sheep that was lost.
Out in the desert He heard its cry,
'Twas sick, and helpless, and ready to die.

4 But all thro' the mountains thunder-riven,
  And up from the rocky steep,
There rose a cry to the gate of heaven;
  "Rejoice! I have found my sheep!"
And the angel echoed around the throne,
  "Rejoice! for the Lord brings back His
      own!"   *Elizabeth C. Clephane.*

141   ST. THEODULPH.   7s & 6s.   *Melchior Teschner.* 1613.
S: *Joyous.*   *Fine.* *The 2d and following verses.*

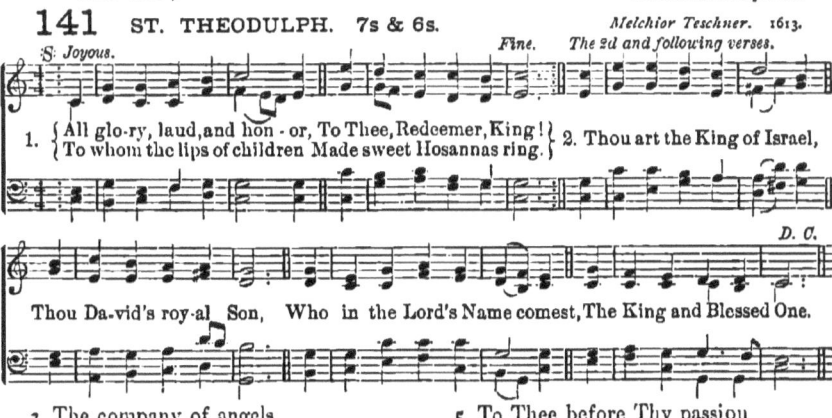

1. All glo-ry, laud, and hon-or, To Thee, Redeemer, King!
   To whom the lips of children Made sweet Hosannas ring. 2. Thou art the King of Israel,

Thou Da-vid's roy-al Son, Who in the Lord's Name comest, The King and Blessed One.

3 The company of angels
    Are praising Thee on high;
  And mortal men and all things
    Created, make reply.
        All glory, etc.

4 The people of the Hebrews
    With palms before Thee went:
  Our praise and prayer and anthems
    Before Thee we present.
        All glory, etc.

5 To Thee before Thy passion
    They sang their hymns of praise:
  To Thee, now high exalted
    Our melody we raise.
        All glory, etc.

6 Thou didst accept their praises;
    Accept the prayers we bring,
  Who in all good delightest,
    Thou good and gracious King.
        All glory, etc.
            Tr. John M. Neale.

CHRIST'S LIFE.

142 THE MASTER HAS COME.
Edwin Pond Parker.

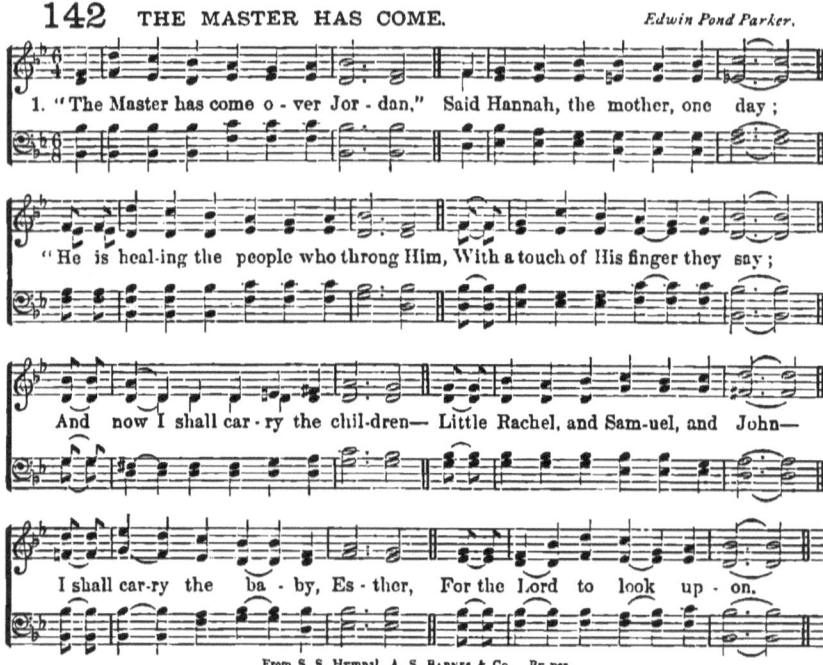

From S. S. Hymnal, A. S. Barnes & Co. By per.

2 "If He lay His hand on the children,
My heart will be lighter, I know;
For a blessing forever and ever
Will follow them as they go."
"Now, why should'st thou hinder the Master,"
Said Peter, "with children like these?
Seest not how from morning till evening
He toucheth and healeth disease?"

3 Then Christ said, "Forbid not the children,
Permit them to come unto me."
And He took in His arms little Esther,
And Rachel He set on His knee.
And the heavy heart of the mother
Was lifted all earth-care above,
As He laid His hands on the brothers,
And blest them with tenderest love.
Julia Gill.

143 COME TO ME FOR REST.
J. E. Rankin. 1883.

CHRIST'S LIFE.

Come to me for rest! Take my yoke up-on you now, Take my seal up-on your brow; Here re-cord your hum-ble vow; Come to me for rest!

2 Ah! how many voices say,
   Come to me for rest!
In a treach'rous, winning way:
   Come to me for rest!
Rest, they have not to bestow:
Rest, man's soul can never know,
Till he hear Christ's accents low:
   Come to me for rest!

3 Yes, poor, weary, laden one,
   Come to me for rest!
Love's atoning work is done,
   Come to me for rest!
'Tis the word of Christ to thee,
He thy Saviour waits to be:
Word death-sealed on Calvary,
   Come to me for rest!
            J. E. Rankin. 1883.

144   EVER WOULD I FAIN BE READING.   8s & 7s.   *I. A. P. Schulz.*

1. Ev-er would I fain be read-ing, In the an-cient Ho-ly Book, Of my Sav-iour's gen-tle plead-ing, Truth in ev-ery word and look

2 How when children came, He blessed them,
   Suffered no man to reprove,
Took them in His arms, and pressed them
   To His heart with words of love.

3 How to all the sick and tearful
   Help was ever gladly shown;
How He sought the poor and fearful,
   Called them brothers and His own.

4 How no contrite soul e'er sought Him
   And was bidden to depart;
How with gentle words He taught him,
   Took the death from out his heart.

5 Let me kneel, my Lord, before Thee,
   Let my heart in tears o'erflow,
Melted by Thy love, adore Thee,
   Blest in Thee, 'mid joy or woe.
    Louise Hensel. 1829.   Tr. *Catherine Winkworth.* 1858.

145 HOSANNA WE SING.

2 Hosanna we sing, for He bends His ear,
And rejoices the hymns of His own to hear;
We know that His heart will never wax cold
To the lambs that He feeds in His earthly fold.
Alleluia we sing in the Church we love,
Alleluia resounds in the Church above;
To Thy little ones, Lord, may such grace be given,
That we lose not our part in the song of heaven. *George S. Hodges.*

CHRIST'S LIFE.

146 RIDE ON, RIDE ON IN MAJESTY.
John B. Dykes.

1. Ride on! ride on in majesty! Hark! all the tribes Ho-san-na cry!
Thine humble beast pur-sues his road, With palms and scattered garments strowed.

2 Ride on! ride on in majesty!
In lowly pomp ride on to die:
O Christ, Thy triumphs now begin
O'er captive death and conquered sin.

3 Ride on! ride on in majesty!
The angel armies of the sky
Look down with sad and wondering eyes
To see the approaching sacrifice.

4 Ride on! ride on in majesty!
The last and fiercest strife is nigh:
The Father on His sapphire throne
Awaits His own anointed Son.

5 Ride on! ride on in majesty!
In lowly pomp ride on to die:
Bow Thy meek head to mortal pain;
Then take, O God, Thy power and reign.
Henry Hart Milman. 1827.

147 WILLIAMS. L. M.
Arr. from "Templi Carmina."

1. When I sur-vey the wondrous cross On which the Prince of glo-ry died,
My rich-est gain I count but loss, And pour contempt on all my pride.

2 Forbid it, Lord, that I should boast
Save in the death of Christ, my God;
All the vain things that charm me most,
I sacrifice them to His blood.

3 See, from His head, His hands, His feet,
Sorrow and love flow mingled down;
Did e'er such love and sorrow meet,
Or thorns compose so rich a crown?

4 His dying crimson, like a robe,
Spreads o'er His body on the tree;
Then I am dead to all the globe,
And all the globe is dead to me.

5 Were the whole realm of nature mine,
That were a present far too small;
Love so amazing, so divine,
Demands my soul, my life, my all.
Isaac Watts. 1709.

CHRIST'S SUFFERINGS AND DEATH.

148 LAMBETH. C. M. *English.*

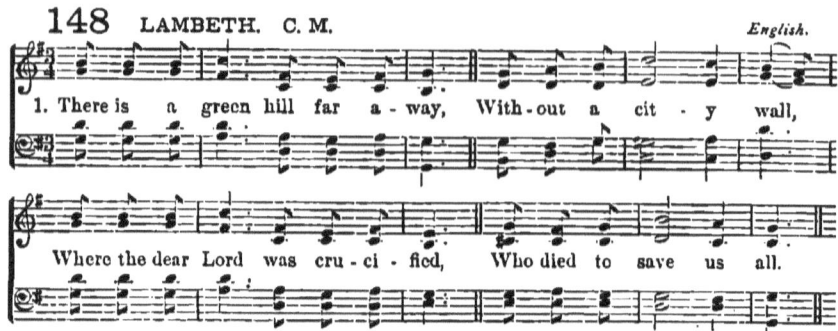

1. There is a green hill far away, With-out a cit-y wall, Where the dear Lord was cru-ci-fied, Who died to save us all.

2 We may not know, we cannot tell,
  What pains He had to bear,
  But we believe it was for us
  He hung and suffered there.

3 He died that we might be forgiven,
  He died to make us good,
  That we might go at last to heaven,
  Saved by His precious blood.

4 There was no other good enough
  To pay the price of sin,
  He only could unlock the gate
  Of heaven, and let us in.

5 O dearly, dearly has He loved,
  And we must love Him too,
  And trust in His redeeming blood,
  And try His works to do.
  Cecil Frances Alexander. 1848.

149 AVON. C. M. *Hugh Wilson. 1768.*

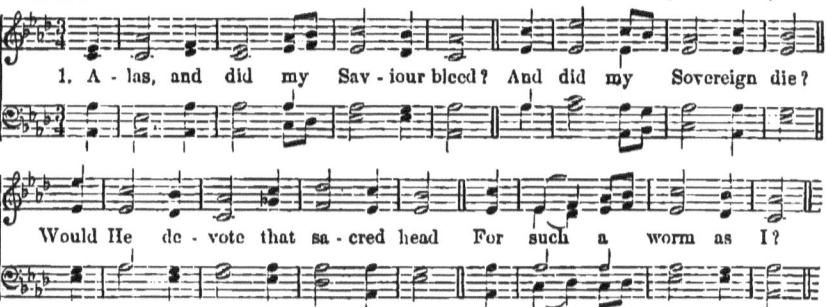

1. A-las, and did my Sav-iour bleed? And did my Sovereign die? Would He de-vote that sa-cred head For such a worm as I?

2 Was it for crimes that I had done
  He groaned upon the tree?
  Amazing pity! grace unknown
  And love beyond degree!

3 Well might the sun in darkness hide,
  And shut his glories in,
  When Christ, the mighty Maker, died
  For man the creature's sin.

4 Thus might I hide my blushing face,
  While His dear cross appears,
  Dissolve my heart in thankfulness,
  And melt mine eyes in tears.

5 But drops of grief can ne'er repay
  The debt of love I owe:
  Here, Lord, I give myself away;
  'Tis all that I can do.
  Isaac Watts. 1709.

CHRIST'S BURIAL.

150 FOUNTAIN. C. M. *Western Air.*

1. There is a fountain fill'd with blood, Drawn from Immanuel's veins; And sinners, plunged beneath that flood, Lose all their guilty stains, Lose all their guilty stains, Lose all their guilty stains.

2 The dying thief rejoiced to see
That fountain in his day;
And there may I, though vile as he,
Wash all my sins away.

3 Dear dying Lamb, Thy precious blood
Shall never lose its power,
Till all the ransomed church of God
Be saved, to sin no more.

4 E'er since, by faith, I saw the stream
Thy flowing wounds supply,
Redeeming love has been my theme,
And shall be, till I die.

5 Then in a nobler, sweeter song,
I'll sing Thy power to save,
When this poor lisping, stammering tongue
Lies silent in the grave.

William Cowper. 1779.

151. REDHEAD. 7s. 6 lines. *Richard Redhead.* 1853.

1. Resting from His work to-day, In the tomb the Saviour lay; Still He slept, from head to feet Shrouded in the winding sheet, Lying in the rock alone, Hidden by the sealed stone.

2 Late at even there was seen
Watching long the Magdalene;
Early, ere the break of day,
Sorrowful she took her way
To the holy garden glade,
Where her buried Lord was laid.

3 So with Thee, till life shall end,
I would solemn vigil spend;
Let me hew Thee, Lord, a shrine
In this rocky heart of mine,
Where in pure embalmèd cell
None but Thee can ever dwell.

4 Myrrh and spices will I bring,
True affection's offering;
Close the door from sight and sound
Of the busy world around;
And in patient watch remain
Till my Lord appear again.

Thomas Whytehead. 1842.

EASTER.

152. EASTER-MORNING.

Wm. F. Sherwin. 1877.

1. Incense from dews of the morning, Caroling voices of birds,
Singing of winds and of waters— (Forest-born songs without words)—
Rise with our hearts' adoration, Join in our morning oblation,
Gather as streams to the sea, O Father of spirits— to Thee!

From "Chatauqua Songs." By permission.

2 Light of the world, Thou hast scattered
   Night from our spirits away;
 Over the pathway before us
   Arches the infinite day;
 Out of the darkness and prison,
   Christ the Redeemer has risen;
 Darkness and dawning are past;
   Lo! Easter is shining at last!

Mary A. Lathbury.

EASTER.

153   CHRIST IS RISEN!   *Arthur S. Sullivan.* 1873.

2 Lo, the chains of death are broken!
   Earth below, and heaven above
Joy anew in every token
   Of Thy triumph, Lord of love!
He o'er heaven and earth shall reign,
   At His Father's side,
Till He cometh once again,
   Bridegroom to His Bride.
      Christ is risen, etc.

3 Angel legions downward thronging,
   Hail the Lord of earth and skies!
Ye who watch'd with holy longing
   Till your sun again should rise:
He is risen! Earth, rejoice!
   Sing, ye starry train!
All things living, find a voice!
   Jesus lives again!
      Christ is risen, etc.
                 Archer T. Gurney. 1862.

EASTER.

154. WELCOME, HAPPY MORNING.

J. Baptiste Calkin.

2 Earth with joy confesses, clothing her for spring,
All good gifts returned with her returning King.
Bloom in every meadow, leaves on every bough,
Speak His sorrows ended, hail His triumph now.—*Refrain.*

3 Maker and Redeemer, Life and Health of all,
Thou from heav'n beholding human nature's fall,
Of the Father's Godhead, True and Only Son,
Manhood to deliver, manhood didst put on.—*Refrain.*

EASTER.

4 Thou, of Life the Author, death didst undergo,
Tread the path of darkness, saving strength to show;
Come then, True and Faithful, now fulfill Thy word,
'Tis Thine own Third Morning, rise, my buried Lord!—*Refrain.*

5 Loose the souls long-prisoned, bound with Satan's chain;
All that now is fallen raise to life again;
Shew Thy face in brightness, bid the nations see,
Bring again our daylight; day returns with Thee!—*Refrain.*

V. Fortunatus. 590. Tr. by *John Ellerton.* 1868.

155 TRIUMPH. 7s & 6s. *Arthur S. Sullivan.*

1. Come, ye faithful, raise the strain Of triumphant gladness; God hath brought His Israel Into joy from sadness; Loosed from Pharaoh's bitter yoke Jacob's sons and daughters; Led them with unmoistened foot Thro' the Red Sea waters.

2 'Tis the spring of souls to-day:
Christ hath burst His prison,
And from three days' sleep in death,
As the sun, hath risen:
All the winter of our sins,
Long and dark, is flying
From His Light, to whom we give
Laud and praise undying.

3 Now the Queen of seasons, bright
With the Day of splendor,
With the royal Feast of Feasts,
Comes its joy to render;
Comes to glad Jerusalem,
Which with true affection
Welcomes in unwearied strains
Jesus' resurrection.

4 Neither might the gates of death,
Nor the tomb's dark portal,
Nor the watchers, nor the seal,
Hold Thee as a mortal:
But to-day amidst the Twelve
Thou didst stand, bestowing
Thine own peace, which evermore
Passeth human knowing.

John of Damascus. 780. Tr. *John M. Neale.* 1862.

EASTER.

156 THE MORNING PURPLES ALL THE SKY.

1. The morning purples all the sky, The air with praises rings; Defeated hell stands sullen by, The world exulting sings: While He, the King, all strong to save, Rends the dark doors away, And thro' the breaches of the grave Strides forth into the day.

Chorus.
ff Glory to God! our glad lips cry, All glory be to God most High! Glory to God! our glad lips cry, All glory be to God, to.... God most High!....
God most High!

2 Death's captive, in his gloomy prison
   Fast fettered He has lain;
But He has mastered death, is risen,
   And death wears now the chain.
The shining angels cry, "Away
   With grief; no spices bring;
Not tears, but songs, this joyful day,
   Should greet the rising King!"
Glory to God! our glad lips cry;
   All glory be to God most High!

Ambrose of Milan. (340-397). *Tr. Alexander Ramsay Thompson.* 1869.

EASTER.

157. ANGELS AT THE TOMB.

1. The angels sat in the garden-tomb On Easter morning fair;
Their radiant smiles dispelled the gloom, [OMIT..........]
And lit up the darksome air; And they said to those, who with sadden'd mind, Had come their crucified Lord to find:

Chorus. "He is ris-en! He is ris-en! Why seek the living among the dead?"....

Allegro. Then banish your sorrow and sadness, And lift up your voices in gladness, For the night of your fear has fled! For the night of your fear has fled!

2 "Come, see the place where the dear Lord lay;"
'Tis vacant now this morn;
And angels come on the Easter-day,
As they did when Christ was born;
And their voices sound in glad refrain,
And they bring glad tidings to earth again.
    Cho.—"He is risen," etc.

3 To-day the angels are standing still
Beside the open graves,
The darksome gloom with their light they fill,
As they speak of the Lord who saves;
Christ conquered Death in that bitter strife,
He will bring us into eternal life.
    Cho.—"He is risen," etc.

(105)

EASTER.

158 ST. ALBINUS. 7s, 8s & 4s. *Henry J. Gauntlett.* 1872.

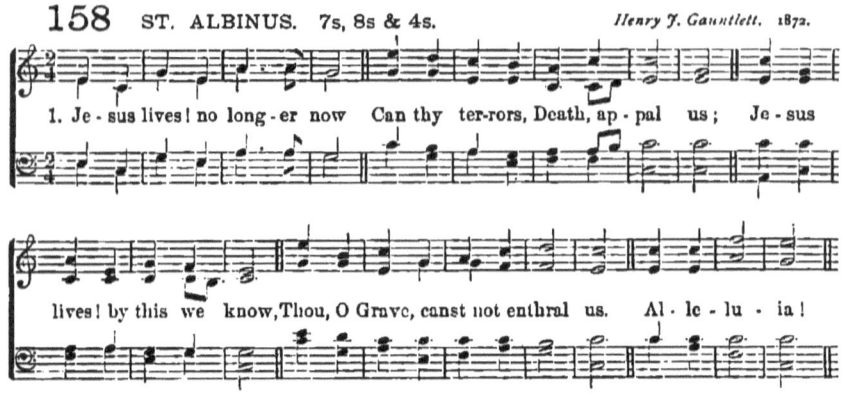

1. Je-sus lives! no long-er now Can thy ter-rors, Death, ap-pal us; Je-sus lives! by this we know, Thou, O Grave, canst not enthral us. Al-le-lu-ia!

2 Jesus lives! henceforth is death
But the gate of life immortal;
This shall calm our trembling breath,
When we pass its gloomy portal.
Alleluia!

3 Jesus lives! for us He died;
Then, alone to Jesus living,
Pure in heart may we abide,
Glory to our Saviour giving.
Alleluia!

4 Jesus lives! our hearts know well
Nought from us His love shall sever;
Life, nor death, nor powers of hell
Tear us from His keeping ever.
Alleluia!

5 Jesus lives! to Him the throne
Over all the world is given;
May we go where He has gone,
Rest and reign with Him in heaven.
Alleluia!

Christian F. Gellert. 1757. Tr. *Frances E. Cox.* 1841. *Alt.*

159 HAIL THE DAY THAT SEES HIM RISE. *Wm. H. Monk.*

1. Hail the day that sees Him rise, Hal-le-lu-jah! To His throne a-bove the skies; Hal-le-lu-jah! Christ, the Lamb for sin-ners given,

CHRIST'S ASCENSION.

Hal - le - lu - jah! En - ters now the brightest heav'n. Hal - le - lu - jah!

2 There for Him high triumph waits; Hallelujah!
Lift your heads, eternal gates! Hallelujah!
He hath conquered death and sin, Hallelujah!
Take the King of Glory in. Hallelujah!

3 Lo, the heaven its Lord receives! Hallelujah!
Yet He loves the earth He leaves; Hallelujah!
Though returning to His throne, Hallelujah!
Still He calls mankind His own. Hallelujah!

4 Still for us He intercedes, Hallelujah!
His prevailing death He pleads; Hallelujah!
Near Himself prepares our place, Hallelujah!
He, the first-fruits of our race. Hallelujah!

5 Lord, though parted from our sight Hallelujah!
Far above the starry height, Hallelujah!
Grant our hearts may thither rise, Hallelujah!
Seeking Thee above the skies. Hallelujah!
Charles Wesley. 1739.

160 ASCENSION HYMN. *Edwin Pond Parker.*

1. Golden harps are sounding, Angel voices ring; Pearly gates are open'd, Open'd for the King.
Cho. All His work is ended, Joy-ful-ly we sing: Je-sus hath as-cend-ed, Glo-ry to our King.

Christ, the King of glory, Je-sus, King of love, Is gone up in triumph To His throne above.

From "Sunday School Hymnal," A. S. Barnes & Co. By per.

2 He who came to save us,
He who bled and died,
Now is crowned with gladness
At His Father's side.
Never more to suffer,
Never more to die;
Jesus, King of glory,
Is gone up on high!—*Chorus.*

3 Praying for His children
In that blessed place,
Calling them to glory,
Sending them His grace;
His bright home preparing,
Little ones, for you;
Jesus ever liveth,
Ever loveth, too.—*Chorus.*
Frances Ridley Havergal.

THE CHURCH.

161 BAVARIA. 8s & 7s. D. *German Melody.*

1. Je - sus spreads His ban - ner o'er us,
   Cheers our fam-ished souls with food,
   He the ban - quet spreads be-fore us,
   Of His mys - tic flesh and blood;
   D. C. May we taste it, kind - ly giv - en
   In re - mem-brance, Lord, of Thee.

Pre-cious ban-quet, bread of heav - en,
Wine of glad - ness, flow - ing free;

2 In Thy holy incarnation,
 When the angels sang Thy birth;
 In Thy fasting and temptation;
 In Thy labors on the earth;
 In Thy trial and rejection;
 In Thy sufferings on the tree;
 In Thy glorious resurrection;
 May we, Lord, remember Thee.
 Roswell Park. 1835.

162 MIDDLETON. 8s & 7s. D. *English Air.*

1. Hail! Thou God of grace and glo - ry!
   Who Thy name hast mag - ni - fied,
   By re-demp-tion's wondrous sto - ry,
   By the Sav - iour cru - ci - fied;
   D. C. Thanks for pre-sent good un-ceas - ing,
   And for hopes of bliss a - bove.

Thanks to Thee for ev - ery bless - ing,
Flow - ing from the Fount of love.

2 Hear us, as thus bending lowly,
 Near Thy bright and burning throne;
 We invoke Thee, God most holy!
 Through Thy well-belovéd Son;
 Send the baptism of Thy Spirit,
 Shed the pentecostal fire;
 Let us all Thy grace inherit,
 Waken, crown each good desire.

3 Bind Thy people, Lord, in union,
 With the sevenfold cord of love;
 Breathe a spirit of communion
 With the glorious hosts above;
 Let Thy work be seen progressing;
 Bow each heart, and bend each knee;
 Till the world Thy truth possessing,
 Celebrates its jubilee.
 Thomas W. Aveling. 1844.

THE CHURCH.

163 ECCLESIA. 8s & 7s. D.

1. Glo-rious things of thee are spo-ken, Zi - on, cit - y of our God!
He, whose word can-not be bro-ken, Formed thee for His own a-bode.
On the Rock of A - ges found-ed, What can shake thy sure re - pose?
With sal - va - tion's walls sur-rounded, Thou may'st smile at all thy foes.

2 See! the streams of living waters,
　Springing from eternal love,
Well supply thy sons and daughters,
　And all fear of want remove:
Who can faint, while such a river
　Ever flows their thirst t' assuage?—
Grace which, like the Lord, the giver,
　Never fails from age to age.

3 Round each habitation hovering,
　See the cloud and fire appear,
For a glory and a covering,
　Showing that the Lord is near!
Thus deriving from their banner,
　Light by night, and shade by day,
Safe they feed upon the manna
　Which He gives them when they pray.
　　　　　　John Newton. 1779.

THE CHURCH.

164 GLADSTONE. L. M. *W. H. Gladstone.*

1. Jesus shall reign where'er the sun Does his successive journeys run; His kingdom stretch from shore to shore, Till moons shall wax and wane no more.

2 For Him shall endless prayer be made,
And endless praises crown His head;
His name, like sweet perfume, shall rise
With every morning-sacrifice.

3 People and realms of every tongue
Dwell on His love with sweetest song;
And infant voices shall proclaim
Their early blessings on His name.

4 Blessings abound where'er He reigns;
The prisoner leaps to loose his chains;
The weary find eternal rest,
And all the sons of want are blest.

5 Let every creature rise and bring
Peculiar honors to our King;
Angels descend with songs again,
And earth repeat the loud Amen!

Isaac Watts. 1719.

165 AURELIA. 7s & 6s. D. *Samuel Sebastian Wesley.* 1868.

1. The Church's one foundation Is Jesus Christ her Lord; She is His new creation By water and the word: From heaven He came and sought her, To be His holy bride; With His own blood He bought her, And for her life He died.

(110)

THE CHURCH.

2 Elect from every nation,
Yet one o'er all the earth,
Her charter of salvation
One Lord, one faith, one birth;
One holy name she blesses,
Partakes one holy food,
And to one hope she presses,
With every grace endued.

3 'Mid toil and tribulation
And tumult of her war,
She waits the consummation
Of peace for evermore;

Till with the vision glorious
Her longing eyes are blest,
And the great church victorious
Shall be the church at rest.

4 The saints their watch are keeping,
Their cry goes up, "How long?"
And soon the night of weeping
Shall be the morn of song.
O happy ones and holy!
Lord, give us grace, that we,
Like them, the meek and lowly,
On high may dwell with Thee.
Samuel J. Stone. 1866.

166 ST. THOMAS. S. M. *William Tansur.* 1768.

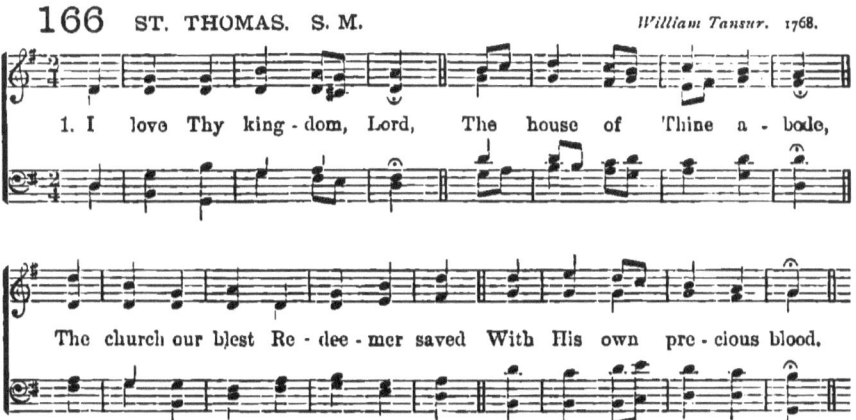

1. I love Thy kingdom, Lord, The house of Thine abode,
The church our blest Redeemer saved With His own precious blood.

2 I love Thy church, O God!
Her walls before Thee stand,
Dear as the apple of Thine eye,
And graven on Thy hand.

3 For her my tears shall fall,
For her my prayers ascend;
To her my cares and toils be given,
Till toils and cares shall end.

4 Beyond my highest joy
I prize her heavenly ways,
Her sweet communion, solemn vows,
Her hymns of love and praise.

5 Jesus, Thou Friend divine,
Our Saviour and our King!
Thy hand from every snare and foe
Shall great deliverance bring.

6 Sure as Thy truth shall last,
To Zion shall be given
The brightest glories earth can yield,
And brighter bliss of heaven.
Timothy Dwight. 1800.

THE CHRISTIAN LIFE.

167 CRUCIFIX. 7s & 6s. *Greek Melody.*

1. We stand in deep repentance, Before Thy throne of love;
   O God of grace, forgive us; The stain of guilt remove; Behold us while with weeping We lift our eyes to Thee; And all our sins sub-du-ing, Our Fa-ther, set us free.

2 O shouldst Thou from us fallen
    Withhold thy grace to guide,
    Forever we should wander
    From Thee, and peace, aside;
    But Thou to spirits contrite
    Dost light and life impart,
    That man may learn to serve Thee
    With thankful, joyous heart.

3 Our souls—on Thee we cast them,
    Our only refuge Thou!
    Thy cheering words revive us,
    When pressed with grief we bow;
    Thou bear'st the trusting spirit
    Upon Thy loving breast,
    And givest all Thy ransomed
    A sweet, unending rest.
    Ray Palmer.

168 HEAVENLY GUEST. 8s & 5s.

1. In the si-lent midnight watches, List—thy bosom door! How it knocketh, knocketh, knock-eth, Knock-eth ev-er-more! Say not 'tis thy pulse is beat-ing: 'Tis thy heart of sin! 'Tis thy Saviour knocks and crieth Rise, and let me in!

INVITATIONS.

2 Death comes down, with reckless footstep,
  To the hall and hut:
Think you Death will stand a-knocking
  Where the door is shut?
Jesus waiteth, waiteth, waiteth;
  But the door is fast!
Grieved, away the Saviour goeth;
  Death breaks in at last!

3 Then 'tis Thine to stand entreating
  Christ to let thee in;
At the gate of heaven beating,
  Wailing for thy sin.
Nay, alas, thou foolish virgin,
  Hast thou then forgot?
Jesus waited long to know thee,
  But He knows thee not!
        Arthur Cleveland Coxe. 1840.

169 COME UNTO ME, YE WEARY. *John B. Dykes.* 1874.

2 "Come unto me, ye fainting,
    And I will give you light."
  O loving voice of Jesus,
    Which comes to cheer the night;
  Our hearts were filled with sadness,
    And we had lost our way;
  But He has brought us gladness
    And songs at break of day.

3 "Come unto me, ye weary,
    And I will give you life."
  O cheering voice of Jesus,
    Which comes to aid our strife;
  The foe is stern and eager,
    The fight is fierce and long;
  But He has made us mighty,
    And stronger than the strong.

4 "And whosoever cometh,
    I will not cast him out."
  O welcome voice of Jesus,
    Which drives away our doubt;
  Which calls us very sinners,
    Unworthy though we be
  Of love so free and boundless,
    To come, dear Lord, to Thee.
          W. C. Dix. 1867.

THE CHRISTIAN LIFE.

170. COME UNTO ME, AND REST.

1. Come ye, come ye! Hear the Saviour sweetly calling, Come ye, come ye! Come unto me, and rest. Ye by sorrow burdened, ye by sin oppressed, Come and find a refuge here upon my breast; I can give you pardon, I can give you peace, Banish all your darkness, bid your trouble cease.

2 Turn ye! turn ye!
I will give you Life eternal;
Turn ye! turn ye!
Turn unto me to-day.
Tho' you long have wandered in the sinful way,
Tho' the powers of evil wait your soul to slay,
I can give deliverance; here for rescue flee;
Take my yoke upon you, meekly learn of me.
Cho.—Come ye, etc.

3 Haste ye! haste ye!
For your life is swiftly fleeting;
Haste ye! haste ye!
Be my disciple true.
Now I gladly open heaven's gates to you,
Press within the portals, heavenly life pursue;
Onward go with singing, with the goal in sight,
For my yoke is easy, and my burden light.
Cho.—Come ye, etc.

INVITATIONS.

171. LANGRAN. 10s.
James Langran.

1. Wea-ry of earth, and lad-en with my sin, I look at heav'n and long to en-ter in. But there no e-vil thing may find a home; And yet I hear a voice that bids me "Come."

2 So vile I am, how dare I hope to stand
In the pure glory of that holy land?
Before the whiteness of that throne appear?
Yet there are hands stretched out to draw me near.

3 It is the voice of Jesus that I hear,
His are the hands stretched out to draw me near,
And His the blood that can for all atone,
And set me faultless there before the throne.

4 'Twas He who found me on the deathly wild,
And made me heir of heaven, the Father's child,
And day by day, whereby my soul may live,
Gives me His grace of pardon, and will give.

5 Yea, Thou wilt answer for me, righteous Lord:
Thine all the merits, mine the great reward;
Thine the sharp thorns, and mine the golden crown,
Mine the life won, and Thine the life laid down.
Samuel J. Stone. 1866.

172. SULLIVAN. 7s.
Arthur S. Sullivan.

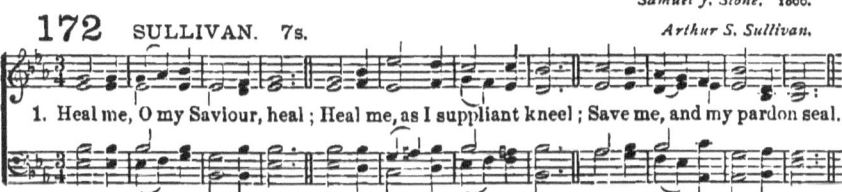

1. Heal me, O my Saviour, heal; Heal me, as I suppliant kneel; Save me, and my pardon seal.

2 Thou the true Physician art,
Thou canst cure the wounded heart,
Thou canst life and health impart.

3 Other comforters are gone:
Thou who didst for sin atone,
Thou canst save, and Thou alone.

4 Hear the prayer I oft have prayed;
Heal the wounds that sin hath made;
And in mercy send Thine aid!

5 Heal me, then, O Saviour, heal!
To Thy mercy I appeal;
Heal me, as I suppliant kneel.
Godfrey Thring. 1866.

173 INVITATION. C. M.
Arr. from Ludwig Spohr. (1784-1859).

1. I heard the voice of Jesus say, "Come unto me and rest; Lay down, thou weary one, lay down Thy head upon my breast." I came to Jesus as I was, Weary and worn and sad; I found in Him a resting-place, And He has made me glad.

2 I heard the voice of Jesus say,
    "Behold, I freely give
  The living water; thirsty one,
    Stoop down, and drink, and live."
  I came to Jesus, and I drank
    Of that life-giving stream :
  My thirst was quenched, my soul revived,
    And now I live in Him.

3 I heard the voice of Jesus say,
    " I am this dark world's light :
  Look unto me; thy morn shall rise,
    And all thy day be bright."
  I looked to Jesus and I found
    In Him my Star, my Sun ;
  And in that light of life I'll walk
    Till all my journey's done.
Horatius Bonar. 1857.

174 MAITLAND. C. M.
Aaron Chapin. 1820.

1. Must Jesus bear the cross alone, And all the world go free? No, there's a cross for every one, And there's a cross for me.

INVITATION AND ACCEPTANCE.

2 How happy are the saints above,
  Who once went sorrowing here!
  But now they taste unmingled love,
  And joy without a tear.

3 The consecrated cross I'll bear,
  Till death shall set me free;
  And then go home my crown to wear,
  For there's a crown for me.

4 Upon the crystal pavement, down
  At Jesus' piercèd feet,
  Joyful, I'll cast my golden crown,
  And His dear name repeat.

5 O precious cross! O glorious crown!
  O resurrection day!
  Ye angels, from the stars come down,
  And bear my soul away.
  G. N. Allen, vs. 1-3. 1849.

175 I AND MY BURDEN.
Edwin Pond Parker.

From S. S. Hymnal, A. S. Barnes & Co. By per.

2 I and my burden; I bore it
  In weakness and weariness long;
  It dimmed all the glory of sunlight,
  It hushed all the gladness of song;
  It hid all the lovelight around me,
  Shed thorns on my weary way;
  It checked all the strength of my striving,
  And banished the beauty of day.

3 I and my burden; I bring it
  In shame and sorrow to Thee;
  I know there is no other refuge,
  Nor succor, nor healing for me.
  I reach out the hands that are failing,
  I lift up my heart so sore;
  I bring Thee my burden, O Master,
  Thy pardon and peace I implore.

THE CHRISTIAN LIFE.

176 BLUMENTHAL. 7s. D. *J. Blumenthal.*

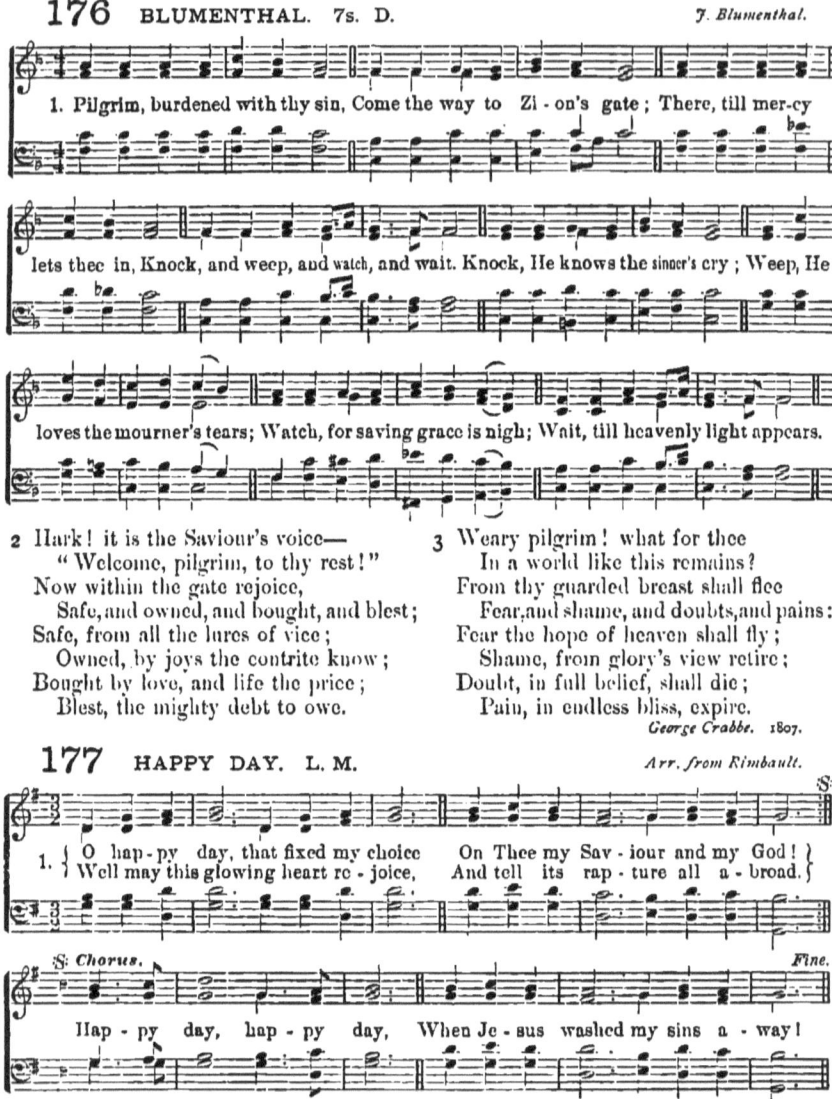

1. Pilgrim, burdened with thy sin, Come the way to Zion's gate; There, till mercy lets thee in, Knock, and weep, and watch, and wait. Knock, He knows the sinner's cry; Weep, He loves the mourner's tears; Watch, for saving grace is nigh; Wait, till heavenly light appears.

2 Hark! it is the Saviour's voice—
"Welcome, pilgrim, to thy rest!"
Now within the gate rejoice,
Safe, and owned, and bought, and blest;
Safe, from all the lures of vice;
Owned, by joys the contrite know;
Bought by love, and life the price;
Blest, the mighty debt to owe.

3 Weary pilgrim! what for thee
In a world like this remains?
From thy guarded breast shall flee
Fear, and shame, and doubts, and pains:
Fear the hope of heaven shall fly;
Shame, from glory's view retire;
Doubt, in full belief, shall die;
Pain, in endless bliss, expire.
George Crabbe. 1807.

177 HAPPY DAY. L. M. *Arr. from Rimbault.*

1. { O happy day, that fixed my choice   On Thee my Saviour and my God! }
   { Well may this glowing heart rejoice, And tell its rapture all abroad. }

Chorus.

Happy day, happy day, When Jesus washed my sins away!

INVITATION AND ACCEPTANCE.

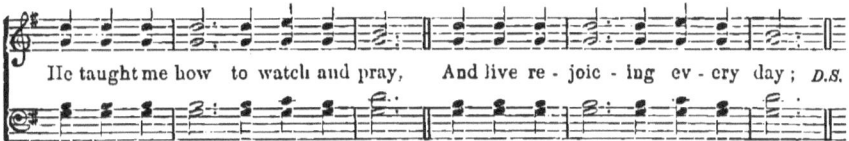

2 O happy bond, that seals my vows
   To Him who merits all my love!
   Let cheerful anthems fill His house,
   While to that sacred shrine I move.
   Cho.—Happy day, etc.

3 'Tis done, the great transaction's done:
   I am my Lord's, and He is mine:
   He drew me, and I followed on,
   Charmed to confess the voice divine.
   Cho.—Happy day, etc.
   Philip Doddridge.

178 "WHOSOEVER WILL." E. S. Lorenz.

2 Whosoever! 'Tis Jesus' word!
   Word that changeth never:
   Sinner lost, hast thou ever heard,
   Whoso, whosoever?—*Refrain.*

3 Whosoever on Christ believes!—
   With His blood He seals it;
   Free forgiveness he there receives:
   'Tis God's Word reveals it.—*Ref.*

4 Whosoever! O wondrous thought!
   Though so high above us;—
   That in spite of sin's crimson spot,
   He, the Lord, can love us.—*Ref.*
   J. E. Rankin.

179. WE COME TO THEE, DEAR SAVIOUR.

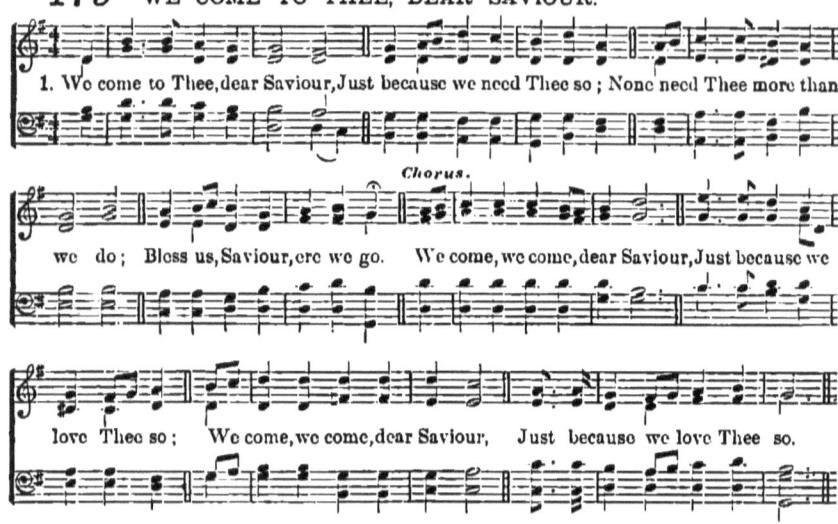

2 We come to Thee, dear Saviour,
  With our broken faith again;
  We know Thou wilt forgive us,
  Nor upbraid us, nor complain.—*Cho.*

3 We come to Thee, dear Saviour,
  For to whom, Lord, can we go;
  The words of life eternal
  From Thy lips forever flow.—*Cho.*

4 We come to Thee, dear Saviour,
  And Thou wilt not ask us why;
  We cannot live without Thee,
  And still less without Thee die.—*Cho.*

F. W. Faber.

180. O JESUS, I HAVE PROMISED. 7s & 6s.

J. W. Elliott.

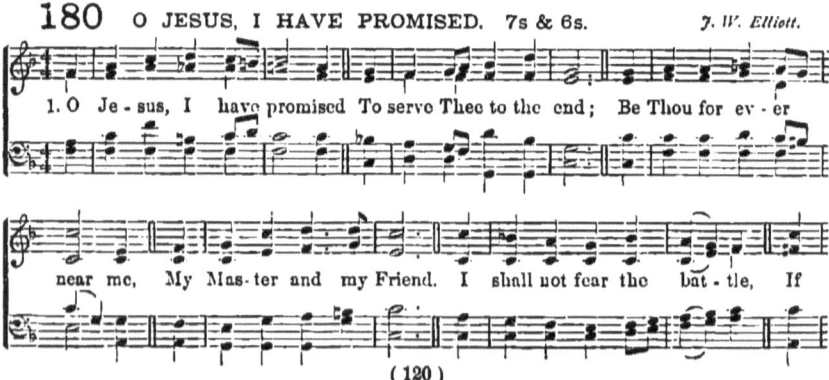

INVITATION AND ACCEPTANCE.

Thou art by my side; Nor wan-der from the pathway, If Thou wilt be my Guide.

2 O let me feel Thee near me,—
The world is ever near;
I see the sights that dazzle,
The tempting sounds I hear.
My foes are ever near me,
Around me and within;
But, Jesus, draw Thou nearer
And shield my soul from sin.

3 O Jesus, Thou hast promised
To all that follow Thee,
That where Thou art in glory
There shall Thy servant be;
And, Jesus, I have promised
To serve Thee to the end;
O, give me grace to follow
My Master and my Friend!
John Ernest Bode. 1860.

181 SOJOURNER'S SONG. 7s & 6s. *Arr. from F. Gumbert.*

1. O Je-sus, Thou art standing Out-side the fast closed door, In low-ly pa-tience wait-ing To pass the threshold o'er; Shame on us, guilt-y mor-tals, Who can His fa-vor share; O shame, thrice shame upon us, To keep Him standing there!

2 O Jesus, Thou art knocking:
And lo! that hand is scarred,
And thorns Thy brow encircle,
And tears Thy face have marred:
O love that passeth knowledge
So patiently to wait!
O sin that hath no equal
So fast to bar the gate!

3 O Jesus, Thou art pleading
In accents meek and low,
"I died for you, poor sinners,
And will ye treat me so?"
O Lord, with shame and sorrow
We open now the door:
Dear Saviour, enter, enter,
And leave us never more.
W. W. How. 1854.

THE CHRISTIAN LIFE.

182 PASCAL. 8s & 6s.   *George J. Elvey.*

1. Just as I am,—with-out one plea, But that Thy blood was shed for me, And that Thou bidd'st me come to Thee, O Lamb of God, I come, I come.

2 Just as I am, and waiting not
To rid my soul of one dark blot,
To Thee, whose blood can cleanse each
  O Lamb of God, I come.   [spot,

3 Just as I am,—though tossed about,
With many a conflict, many a doubt,
Fightings and fears, within, without,
  O Lamb of God, I come.

4 Just as I am,—poor, wretched, blind—
Sight, riches, healing of the mind,
Yea, all I need, in Thee to find,
  O Lamb of God, I come.

5 Just as I am,—Thou wilt receive,
Wilt welcome, pardon, cleanse, relieve;
Because Thy promise I believe,
  O Lamb of God, I come.

6 Just as I am,—Thy love unknown
Has broken every barrier down;
Now to be Thine, yea, Thine alone,
  O Lamb of God, I come.

Charlotte Elliott. 1836.

183 STEPHANOS. P. M.   *Henry W. Baker.* 1801.

1. Art thou weary, art thou languid, "Come to me," saith One,
Art thou sore distressed? "and coming, Be at rest!"

2 Hath He marks to lead me to Him,
  If He be my Guide?—
"In His feet and hands are wound-prints,
  And His side."

3 Is there diadem as Monarch,
  That His brow adorns?—
"Yea, a crown, in very surety;
  But of thorns."

4 If I find Him, if I follow,
  What His guerdon here?—
"Many a sorrow, many a labor,
  Many a tear."

5 If I still hold closely to Him,
  What hath He at last?—
"Sorrow vanquished, labor ended,
  Jordan passed."

6 If I ask Him to receive me,
  Will He say me nay?
"Not till earth, and not till heaven
  Pass away."

7 Finding, following, keeping, struggling,
  Is He sure to bless?—
"Saints, apostles, prophets, martyrs,
  Answer, Yes."

Stephen of St. Sabas. (725-794.)   *Tr., John M. Neale.* 1851.

CONSECRATION.

184 ONE THERE IS ABOVE ALL OTHERS. 8s & 7s.

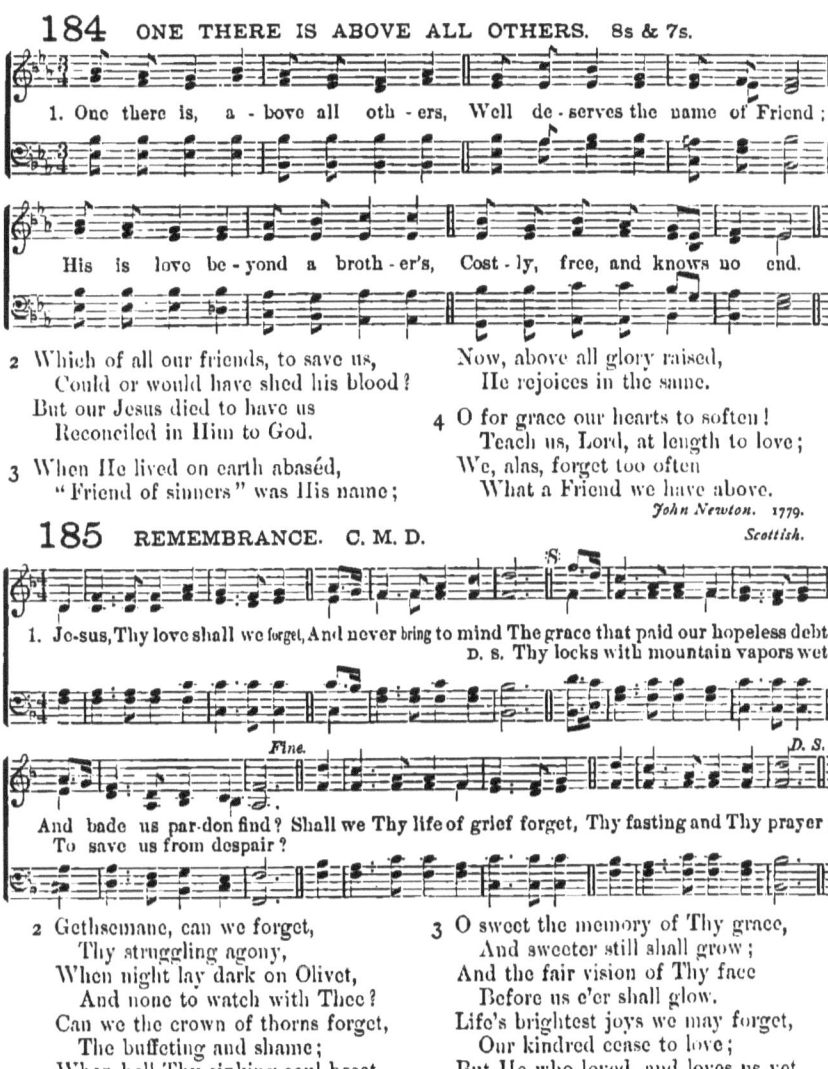

1. One there is, a-bove all oth-ers, Well de-serves the name of Friend;
His is love be-yond a broth-er's, Cost-ly, free, and knows no end.

2 Which of all our friends, to save us,
Could or would have shed his blood?
But our Jesus died to have us
Reconciled in Him to God.

3 When He lived on earth abaséd,
"Friend of sinners" was His name;
Now, above all glory raised,
He rejoices in the same.

4 O for grace our hearts to soften!
Teach us, Lord, at length to love;
We, alas, forget too often
What a Friend we have above.

John Newton. 1779.

185 REMEMBRANCE. C. M. D.
Scottish.

1. Je-sus, Thy love shall we forget, And never bring to mind The grace that paid our hopeless debt,
D. S. Thy locks with mountain vapors wet,
And bade us par-don find? Shall we Thy life of grief forget, Thy fasting and Thy prayer;
To save us from despair?

2 Gethsemane, can we forget,
Thy struggling agony,
When night lay dark on Olivet,
And none to watch with Thee?
Can we the crown of thorns forget,
The buffeting and shame;
When hell Thy sinking soul beset,
And earth reviled Thy name?

3 O sweet the memory of Thy grace,
And sweeter still shall grow;
And the fair vision of Thy face
Before us e'er shall glow.
Life's brightest joys we may forget,
Our kindred cease to love;
But He who loved, and loves us yet,
Our constancy shall prove.

W. Mitchell. 1831.

186 LOVING-KINDNESS. L. M.
Christian Lyre. 1830.

1. A-wake, my soul, to grate-ful lays, And sing the great Redeemer's praise;
He just-ly claims a song from me, His lov-ing-kind-ness, O how free!
Lov-ing-kind-ness, lov-ing-kind-ness, His lov-ing-kind-ness, O how free!

2 He saw me ruined in the fall,
Yet loved me notwithstanding all,
And saved me from my lost estate,
His loving-kindness is so great.

3 Through mighty hosts of cruel foes,
Where earth and hell my way oppose,
He safely leads my soul along,
His loving-kindness is so strong.

4 So when I pass death's gloomy vale,
And life and mortal powers shall fail,
O may my last expiring breath
His loving-kindness sing in death.

5 Then shall I mount, and soar away
To the bright world of endless day;
There shall I sing, with sweet surprise,
His loving-kindness in the skies.

Samuel Medley. 1787.

187 SAVIOUR, THY DYING LOVE.
Arthur S. Sullivan.

1. Saviour, Thy dying love Thou gavest me, Nor should I aught withhold, Dear Lord, from Thee;
In love my soul would bow, My heart fulfil its vow, Some offering bring Thee now, Something for Thee.

CONSECRATION.

2 At the blest mercy-seat,
  Pleading for me,
My feeble faith looks up,
  Jesus, to Thee:
Help me the cross to bear,
Thy wondrous love declare,
Some song to raise, or prayer,
  Something for Thee.

3 Give me a faithful heart,—
  Likeness to Thee,—
That each departing day
  Henceforth may see
Some work of love begun,
Some deed of kindness done,
Some wanderer sought and won,
  Something for Thee.

4 All that I am and have,—
  Thy gifts so free,—
In joy, in grief, through life,
  Dear Lord, for Thee!
And when Thy face I see,
My ransomed soul shall be
Through all eternity
  Something for Thee.
                       S. D. Phelps.

188 OAK. 6s & 4s.   *Lowell Mason.* 1854.

1. More love to Thee, O Christ, More love to Thee! Hear Thou the prayer I make On bend-ed knee. This is my earnest plea, More love, O Christ, to Thee, More love, O Christ, to Thee, More love to Thee.

2 Once earthly joy I craved,
    Sought peace and rest;
  Now Thee alone I seek,
    Give what is best:
  This all my prayer shall be,
  More love, O Christ, to Thee,
  More love to Thee?

3 Let sorrow do its work,
    Send grief and pain;
  Sweet are Thy messengers,
    Sweet their refrain,
  When they can sing with me,
  More love, O Christ, to Thee,
  More love to Thee!

4 Then shall my latest breath
    Whisper Thy praise;
  This be the parting cry
    My heart shall raise,
  This still its prayer shall be,
  More love, O Christ, to Thee,
  More love to Thee!
           Elizabeth Payson Prentiss. 1869.

(125)

THE CHRISTIAN LIFE.

189 HOWARD. C. M.
S. Howard. 1760.

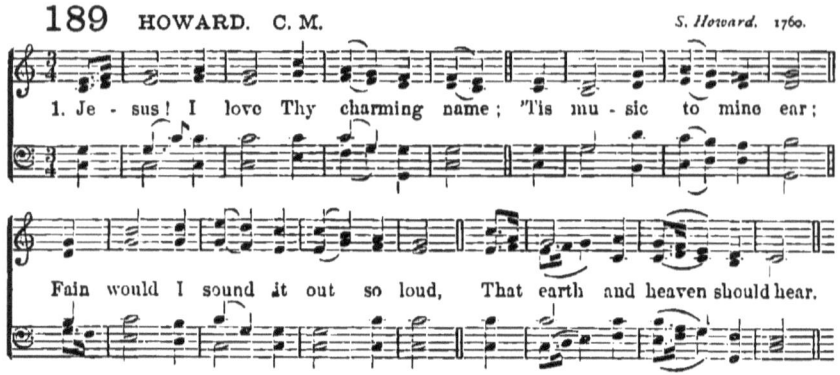

1. Jesus! I love Thy charming name;
'Tis music to mine ear;
Fain would I sound it out so loud,
That earth and heaven should hear.

2 All that my loftiest powers can wish,
In Thee doth richly meet;
Not to mine eyes is light so dear,
Nor friendship half so sweet.

3 Thy grace still dwells upon my heart,
And sheds its fragrance there;
The noblest balm of all my wounds,
The cordial of my care.

4 I'll speak the honors of Thy name
With my last laboring breath;
Then, speechless, clasp Thee in mine arms,
The Conqueror of death.
Philip Doddridge. 1755.

190 SPANISH HYMN. 7s. 6 lines.
Spanish Melody.

1. Blessed Saviour, Thee I love,
All my other joys above;
All my hopes in Thee abide,
Thou my hope, and naught beside:
D. C. Ever let my glory be,
Only, only, only Thee.

2 Once again beside the cross,
All my gain I count but loss;
Earthly pleasures fade away,—
Clouds they are that hide my day
Hence, vain shadows! let me see
Jesus, crucified for me.

3 Blesséd Saviour, Thine am I,
Thine to live, and Thine to die;
Height, or depth, or earthly power,
Ne'er shall hide my Saviour more:
Ever shall my glory be,
Only, only, only Thee.
George Duffield. 1859.

(126)

CONSECRATION.

191 MIDDLETON. 8s & 7s. *English.*

1. Jesus, I my cross have taken, All to leave and follow Thee;
   Destitute, despised, forsaken, Thou, from hence, my all shalt be:
D.C. Yet how rich is my condition! God and heav'n are still my own!

Perish ev'ry fond ambition, All I've sought, or hoped, or known;

2 Let the world despise and leave me,
   They have left my Saviour, too;
   Human hearts and looks deceive me;
   Thou art not, like man, untrue;
   And while Thou shalt smile upon me,
   God of wisdom, love, and might,
   Foes may hate, and friends may shun me,
   Show Thy face, and all is bright.

3 Man may trouble and distress me,
   'Twill but drive me to Thy breast;
   Life with trials hard may press me,
   Heaven will bring me sweeter rest.
   O 'tis not in grief to harm me,
   While Thy love is left to me;
   O 'twere not in joy to charm me,
   Were that joy unmixed with Thee.
   Henry Francis Lyte. 1825.

192 COME, MY REDEEMER, COME. *Johanna Kinkel.*

1. Come, my Redeemer, come, And deign to dwell with me, Come, make my heart Thy home, And bid Thy rivals flee; Come, my Redeemer, quickly come, And make my heart thy lasting home.

2 Rule Thou in every thought
   And passion of my soul,
   Till all my powers are brought
   Beneath Thy full control:
   Come, my Redeemer, quickly come,
   And make my heart Thy lasting home.

3 Then shall my days be Thine,
   And all my heart be love;
   And joy and peace be mine,
   Such as are known above:
   Come, my Redeemer, quickly come,
   And make my heart Thy lasting home.
   Andrew Reed. 1842.

THE CHRISTIAN LIFE.

193 ROOM IN MY HEART FOR THEE.

1. Thou didst leave Thy throne and Thy kingly crown When Thou camest to earth for me; But in Bethlehem's home was there found no room For Thy ho-ly na-tiv-i-ty.

Refrain.
O come to my heart, Lord Je-sus! There is room in my heart for Thee!
O come to my heart, Lord Je-sus, come! There is room in my heart for Thee!

2 Heaven's arches rang when the Angels sang,
   Proclaiming Thy royal degree;
But in lowly birth didst Thou come to earth,
   And in great humility.—*Refrain.*

3 The foxes found rest, and the bird had its nest
   In the shade of the cedar tree;
But Thy couch was the sod, O Thou Son of God,
   In the desert of Galilee.—*Refrain.*

4 Thou camest, O Lord, with the living word
   That should set Thy people free;
But with mocking scorn, and with crown of thorn,
   They bore Thee to Calvary.—*Refrain.*

5 When the heavens shall ring and the Angels sing
   At Thy coming to victory,
Let Thy voice call me home, saying, "Yet there is room,
   There is room at my side for Thee."—*Refrain.*

Frances Ridley Havergal.

CONSECRATION.

194 SILOAM. C. M.

1 Jesus, the very thought of Thee
  With sweetness fills the breast;
  But sweeter far Thy face to see,
  And in Thy presence rest.

2 Nor voice can sing, nor heart can frame,
  Nor can the memory find
  A sweeter sound than Thy blest name,
  O Saviour of mankind!

3 O Hope of every contrite heart!
  O joy of all the meek!
  To those who fall, how kind Thou art!
  How good to those who seek!

4 But what to those who find? Ah! this
  Nor tongue nor pen can show:
  The love of Jesus,—what it is,
  None but His loved ones know.

5 Jesus, our only joy be Thou!
  As Thou our prize wilt be;
  Jesus, be Thou our glory now,
  And through eternity!
      Bernard of Clairvaux. 1140.
      Tr. *Edward Caswall.* 1849.

195 LABAN. S. M.

1 My soul, be on thy guard;
  Ten thousand foes arise,
  And hosts of sin are pressing hard
  To draw thee from the skies.

2 O watch, and fight, and pray,
  The battle ne'er give o'er;
  Renew it boldly every day,
  And help divine implore.

3 Fight on, my soul, till death
  Shall bring thee to thy God;
  He'll take thee at thy parting breath,
  To His divine abode.
      George Heath. 1806.

196 MANOAH. C. M.

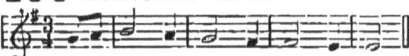

1 Walk in the light! so shalt thou know
  That fellowship of love,
  His Spirit only can bestow,
  Who reigns in light above.

2 Walk in the light! and thou shalt find
  Thy heart made truly His,
  Who dwells in cloudless light enshrined;
  In whom no darkness is.

3 Walk in the light! and thou shalt see
  Thy path, though thorny, bright,
  For God by grace shall dwell in thee,
  And God himself is Light.
      Bernard Barton.

197 ARIEL. C. P. M.

1 O, could I speak the matchless worth,
  O, could I sound the glories forth,
    Which in my Saviour shine!
  I'd soar and touch the heavenly strings,
  And vie with Gabriel, while he sings,
    In notes almost divine.

2 I'd sing the precious blood He spilt,
  My ransom from the dreadful guilt
    Of sin and wrath divine:
  I'd sing His glorious righteousness,
  In which all-perfect, heavenly dress
    My soul shall ever shine.

3 I'd sing the characters He bears,
  And all the forms of love He wears,
    Exalted on His throne;
  In loftiest songs of sweetest praise,
  I would to everlasting days
    Make all His glories known.

4 Well, the delightful day will come,
  When my dear Lord will bring me home,
    And I shall see His face:
  Then, with my Saviour, Brother, Friend,
  A blest eternity I'll spend,
    Triumphant in His grace.
      Samuel Medley. 1789.

THE CHRISTIAN LIFE.

198 SICILY. 8s & 7s. *Sicilian Melody.*

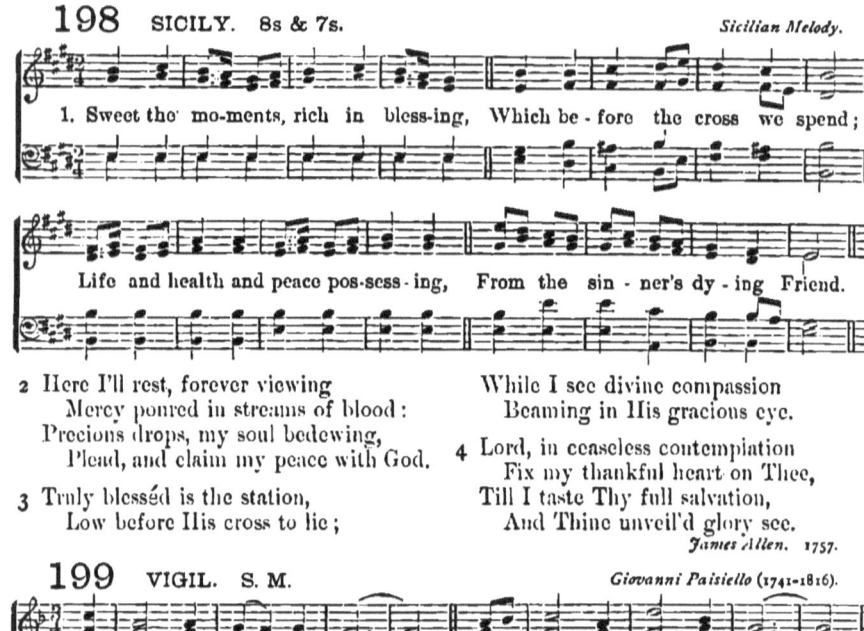

1. Sweet the moments, rich in bless-ing, Which be-fore the cross we spend;
Life and health and peace pos-sess-ing, From the sin-ner's dy-ing Friend.

2 Here I'll rest, forever viewing
  Mercy poured in streams of blood:
Precious drops, my soul bedewing,
  Plead, and claim my peace with God.

3 Truly blessèd is the station,
  Low before His cross to lie;
While I see divine compassion
  Beaming in His gracious eye.

4 Lord, in ceaseless contemplation
  Fix my thankful heart on Thee,
Till I taste Thy full salvation,
  And Thine unveil'd glory see.

James Allen. 1757.

199 VIGIL. S. M. *Giovanni Paisiello* (1741-1816).

1. Since Je-sus is my Friend, And I to Him be-long,
It mat-ters not what foes in-tend, How-ev-er fierce and strong.

2 He whispers, in my breast,
  Sweet words of holy cheer,
How he, who seeks in God his rest,
  Shall ever find Him near;

3 How God hath built above
  A city fair and new,   [prove
Where eye and heart shall see and
  What faith has counted true.

4 My heart for gladness springs,
  It cannot more be sad;
For very joy it laughs and sings,
  Sees naught but sunshine glad.

5 The sun, that glads mine eyes,
  Is Christ, the Lord I love;
I sing for joy of that, which lies
  Stored up for me above.

Ger., Paul Gerhardt. 1650. *Tr., Catherine Winkworth.* 1855.

200 TRUST. 7s. D.
George F. Root. 1872.

1. Sav-iour, hap-py should I be, If I could but trust in Thee;
Trust Thy wis-dom me to guide, Trust Thy good-ness to pro-vide;
Sav-iour, hap-py shoul I be, If I could but trust in Thee.
Trust Thy sav-ing love and power, Trust Thee ev-ery day and hour;

Copyright. By per. J. Church & Co.

2 Trust Thee as the only light
In the darkest hour of night;
Trust in sickness, trust in health;
Trust in poverty and wealth;
Trust in joy, and trust in grief;
Trust Thy promise for relief:
Saviour, happy should I be,
If I could but trust in Thee.

3 Trust Thy blood to cleanse my soul;
Trust Thy grace to make me whole;
Trust Thee living, dying, too;
Trust Thee all my journey through;
Trust Thee till my feet shall be
Planted on the crystal sea!
Saviour, happy should I be,
If I could but trust in Thee.
Edward H. Nevin. 1858.

201 GENTLE SHEPHERD.
German.

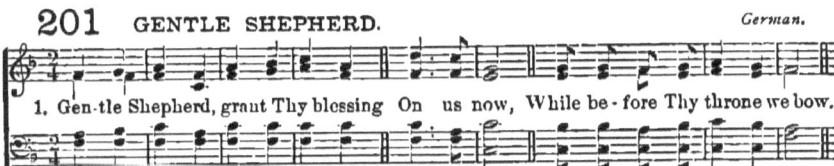

1. Gen-tle Shepherd, grant Thy blessing On us now, While be-fore Thy throne we bow.

2 Gentle Shepherd, we Thy children
Seek Thy face:
Give us now Thy heavenly grace.

3 Gentle Shepherd, bless the children
Of this fold:
Cleanse the hearts of young and old.

4 Gentle Shepherd, when life's ended,
Take us home,
Never from Thy side to roam.

202 WAS THERE EVER KINDEST SHEPHERD. *Henry Smart.*

1. Was there ever kindest shepherd, Half so gentle, half so sweet, As the Saviour, who would have us Come and gather at His feet? There's a wideness in God's mercy, Like the wideness of the sea; There's a kindness in His justice, Which is more than lib-er-ty.

2 There is no place where earth's sorrows
　Are more felt than up in heaven;
There is no place where earth's failings
　Have such kindly judgment given;
For the love of God is broader
　Than the measure of man's mind,
And the heart of the Eternal
　Is most wonderfully kind.

3 There is grace enough for thousands
　Of new worlds as bright as this;
There is room for fresh creations
　In that upper world of bliss.
There is welcome for the sinner,
　And more graces for the good;
There is mercy with the Saviour,
　There is healing in His blood.
　　　　　　　Frederick W. Faber.

203 BENTLEY. 7s & 6s. D. *John Hullah.* 1865.

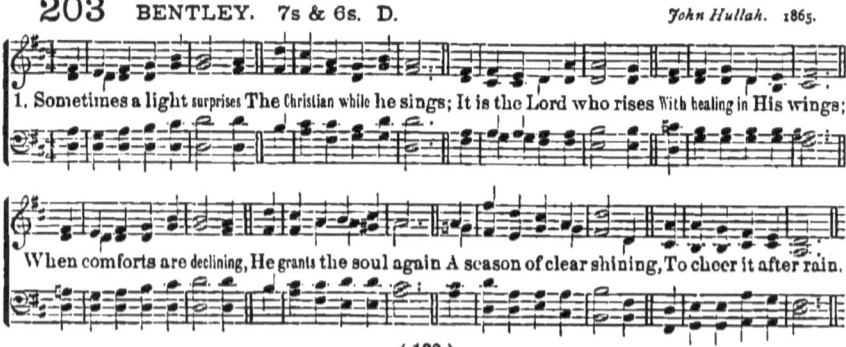

1. Sometimes a light surprises The Christian while he sings; It is the Lord who rises With healing in His wings; When comforts are declining, He grants the soul again A season of clear shining, To cheer it after rain.

TRUST.

2 In holy contemplation,
   We sweetly then pursue
  The theme of God's salvation,
   And find it ever new:
  Set free from present sorrow,
   We cheerfully can say,
  Let the unknown to-morrow
   Bring with it what it may.

3 It can bring with it nothing
   But He will bear us through;
  Who gives the lilies clothing
   Will clothe His people too;

Beneath the spreading heavens,
 No creature but is fed;
And He who feeds the ravens
 Will give His children bread.

4 Though vine nor fig-tree neither
   Their wonted fruit shall bear,
  Though all the field should wither,
   Nor flocks nor herds be there;
  Yet God the same abiding,
   His praise shall tune my voice,
  For, while in Him confiding,
   I cannot but rejoice.
               William Cowper. 1779.

204 LOVE DIVINE.   *Himmel.*

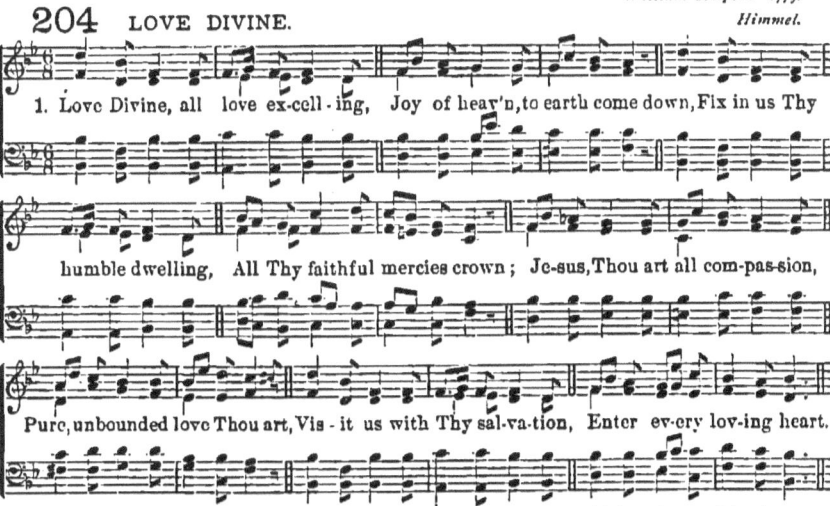

1. Love Divine, all love ex-cell-ing, Joy of heav'n, to earth come down, Fix in us Thy humble dwelling, All Thy faithful mercies crown; Je-sus, Thou art all com-pas-sion, Pure, unbounded love Thou art, Vis-it us with Thy sal-va-tion, Enter ev-ery lov-ing heart.

2 Breathe, O breathe, Thy loving Spirit
   Into every troubled breast;
  Let us all in Thee inherit,
   Let us find Thy promised rest;
  Take away the love of sinning,
   Alpha and Omega be,
  End of faith, as its beginning,
   Set our hearts at liberty.

3 Come, almighty to deliver,
   Let us all Thy grace receive;
  Suddenly return, and never,
   Never more Thy temples leave.

Thee we would be always blessing,
 Serve Thee as Thy hosts above;
Pray, and praise Thee without ceasing;
 Glory in Thy precious love.

4 Finish, then, Thy new creation;
   Pure, unspotted may we be;
  Let us see our whole salvation
   Perfectly secured by Thee:
  Changed from glory into glory,
   Till in heaven we take our place;
  Till we cast our crowns before Thee,
   Lost in wonder, love, and praise.
               Charles Wesley. 1747.

THE CHRISTIAN LIFE.

205 THERE IS A NAME I LOVE TO HEAR.

1. There is a name I love to hear, I love to sing its worth; It sounds like music in mine ear,
D. S. It tells me of His precious blood,

The sweetest name on earth. It tells me of a Saviour's love, Who died to set me free;
The sinner's perfect plea.

2 It tells me what my Father hath
In store for every day,
And, though I tread a darksome path,
Yields sunshine all the way.

It tells of One, whose loving heart
Can feel my deepest woe;
Who in each sorrow bears a part
That none can bear below.
Frederick Whitfield. 1859.

206 THE LOVE OF JESUS.

1. There is no love like the love of Jesus, Never to fade or fall, Till into the fold of the peace of God He has gathered us all.

Chorus.
No love like the love of Jesus, Never to fade or fall, Till into the fold of the peace of God He has gathered us all.

(134)

TRUST.

2 There is no voice like the voice of Jesus,
  Ah! how sweet its chime, [spring
  Like the musical ring of some rushing
  In the summer time.—*Chorus.*

3 O, might we list to the voice of Jesus!
  O, might we never roam! [breast,
  Our souls should rest in peace on His
  In the heavenly home.—*Chorus.*
  F. *Littlewood.*

207 THE ROCK THAT IS HIGHER. W. G. Fischer.

1. O, sometimes the shadows are deep, And rough seems the path to the goal,
And sorrows, sometimes how they sweep Like tempests down over the soul.

Chorus.
O, then, to the Rock let me fly, To the Rock that is higher than I;
  let me fly   is higher than I;
O, then, to the Rock let me fly, let me fly, To the Rock that is higher than I.

2 O, sometimes how long seems the day,
  And sometimes how weary my feet;
  But toiling in life's dusty way,
  The Rock's blessed shadow how sweet!
  O, then, to the Rock let me fly,
  To the Rock that is higher than I.

3 O, near to the Rock let me keep,
  If blessings, or sorrows prevail;
  Or climbing the mountain way steep,
  Or walking the shadowy vale.
  Then quick to the Rock I can fly,
  To the Rock that is higher than I.
  E. *Johnson.*

THE CHRISTIAN LIFE.

208. I LOVE TO TELL THE STORY.

W. G. Fischer. 1869.

1. I love to tell the story Of unseen things above; Of Jesus and His glory, Of Jesus and His love. I love to tell the story, Because I know 'tis true, It satisfies my longings, As nothing else can do.

Chorus.
I love to tell the story, 'Twill be my theme in glory, To tell the old, old story Of Jesus and His love.

2 I love to tell the story;
   More wonderful it seems
   Than all the golden fancies
   Of all our golden dreams.
I love to tell the story,
   It did so much for me!
   And that is just the reason
   I tell it now to thee.—*Cho.*

3 I love to tell the story;
   'Tis pleasant to repeat
   What seems, each time I tell it,
   More wonderfully sweet.
I love to tell the story,
   For some have never heard
   The message of salvation
   From God's own holy word.

4 I love to tell the story;
   For those who know it best
   Seem hungering and thirsting
   To hear it like the rest.
And when, in scenes of glory,
   I sing the New, New Song,
   'Twill be the Old, Old Story
   That I have loved so long.—*Cho.*

Kate Hankey. 1865.

TRUST.

209 "THE OLD, OLD STORY."

1 Tell me the old, old story
  Of unseen things above,
  Of Jesus and His glory,
  Of Jesus and His love;
  Tell me the story simply,
    As to a little child,
  For I am weak and weary,
    And helpless and defiled.

2 Tell me the story softly,
    With earnest tones, and grave:
  Remember, I'm the sinner
    Whom Jesus came to save;
  Tell me the story always,
    If you would really be,
  In any time of trouble,
    A comforter to me.

3 Tell me same old story,
    When you have cause to fear
  That this world's empty glory
    Is costing me too dear;
  Yes, and when that world's glory
    Is dawning on my soul,
  Tell me the old, old story;
    "Christ Jesus makes thee whole."
      Kate Hankey. 1865.

210 VARINA. Copyright. By per. O. Ditson & Co. C. M. D.

1 There is a land of pure delight
    Where saints immortal reign;
  Infinite day excludes the night,
    And pleasures banish pain.
  There everlasting spring abides,
    And never-with'ring flow'rs;
  Death, like a narrow sea, divides
    This heav'nly land from ours.

2 Sweet fields beyond the swelling flood
    Stand dressed in living green;
  So to the Jews old Canaan stood,
    While Jordan rolled between.
  But timorous mortals start and shrink
    To cross this narrow sea;
  And linger, shivering on the brink,
    And fear to launch away.

3 O, could we make our doubts remove,
    These gloomy doubts that rise,
  And see the Canaan that we love
    With unbeclouded eyes,—
  Could we but climb where Moses stood,
    And view the landscape o'er, [flood,
  Not Jordan's stream, nor death's cold
    Should fright us from the shore.
      Isaac Watts. 1709.

211 OLIVET. 6s & 4s.

1 My faith looks up to Thee,
  Thou Lamb of Calvary,
    Saviour divine;
  Now hear me while I pray,
  Take all my guilt away,
  O, let me from this day
    Be wholly Thine.

2 May Thy rich grace impart
  Strength to my fainting heart;
    My zeal inspire;
  As Thou hast died for me,
  O, may my love to Thee
  Pure, warm and changeless be,
    A living fire!

3 While life's dark maze I tread,
  And griefs around me spread,
    Be Thou my Guide;
  Bid darkness turn to day,
  Wipe sorrow's tears away,
  Nor let me ever stray
    From Thee aside.

4 When ends life's transient dream,
  When death's cold, sullen stream
    Shall o'er me roll,
  Blest Saviour! then, in love,
  Fear and distrust remove
  O bear me safe above,
    A ransomed soul!
      Ray Palmer. 1830.

212 ALL'S WELL.

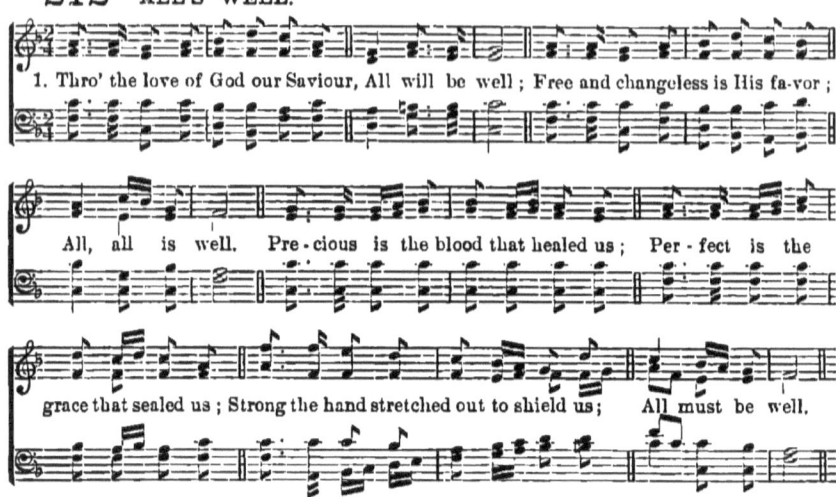

1. Thro' the love of God our Saviour, All will be well; Free and changeless is His fa-vor; All, all is well. Pre-cious is the blood that healed us; Per-fect is the grace that sealed us; Strong the hand stretched out to shield us; All must be well.

2 Though we pass through tribulation,
    All will be well:
  Ours is such a full salvation;
    All, all is well.
  Happy still in God confiding,
  Fruitful, if in Christ abiding,
  Holy, through the Spirit's guiding,
    All must be well.

3 We expect a bright to-morrow;
    All will be well;
  Faith can sing through days of sorrow,
    All, all is well.
  On our Father's love relying,
  Jesus every need supplying,
  Or in living, or in dying,
    All must be well.
              Mary B. Peters. 1847.

213 MACDONALD. 7s & 6s.

1. In heavenly love a-bid-ing, No change my heart shall fear; And safe is such con-fid-ing, For noth-ing changes here. The storm may roar with-out me, My

TRUST.

heart may low be laid, But God is round a-bout me, And can I be dis-mayed?

2 Wherever He may guide me,
No want shall turn me back;
My Shepherd is beside me,
And nothing can I lack.
His wisdom ever waketh,
His sight is never dim,
He knows the way He taketh,
And I will walk with Him.

3 Green pastures are before me,
Which yet I have not seen;
Bright skies will soon be o'er me,
Where darkest clouds have been.
My hope I cannot measure,
My path to life is free,
My Saviour has my treasure,
And He will walk with me.
Anna Latitia Waring. 1850.

214 PORTUGUESE HYMN. 11s.

1 How firm a foundation, ye saints of the Lord,
Is laid for your faith in His excellent word!
What more can He say than to you He hath said,
To you who for refuge to Jesus have fled?

2 "Fear not, I am with thee, O be not dismayed,
For I am thy God; I will still give thee aid:
I'll strengthen thee, help thee, and cause thee to stand,
Upheld by my gracious, omnipotent hand.

3 "When through the deep waters I call thee to go,
The rivers of sorrow shall not overflow;
For I will be with thee thy trials to bless,
And sanctify to thee thy deepest distress.

4 "The soul that on Jesus hath leaned for repose,
I will not, I will not desert to his foes;
That soul, though all hell should endeavor to shake,
I'll never, no never, no never forsake!"
George Keith. 1787.

215 TOPLADY. 7s. 6 lines.

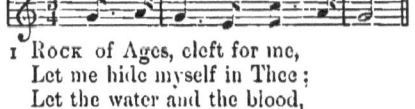

1 Rock of Ages, cleft for me,
Let me hide myself in Thee;
Let the water and the blood,
From Thy wounded side which flowed,
Be of sin the double cure,
Cleanse me from its guilt and power.

2 Could my tears forever flow,
Could my zeal no languor know,
These for sin could not atone;
Thou must save and Thou alone;
In my hand no price I bring;
Simply to Thy cross I cling.

3 While I draw this fleeting breath,
When my eyelids close in death,
When I soar to worlds unknown,
And behold Thee on Thy throne,—
Rock of Ages, cleft for me,
Let me hide myself in Thee.
Augustus M. Toplady. 1776.

THE CHRISTIAN LIFE.

216 BELMONT. C. M.
Johann C. W. A. Mozart. 1805.

1. O for a faith that will not shrink, Tho' press'd by ev - ery foe; That will not trem - ble on the brink Of an - y earth - ly woe;

2 That will not murmur nor complain
  Beneath the chastening rod;
  But, in the hour of grief or pain,
  Will lean upon its God;

3 A faith that shines more bright and clear
  When tempests rage without;

That when in danger knows no fear,
  In darkness feels no doubt.

4 Lord, give us such a faith as this,
  And then, whate'er may come,
  We'll taste, e'en here, the hallowed bliss
  Of an eternal home.

W. H. Bathurst. 1831.

217 THE SHADOW OF THE ROCK.

1. In the shadow of the Rock, Let me rest, Let me rest! When I feel the tempest's shock Thrill my breast, Thrill my breast; All in vain the storm shall sweep, While I hide, While I hide; And my tran - quil sta-tion keep By Thy side, By Thy side.

TRUST.

2 On the parched and desert way, Where I tread,
With the noontide scorching ray O'er my head,
Let me find the welcome shade, Cool and still,
And my weary steps be staid Where I will.

3 I in peace will rest me there Till I see
That the skies again are fair Over me;
That the burning heats are past, And the day
Bids the weary one at last Go his way.

4 Then my pilgrim staff I'll take, And once more
I'll my onward journey make, As before;
And with joyous heart and strong I will raise
Unto thee, O Rock, a song Glad with praise.

Ray Palmer.

218 TRUST HIM STILL.

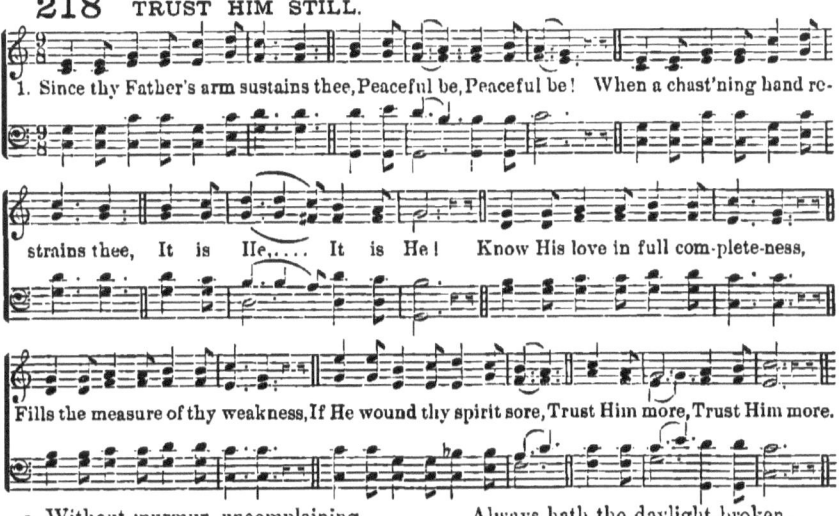

1. Since thy Father's arm sustains thee, Peaceful be, Peaceful be! When a chast'ning hand restrains thee, It is He.... It is He! Know His love in full com-plete-ness, Fills the measure of thy weakness, If He wound thy spirit sore, Trust Him more, Trust Him more.

2 Without murmur, uncomplaining,
In His hand
Leave whatever things thou canst not
Understand.
Though the world thy folly spurneth,
From thy faith in pity turneth,
In His love if thou abide,
He will guide.

3 Fearest sometimes that thy Father
Hath forgot?
When the clouds around thee gather,
Doubt Him not!

Always hath the daylight broken,
Always hath He comfort spoken,
Better hath He been for years
Than thy fears.

4 Therefore, whatsoe'er betideth,
Night or day,
Know His love for thee provideth
Good alway.
Journey on, His mercy sharing,
Every cross He gives thee bearing,
Humbly bending to His will,
Trust Him still.

Anon.

THE CHRISTIAN LIFE.

219 PLEYEL'S HYMN. 7s. *Ignace Pleyel.* 1800.

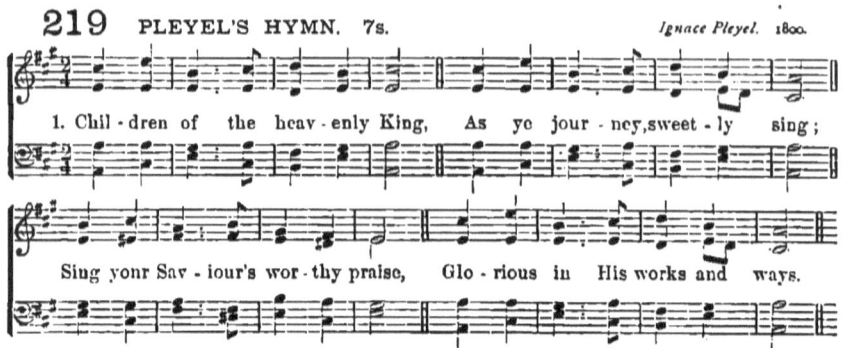

1. Chil-dren of the heav-enly King, As ye jour-ney, sweet-ly sing; Sing your Sav-iour's wor-thy praise, Glo-rious in His works and ways.

2 Ye are traveling home to God
In the way the fathers trod;
They are happy now, and ye
Soon their happiness shall see.

3 Shout, ye little flock, and blest!
You on Jesus' throne shall rest;
There your seat is now prepared;
There your kingdom and reward.

4 Fear not, brethren; joyful stand
On the borders of your land;
Jesus Christ, your Father's Son,
Bids you undismayed go on.

5 Lord, obediently we go,
Gladly leaving all below;
Only Thou our Leader be,
And we still will follow Thee.
John Cennick. 1742.

220 HALLE. 7s. *Francis Joseph Haydn.* 1798.

1. "As thy day, thy strength shall be!" This should be e-nough for thee; He who knows thy frame will spare Bur-dens more than thou canst bear.

2 When thy days are veiled in night,
Christ shall give thee heavenly light;
Seem they wearisome and long,
Yet in Him thou shalt be strong.

3 Cold and wintry though they prove,
Thine the sunshine of His love;

Or with fervid heat opprest,
In His shadow thou shalt rest.

4 When thy days on earth are past,
Christ shall call thee home at last,
His redeeming love to praise,
Who hath strengthened all thy days.
Frances Ridley Havergal. 1872.

TRUST.

221 WAITING. 7s.
Helen M. Herrick.

1. Wait, my soul, up-on the Lord, To His gra-cious prom-ise flee; Lay-ing hold up-on His word, "As thy days thy strength shall be!"

2 If the sorrows of thy case
  Seem peculiar still to thee,
God has promised needful grace—
  "As thy days thy strength shall be."

3 Days of trial, days of grief,
  In succession thou mayst see;
This is still thy sweet relief—
  "As thy days thy strength shall be."

4 Rock of Ages, I'm secure,
  With Thy promise full and free;
Faithful, positive, and sure—
  "As thy days thy strength shall be."
  William F. Lloyd. 1830.

222 EVAN. C. M.
W. H. Havergal. 1849.

1. O for a heart to praise my God! A heart from sin set free; A heart that al-ways feels Thy blood, So free-ly shed for me;

2 A heart resigned, submissive, meek,
  My great Redeemer's throne,
Where only Christ is heard to speak,
  Where Jesus reigns alone.

3 An humble, lowly, contrite heart,
  Believing, true and clean;
Which neither life nor death can part,
  From Him that dwells within!

4 A heart in every thought renewed,
  And filled with love divine;
Perfect and right and pure and good,
  A copy, Lord, of Thine.
  Charles Wesley. 1742.

THE CHRISTIAN LIFE.

223 ST. LEONARD. L. M. D. *Henry Hiles.*

1. Lord, Thou hast taught our hearts to glow With love's undying flame ; But more of Thee we long to know, And more would love Thy name. Thy life, Thy death, inspire our song, Thy Spirit breathes thro' all ; And here our feet would lin-ger long, But we o - bey Thy call.

2 Thou bid'st us go, with Thee to stand
   Against hell's marshaled powers ;
And heart to heart, and hand to hand,
   To make Thine honor ours.
With Thine own pity, Saviour, see
   The thronged and darkening way :
We go to win the lost to Thee,
   O help us, Lord, we pray.

3 Teach Thou our lips of Thee to speak,
   Of Thy sweet love to tell ;
Till they who wander far shall seek
   And find and serve Thee well.
O'er all the world Thy Spirit send,
   And make Thy goodness known,
Till earth and heaven together blend
   Their praises at Thy throne.
            Ray Palmer. 1865.

224 MORE LIKE JESUS. *J. M. Stillman. By per.*

1. I want to be more like Je - sus, And follow Him day by day ; I want to be true and faith - ful, And ev - 'ry command o - bey.   *Refrain.*   More and more like Je - sus,

CHRIST-LIKE SERVICE.

I would ev-er be.... ev-er be; More and more like Je-sus, My Saviour who died for me.

2 I want to be kind and gentle
  To those who are in distress;
  To comfort the broken-hearted
  With sweet words of tenderness.—*Ref.*

3 I want to be meek and lowly,
  Like Jesus, our Friend and King;

I want to be strong and earnest,
  And souls to the Saviour bring.—*Ref.*

4 I want to be pure and holy,
  As pure as the crystal snow;
  I want to love Jesus dearly,
  For Jesus loves me, I know.—*Ref.*

J. M. Stillman.

225 SMYRNA. 8s & 7s. D. *Johann C. W. A. Mozart.* (1756-1791.)

1. Christians, up! the day is breaking, Gird your ready ar-mor on; Slumb'ring hosts around are wak-ing, Rouse ye! in the Lord be strong! While ye sleep or i-dly lin-ger, Thousands sink, with none to save; Hasten! time's un-err-ing fin-ger Points to many an o-pen grave.

2 Hark! unnumbered voices crying,
  "Save us, or we droop and die!"
  Succor bear the faint and dying,
  On the wings of mercy fly:
  Lead them to the crystal fountain
  Gushing with the streams of life;
  Guide them to the sheltering mountain,
  For the gale with death is rife.

3 See the blest millennial dawning!
  Bright the beams of Bethlehem's star;
  Eastern lands behold the morning;
  Lo! it glimmers from afar;
  O'er the mountain-top ascending,
  Soon the scattered light shall rise,
  Till, in radiant glory blending,
  Heaven's high noon shall greet our eyes.

E. S. Porter.

THE CHRISTIAN LIFE.

226 THE SOUL'S DESIRE. 6s & 5s.
Edwin Pond Parker.

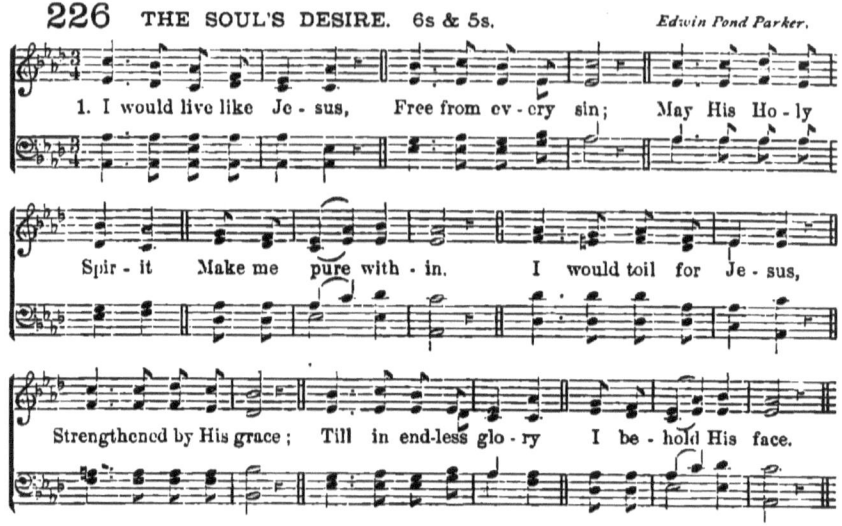

1. I would live like Jesus, Free from every sin; May His Holy Spirit Make me pure within. I would toil for Jesus, Strengthened by His grace; Till in endless glory I behold His face.

2 I would tell to Jesus
   Every grief and care,
  He delights to answer
   Humble, fervent prayer.
  Through the changeful future,
   Jesus, be my guide;
  In Thy great compassion
   Keep me near Thy side.

3 I would trust in Jesus
   All my journey through;
  He is ever faithful,
   He is ever true.
  Saviour, in my spirit
   Shed abroad Thy love;
  When I die, receive me
   To Thy home above.

227 TAINTOR. 6s & 5s.
John B. Dykes.

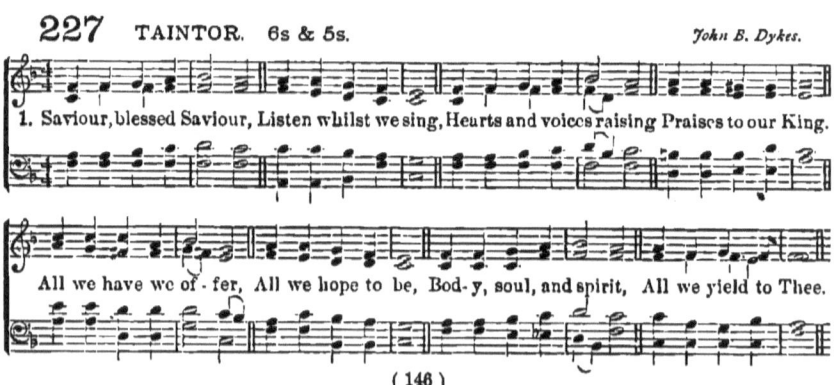

1. Saviour, blessed Saviour, Listen whilst we sing, Hearts and voices raising Praises to our King. All we have we offer, All we hope to be, Body, soul, and spirit, All we yield to Thee.

CHRIST-LIKE SERVICE.

2 Nearer, ever nearer,
　　Christ, we draw to Thee,
　Deep in adoration
　　Bending low the knee:
　Thou for our redemption
　　Cam'st on earth to die;
　Thou, that we might follow,
　　Hast gone up on high.

3 Great and ever greater
　　Are Thy mercies here,
　True and everlasting
　　Are the glories there,

Where no pain, or sorrow,
　Toil, or care, is known,
Where the angel-legions
　Circle round Thy throne.

4 Dark and ever darker
　　Was the wintry past,
　Now a ray of gladness
　　O'er our path is cast;
　Every day that passeth,
　　Every hour that flies,
　Tells of love unfeignéd,
　　Love that never dies.
　　　　　　Godfrey Thring. 1866.

228　THE HARVEST IS WHITE.

1. Reapers! O reapers! the harvest is white, And waiting the sickle to-day, The shadows are falling and soon comes the night, Bear the sheaves to the garner away. Reapers, reapers, great your reward, When life's labors are done; At the last day, day of our Lord, You will shine for aye as the sun.

2 Reapers! O reapers! the harvest still waits,
　　And soon will the winter begin;
　The Husbandman asks, what the work so belates,
　　O come, and the sheaves gather in.—*Chorus.*

3 Reapers! O reapers! then enter the field,
　　And save for the Master His grain;
　For idleness surely to you can but yield
　　A harvest of sorrow and pain.—*Chorus.*
　　　　　　　　　　　　　　　J. E. Rankin.

THE CHRISTIAN LIFE.

229 CARITAS. 8s & 7s. D.

1. Is thy cruse of comfort failing? Rise and share it with another,
And thro' all the years of famine, It shall serve thee and thy brother.
Love divine will fill thy store-house, Or thy handful still renew;
Scanty fare for one will often, Make a royal feast for two.

2 For the heart grows rich in giving;
   All its wealth is living grain;
Seeds which mildew in the garner,
   Scattered, fill with gold the plain.
Is thy burden hard and heavy?
Do thy steps drag wearily?
Help to bear thy brother's burden,
   God will bear both it and thee.

3 Numb and weary on the mountains,
   Would'st thou sleep amidst the snow?
Chafe that frozen form beside thee,
   And together both shall glow.
Art thou stricken in life's battle?
   Many wounded round thee moan;
Lavish on their wounds thy balsams,
   And that balm shall heal thine own.

4 Is the heart a well left empty?
   None but God its void can fill;
Nothing but a ceaseless Fountain
   Can its ceaseless longings still.
Is the heart a living power?
Self-inclined, its strength sinks low,
It can only live in loving, -
   And by serving love will grow.
                                Elizabeth Charles.

OVERCOMING TEMPTATION.

230 TEMPTED AND TRIED.

1. Tempted and tried! There's One at thy side, And never in vain shall His children confide, He'll save and defend, for He loves to the end, The a-dor-a-ble Master and glo-ri-ous Friend.

Chorus.
Tempted and tried! Tempted and tried! The Saviour is near thee, He walks by thy side;
Tempted and tried! Tempted and tried! He'll guard thee and guide thee whatever betide.

2 Tempted and tried! There's One at thy side,
Thy faithful Redeemer, thy Keeper and Guide;
Thy shield and thy sword, thine exceeding reward;
Then enough for the servant to be as his Lord.—*Chorus.*

3 Tempted and tried! The Saviour that died
Hath called thee to suffer and reign at His side;
His cross thou shalt bear, and His crown thou shalt wear,
And forever and ever His glory shalt share.—*Chorus.*

Frances Ridley Havergal.

THE CHRISTIAN LIFE.

231. TO THE RESCUE.
Arr. from F. Mohring.

1. To the rescue! to the rescue! For our friends in danger stand! Now a deadly foe and daring, With his subtle wiles ensnaring, Neither age nor beauty sparing, Spreads death on every hand; But a-

D.S. gainst him we are striving, For His overthrow contriving, And we rest not in our driving The foe from out our [OMIT.].......... land.

D.S. striving, striving,

2 Let us rally, let us rally,
For the battle we shall win;
Break the chains of vice enslaving,
All the blows of conflict braving,
For the souls of men we're saving

But against him we are
From the power of deadly sin.
And the Lord shall give His blessing
On His army forward pressing,
And, with them all wrongs redressing,
His glorious reign begin.

232. ARISE! FOR CHRIST ARISE.
Roguet De Lisle. 1792.

1. Friends of the tempted! Christ is calling, It is His voice, heard from the skies; No longer to this curse appalling, Be deaf of ears, be blind of eyes,

HELP FOR THE TEMPTED.

2 Ten thousand hearts are torn and bleeding!
   Ten thousand homes lie waste and lone;
Shall blood-bought souls live on, unheed-
    ing,
   As tho' this work were not Christ's own?
   As tho' this work were not Christ's own?
O Thou, whose cause we've sworn to
    cherish, [pow'rs
How long, how long shall hell's dark
Weigh down with woe this land of ours,
While year by year ten thousand perish?
    Cho.—Arise! etc.

3 Friends of the tempted! Hearts all glow-
    ing,
   Lift up, lift up again, your voice;
The Lord is come, His grace bestowing;
   The Lord is come! rejoice! rejoice!
   The Lord is come! rejoice! rejoice!
Like the fleet hart, the lame are leap-
    ing;
Forth from the prison captives come!
While in full many an humble home,
There is rejoicing, where was weeping.
    Cho.—Arise! etc.

J. E. Rankin.

THE CHRISTIAN LIFE.

233 MAN'S WRONGS, WE WILL RIGHT THEM.
J. E. Rankin.

1. We will not faint or fal-ter now, Tho' oth-er toils there are; We lift to heaven an unblenched brow, And thus we sol-emn swear:

Chorus.
Man's wrongs, we still will right them, Man's burdens help him bear; Man's foes, we still will fight them, And make his cause our care, And make his cause our care.

2 Millions for this have shed their blood,
 In every age allied:
 Shall we not keep the cause still good
 For which the martyrs died!—*Cho.*

3 The sun has seen, on many a field,
 The flag, man loved, go down:
 And yet His cause with blood thus sealed,
 Has won, at last, the crown.—*Cho.*

4 When God incarnate, came to earth,
 And stooped to lift the race;
 He wrote in blood man's native worth,
 And died, to make him place.—*Cho.*

5 So long as God shall give us life,
 Fresh toils we will not spare:
 Whate'er the field, the same the strife,
 The same the vow we swear.
 J. E. Rankin.

HELP FOR THE TEMPTED.

234 ST. ANDREW. 6s & 5s. *John B. Dykes.* 1868.

1. Christian, dost thou see them On the holy ground, How the powers of darkness Rage thy steps around? Christian, up and smite them, Counting gain but loss; In the strength that cometh By the holy Cross.

2 Christian, dost thou feel them,
  How they work within,
 Striving, tempting, luring,
  Goading into sin?
 Christian, never tremble;
  Never be downcast;
 Gird thee for the battle;
  Thou shalt win at last.

3 Christian, dost thou hear them,
  How they speak thee fair?
 "Always fast and vigil?
  Always watch and prayer:"

Christian, answer boldly,
 "While I breathe I pray:"
Peace shall follow battle,
 Night shall end in day.

4 "Well I know thy trouble,
  O my servant true;
 Thou art very weary,
  I was weary too;
 But that toil shall make thee
  Some day all mine own,
 And the end of sorrow
  Shall be near my throne."

Andrew of Crete, 8th century. Tr., *John M. Neale*. 1862.

235 PARACLETE. 7s & 3s. *U. C. Burnap.* 1869.

1. Christian, seek not yet repose,
 Cast thy dreams of ease away;
 Thou art in the midst of foes:
  Watch and pray.

2 Gird thy heavenly armor on,
 Wear it ever night and day;
 Ambushed lies the evil one:
  Watch and pray.

3 Hear the victors who o'ercame;
 Still they mark each warrior's way;
 All with warning voice exclaim,—
  Watch and pray.

4 Hear, above all, hear thy Lord;
 Him thou lovest to obey;
 Hide within thy heart His word,—
  Watch and pray.

5 Watch, as if on that alone
 Hung the issues of the day;
 Pray that help may be sent down:
  Watch and pray.

William Walsham How. 1872.

THE CHRISTIAN LIFE.

236 LUDWIG. 7s. D.
Ludwig von Beethoven. 1824.

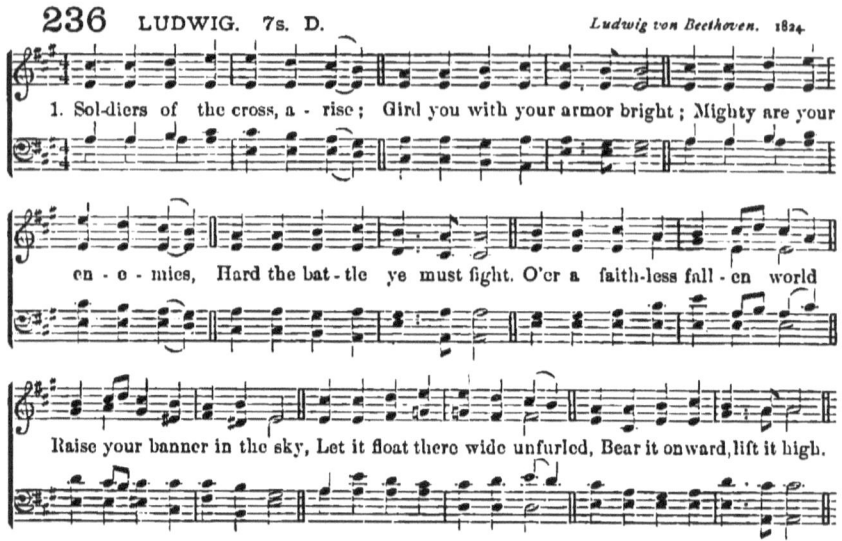

1. Soldiers of the cross, arise; Gird you with your armor bright; Mighty are your enemies, Hard the battle ye must fight. O'er a faithless fallen world Raise your banner in the sky, Let it float there wide unfurled, Bear it onward, lift it high.

2 'Mid the homes of want and woe,
   Strangers to the living Word,
Let the Saviour's herald go,
   Let the voice of hope be heard.
Where the shadows deepest lie,
   Carry truth's unsullied ray;
Where are crimes of darkest dye,
   There the saving sign display.

3 To the weary and the worn
   Tell of realms where sorrows cease;
To the outcast and forlorn
   Speak of mercy and of peace.
Be the banner still unfurled,
   Bear it bravely still abroad,
Till the kingdoms of the world
   Are the kingdoms of the Lord.
William Walsham How. 1854.

237 HARK! THE VOICE OF JESUS CALLING.

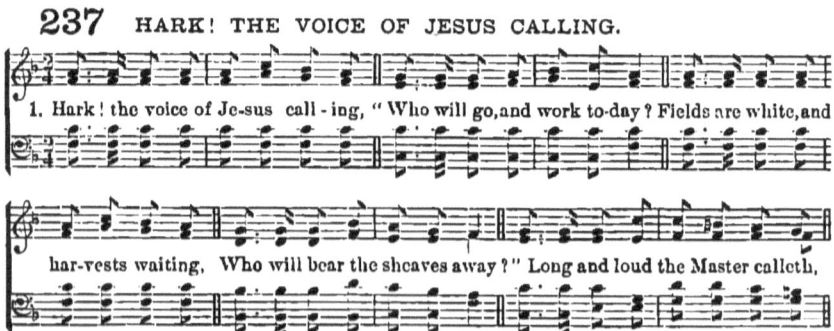

1. Hark! the voice of Jesus calling, "Who will go, and work to-day? Fields are white, and harvests waiting, Who will bear the sheaves away?" Long and loud the Master calleth,

ACTIVITY.

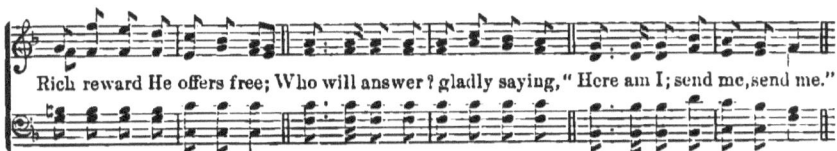

2 If you cannot cross the ocean
   And the heathen lands explore,
  You can find the heathen nearer,
   You can help them at your door;
  If you cannot give your thousands,
   You can give the widow's mite,
  And the least you give for Jesus
   Will be precious in His sight.

3 If you cannot speak like angels,
   If you cannot preach like Paul,
  You can tell the love of Jesus,
   You can say He died for all.

  If you cannot rouse the wicked
   With the judgment's dread alarms,
  You can lead the little children
   To the Saviour's waiting arms.

4 While the souls of men are dying,
   And the Master calls for you,
  Let none hear you idly saying,
   "There is nothing I can do!"
  Take the task He gives you gladly,
   Let His work your pleasure be;
  Answer quickly when He calleth,
   "Here am I; send me, send me."
                        D. March.

238   THE VOYAGE OF LIFE.   *W. O. Perkins.*

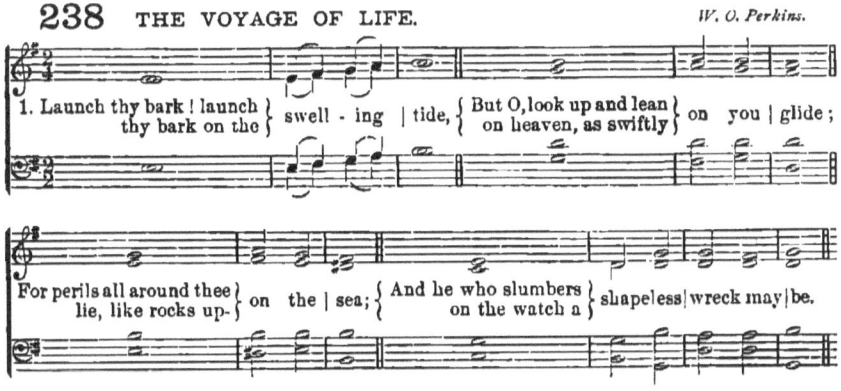

2 Hoist thy flag! hoist thy flag! nail it | to the | mast;
   The flag of justice and of truth upon the | breezes | cast;
   And 'neath that banner's glorious folds spread out thy | flowing | sail;
   Press onward to the destined port be- | fore the | fav'ring | gale.

3 Speed thee on! speed thee on o'er the | troubled | sea;
   But O, let wisdom steer thy bark, and truth thy | compass | be.
   Unloose thy sail; God speed thee now, thy vigil | never | cease,
   Till, anchored in the heavenly port, thou | find e- | ternal | peace.

THE CHRISTIAN LIFE.

239 GREATHEART.
Joseph Barnby.

1. We march, we march to vic-to-ry! With the cross of the Lord be-fore us,
D. S. march, we march, etc.

With His lov-ing eye looking down from the sky, And His ho-ly arm spread o'er us,

His ho-ly arm spread o'er us, o'er us. 2. We come in the might of the Lord of light,

A joy-ful host to meet Him: And we put to flight the ar-mies of night,

That the sons of the day may greet Him, The sons of the day may greet Him. We

3 The bands of the alien flee away,
And our chant goes up like thunder;
And the van of the Lord, in serried array,
Cleaves Satan's ranks asunder.
We march, we march, etc.

4 Our sword is the Spirit of God on high,
Our helmet is His salvation,
Our banner the Cross of Calvary,
Our watchword—The Incarnation.
We march, we march, etc.

SOLDIERS OF THE CROSS.

5 We tread in the might of the Lord of Hosts,
   And we fear not man nor devil;
   For our Captain himself guards well our coasts,
     To defend His church from evil.
      We march, we march, etc.

6 And the choir of angels with song awaits
   Our march to the Golden Zion;
   For our Captain has broken the brazen gates,
     And burst the bars of iron.
      We march, we march, etc.

7 Then onward we march, our arms to prove,
   With the banner of Christ before us,
   With His eye of love looking down from above,
     And His holy arm spread o'er us,
      We march, we march, etc. *Gerard Moultrie.*

240   ST. GERTRUDE.   6s & 5s.   *Arthur S. Sullivan.* 1872.

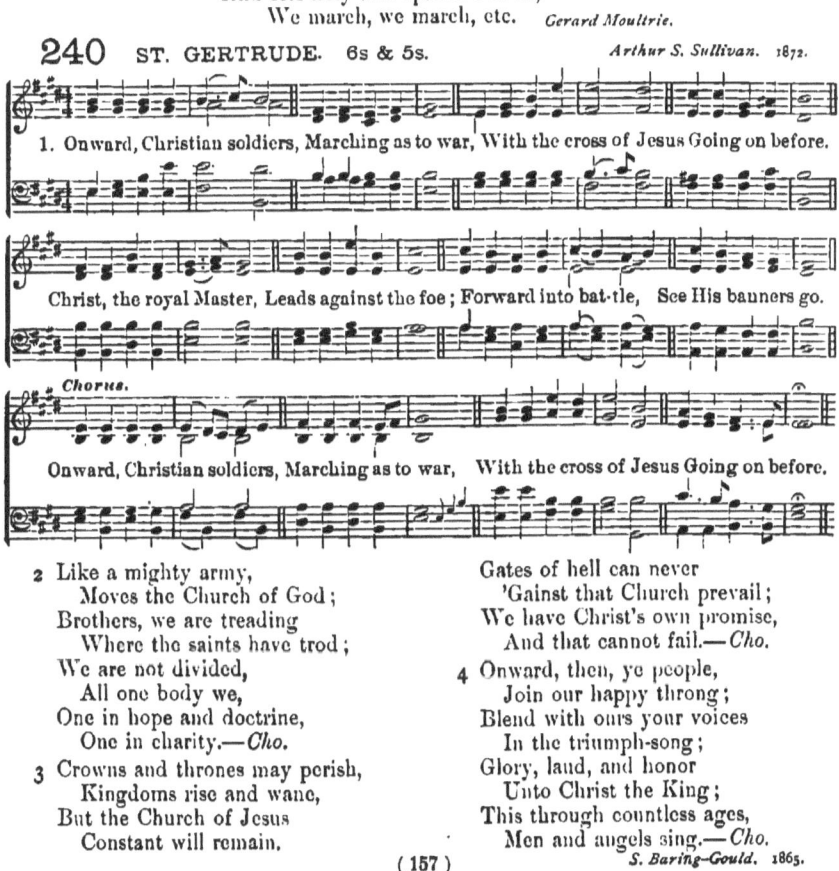

1. Onward, Christian soldiers, Marching as to war, With the cross of Jesus Going on before.
Christ, the royal Master, Leads against the foe; Forward into bat-tle, See His banners go.

Chorus.
Onward, Christian soldiers, Marching as to war, With the cross of Jesus Going on before.

2 Like a mighty army,
   Moves the Church of God;
  Brothers, we are treading
   Where the saints have trod;
  We are not divided,
   All one body we,
  One in hope and doctrine,
   One in charity.—*Cho.*

3 Crowns and thrones may perish,
   Kingdoms rise and wane,
  But the Church of Jesus
   Constant will remain.

Gates of hell can never
   'Gainst that Church prevail;
We have Christ's own promise,
   And that cannot fail.—*Cho.*

4 Onward, then, ye people,
   Join our happy throng;
  Blend with ours your voices
   In the triumph-song;
  Glory, laud, and honor
   Unto Christ the King;
  This through countless ages,
   Men and angels sing.—*Cho.*
        S. Baring-Gould. 1865.

THE CHRISTIAN LIFE.

241 BRETHREN, WHILE WE SOJOURN HERE.

1. Brethren, while we sojourn here, Fight we must but should not fear; Foes we have, but we've a Friend, One that loves us to the end. Forward, then, with courage go, Long we shall not dwell below; Soon the joyful news will come, "Child, your Father calls—come home!"

2 In the way a thousand snares
Lie, to take us unawares;
Satan, with malicious art,
Watches each unguarded part:
But, from Satan's malice free,
Saints shall soon victorious be;
Soon the joyful news will come,
" Child, your Father calls—come home!"

3 But of all the foes we meet,
None so oft mislead our feet,
None betray us into sin
Like the foes that dwell within;
Yet let nothing spoil our peace,
Christ shall also conquer these;
Soon the joyful news will come,
" Child, your Father calls—come home!"

Joseph Swain. 1792.

242 LA CROSSE. *English. Adapted by Robert Nourse.*

1. Let our choir new anthems raise, God Himself to joy and praise
    Wake the morn with gladness;   Turns the martyr's sadness.

2 Never flinched they from the flame,
    From the torture never;
  Vain the foeman's sharpest aim,
    Satan's best endeavor;

3 For by faith they saw the Land,
    Decked in all its glory,
  Where triumphant now they stand
    With the victor's story.

4 Up and follow, Christian men!
    Press through toil and sorrow;
  Spurn the night of fear, and then,
    O, the glorious morrow!

5 Who will venture on the strife?
    Who will first begin it?
  Who will gain the Land of Life?
    Warriors, up and win it!

St. Joseph of the Studium. 830.   *Tr., John Mason Neale.* 1862.

243 CHRISTMAS. C. M.
George Frederick Handel.

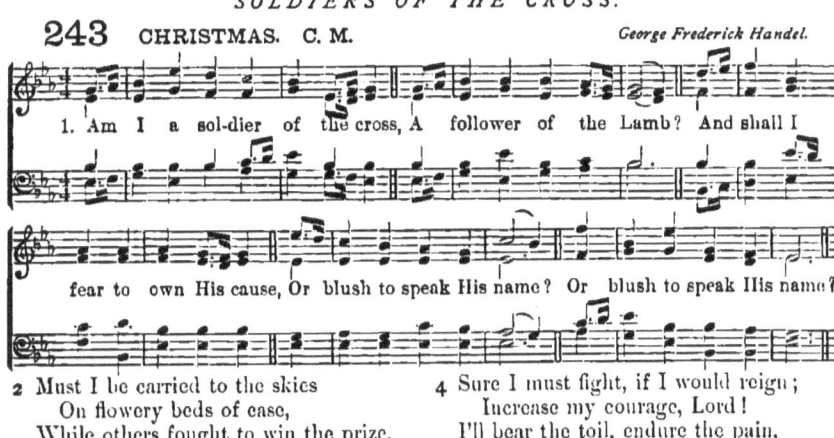

1. Am I a sol-dier of the cross, A follower of the Lamb? And shall I fear to own His cause, Or blush to speak His name? Or blush to speak His name?

2 Must I be carried to the skies
  On flowery beds of ease,
While others fought to win the prize,
  And sailed through blood seas?

3 Are there no foes for me to face?
  Must I not stem the flood?
Is this vile world a friend to grace,
  To help me on to God?

4 Sure I must fight, if I would reign;
  Increase my courage, Lord!
I'll bear the toil, endure the pain,
  Supported by Thy word.

5 Thy saints, in all this glorious war,
  Shall conquer, though they die;
They view the triumph from afar,
  And seize it with their eye.

Isaac Watts. 1723.

244 ITALIAN HYMN. 6s & 4s.
F. Giardini. 1760.

1. Christ for the world we sing; The world to Christ we bring, With loving zeal; The poor, and them that mourn, The faint and overborne, Sin-sick and sorrow-worn, Whom Christ doth heal.
2. Christ for the world we sing; The world to Christ we bring, With fervent pray'r; The wayward and the lost, By restless passions tossed, Redeemed, at countless cost, From dark despair.

3 Christ for the world we sing;
  The world to Christ we bring,
    With one accord;
  With us the work to share,
  With us reproach to dare,
  With us the cross to bear,
    For Christ our Lord.

4 Christ for the world we sing;
  The world to Christ we bring,
    With joyful song;
  The new-born souls, whose days,
  Reclaimed from error's ways,
  Inspired with hope and praise,
    To Christ belong.

Samuel Wolcott.

THE CHRISTIAN LIFE.

245 UPLIFT THE BANNER.
J. Baptiste Calkin. 1872.

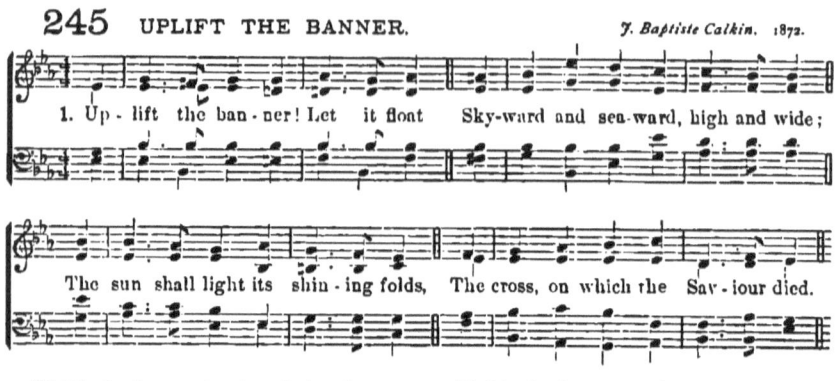

1. Up-lift the ban-ner! Let it float Sky-ward and sea-ward, high and wide; The sun shall light its shin-ing folds, The cross, on which the Sav-iour died.

2 Uplift the banner! Angels bend
In anxious silence o'er the sign,
And vainly seek to comprehend
The wonder of the love Divine.

3 Uplift the banner! Heathen lands
Shall see from far the glorious sight,
And nations, gathering at the call,
Their spirits kindle in its light.

4 Uplift the banner! Let it float
Skyward and seaward, high and wide;
Our glory only in the Cross,
Our only hope the Crucified.

5 Uplift the banner! Wide and high,
Seaward and skyward let it shine;
Nor skill, nor might, nor merit ours;
We conquer only in that sign.
Geo. W. Doane. 1824.

246 WEBB.
George James Webb. 1830.

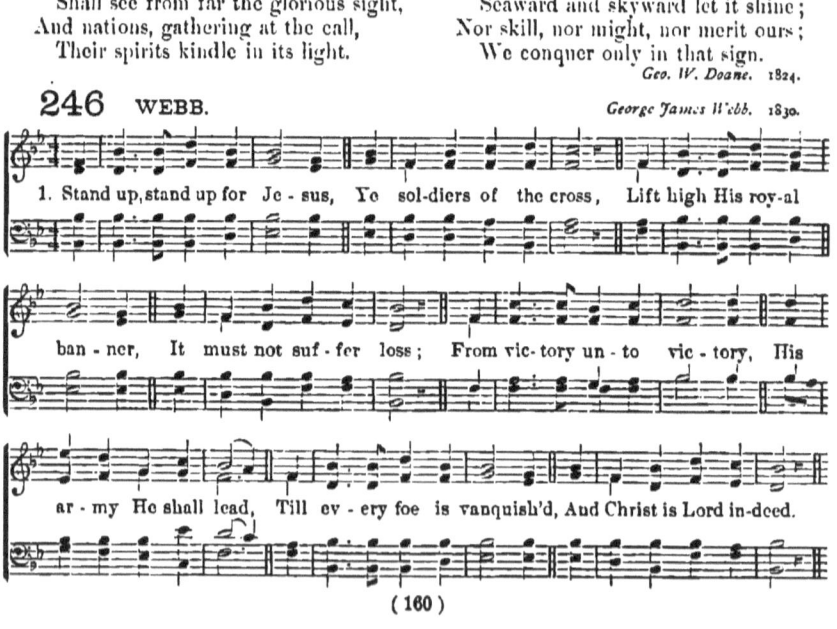

1. Stand up, stand up for Je-sus, Ye sol-diers of the cross, Lift high His roy-al ban-ner, It must not suf-fer loss; From vic-tory un-to vic-tory, His ar-my He shall lead, Till ev-ery foe is vanquish'd, And Christ is Lord in-deed.

SOLDIERS OF THE CROSS.

2 Stand up, stand up for Jesus,
　　The trumpet call obey;
　Forth to the mighty conflict,
　　In this His glorious day:
　"Ye that are men, now serve Him"
　　Against unnumbered foes;
　Let courage rise with danger,
　　And strength to strength oppose.

3 Stand up, stand up for Jesus,
　　Stand in His strength alone;
　The arm of flesh will fail you,
　　Ye dare not trust your own;
　Put on the gospel armor,
　　And watching unto prayer,
　Where duty calls, or danger,
　　Be never wanting there.

4 Stand up, stand up for Jesus,
　　The strife will not be long;
　This day the noise of battle,
　　The next the victor's song:
　To him that overcometh,
　　A crown of life shall be;
　He with the King of Glory
　　Shall reign eternally.
　　　　　　　George Duffield. 1858.

247　VICTORIA. L. M. D.　　*Henry Lahee.* 1861.

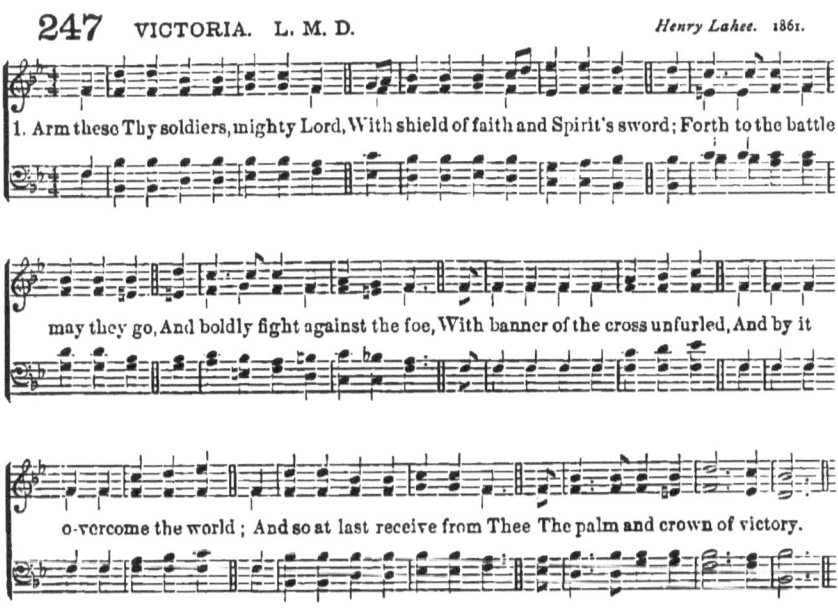

1. Arm these Thy soldiers, mighty Lord, With shield of faith and Spirit's sword; Forth to the battle may they go, And boldly fight against the foe, With banner of the cross unfurled, And by it o-vercome the world; And so at last receive from Thee The palm and crown of victory.

2 Come, ever-blessed Spirit, come,
　And make thy servants' hearts thy home;
　May each a living temple be,
　Hallowed forever, Lord, to thee;
　Enrich that temple's holy shrine
　With sevenfold gifts of grace divine;
　With wisdom, light, and knowledge bless,
　Strength, counsel, fear, and godliness.
　　　　　Christopher Wordsworth. 1863.

THE CHRISTIAN LIFE.

248 MISSIONARY CHANT. L. M. — Charles Zeuner. 1832.

1. Ye Christian heralds! go, proclaim
Salvation thro' Immanuel's name,
To distant climes the tidings bear,
And plant the Rose of Sharon there.

2 He'll shield you with a wall of fire,
With flaming zeal your breast inspire;
Bid raging winds their fury cease,
And hush the tempest into peace.

3 And when our labors all are o'er,
Then we shall meet to part no more,—
Meet with the blood-bought throng, to fall,
And crown our Jesus—Lord of all!

Winchell's Coll. 1817.

249 WORK, FOR THE NIGHT.

Copyright. Used by per. of O. Ditson & Co.

1 Work, for the night is coming,
Work through the morning hours;
Work while the dew is sparkling,
Work 'mid springing flowers;
Work when the day grows brighter,
Work in the glowing sun;
Work, for the night is coming,
When man's work is done.

2 Work, for the night is coming,
Work through the sunny noon;
Fill brightest hours with labor,
Rest comes sure and soon.
Give every flying minute
Something to keep in store;
Work, for the night is coming,
When man works no more.

3 Work, for the night is coming,
Under the sunset skies;
While their bright tints are glowing,
Work, for daylight flies.
Work till the last beam fadeth,
Fadeth to shine no more;
Work while the night is darkening,
When man's work is o'er.   *S. Dyer.*

250 MISSIONARY HY. 7s & 6s. D.

1 From Greenland's icy mountains,
From India's coral strand,
Where Afric's sunny fountains
Roll down their golden sand;
From many an ancient river,
From many a palmy plain,
They call us to deliver
Their land from error's chain.

2 What though the spicy breezes
Blow soft o'er Ceylon's isle,
Though every prospect pleases,
And only man is vile?
In vain with lavish kindness
The gifts of God are strown;
The heathen, in his blindness,
Bows down to wood and stone.

3 Shall we whose souls are lighted
With wisdom from on high,
Shall we to men benighted
The lamp of life deny?
Salvation! O, salvation!
The joyful sound proclaim,
Till earth's remotest nation
Has learned Messiah's name,

MISSIONS.

4 Waft, waft, ye winds! His story,
   And you, ye waters! roll
Till, like a sea of glory,
   It spreads from pole to pole;
Till o'er our ransomed nature
   The Lamb for sinners slain,
Redeemer, King, Creator,
   In bliss returns to reign.
                    Reginald Heber. 1819.

251 WEBB. 7s & 6s. D

1 The morning light is breaking;
   The darkness disappears;
The sons of earth are waking
   To penitential tears.
Each breeze that sweeps the ocean
   Brings tidings from afar
Of nations in commotion,
   Prepared for Zion's war.

2 Blest river of salvation,
   Pursue thy onward way;
Flow thou to every nation,
   Nor in thy richness stay:
Stay not till all the lowly
   Triumphant reach their home;
Stay not till all the holy
   Proclaim, "The Lord is come!"
                    S. F. Smith. 1832.

252 ZION. 8s, 7s & 4s.

1 O'er the gloomy hills of darkness,
   Cheered by no celestial ray,
Sun of righteousness! arising,
   Bring the bright, the glorious day;
      Send the gospel
   To the earth's remotest bounds.

2 Kingdoms wide that sit in darkness,
   Grant them, Lord! the glorious light;
And from eastern coast to western,
   May the morning chase the night;
      And redemption,
   Freely purchased, win the day.

3 Fly abroad, thou mighty Gospel!
   Win and conquer, never cease;

May Thy lasting, wide dominions
   Multiply and still increase;
      Sway Thy sceptre,
   Saviour! all the world around.
                    W. Williams. 1772.

253 STOCKWELL. 8s & 7s.

Copyright. By per. of O. Ditson & Co.

1 Cast thy bread upon the waters,
   Thinking not 'tis thrown away;
God himself saith, thou shalt gather
   It again some future day.

2 As the seed by billows floated,
   To some distant island lone,
So to human souls benighted,
   That thou flingest may be borne.

3 Cast thy bread upon the waters;
   Why wilt thou still doubting stand?
Bounteous shall God send the harvest,
   If thou sow'st with liberal hand.
                    Mrs. J. H. Hanaford. 1852.

254 BOYLSTON. S. M.

1 The harvest dawn is near,
   The year delays not long;
And he who sows with many a tear,
   Shall reap with many a song.

2 Sad to his toil he goes,
   His seed with weeping leaves;
But he shall come at twilight's close,
   And bring his golden sheaves.
                    George Burgess. 1840.

255 DUKE STREET. L. M.

1 Soon may the last glad song arise
Through all the millions of the skies—
That song of triumph which records
That all the earth is now the Lord's!

2 Let thrones and powers and kingdoms be
Obedient, mighty God, to Thee!
And, over land and stream and main,
Wave Thou the sceptre of Thy reign.
                    Mrs. Voke. 1816.

THE CHRISTIAN LIFE.

256 CHRISTIAN SISTER O'ER THE SEA. 7s. D. *T. Corben.* 1882.

1. Christian sis-ter o'er the sea, This has Jesus done for thee: Thine a country fair and strong, Where God's blessings thickly throng; Where in peace God's people dwell; Where is heard the Sabbath-bell; Christian sis-ter o'er the sea, Canst thou nothing do for me?

2 Christian sister o'er the sea,
This has Jesus done for thee:
Thine the comforts sweet, that come
From a hallowed Christian home:
Where thy mother tongue can teach
Jesus' love with infant speech.
Christian sister o'er the sea,
Canst thou nothing do for me?

3 Christian sister o'er the sea,
This has Jesus done for thee!—
Mine a country dark as night,
Where unknown is Gospel light;
Where we pass life's weary days,
Never heard the voice of praise;
Christian sister o'er the sea,
Canst thou nothing do for me?

J. E. Rankin. 1882.

257 HARK, THE MACEDODIAN CRY. 7s. D.

1. Hark, the Macedonian cry, Come and help us, lest we die; Wing of morning quickly take, Our long night of woe to break; Hush for once the roar of gain, Like the

MISSIONS.

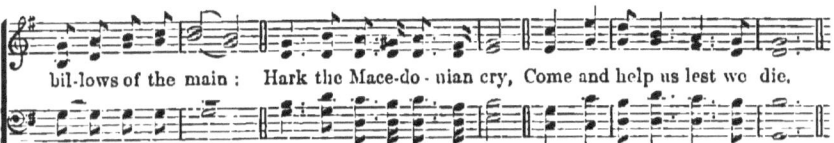
bil-lows of the main : Hark the Mace-do-nian cry, Come and help us lest we die.

2 Hark! I hear it yet again,
Voice of sinful, dying men!
Hush, for once life's busy hum,
Let the voice of joy be dumb:
Cease from pray'r, and cease from song,
While ye pass the cry along:
Ah! that bitter, bitter cry:
Come and help us, lest we die.

3 From Christ's empires yet to be,
In wild realms beyond the sea;
From the hills and from the plain,
From the island and the main;
Where'er man in sin is found,
Comes that voice, the earth around;
Voice that reaches to the sky;
Come and help us, lest we die.
J. E. Rankin. 1882.

258 DAUGHTER OF ZION, AWAKE! 11s. *Samuel S. Wesley.* 1864.

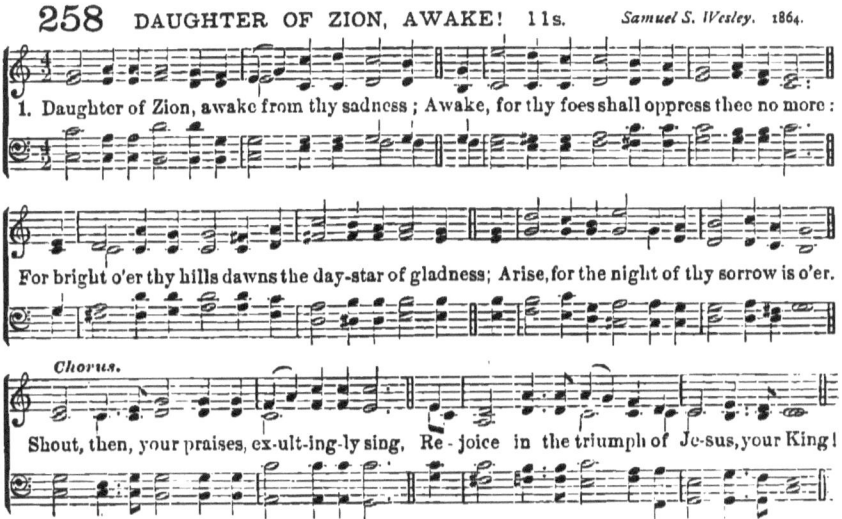

1. Daughter of Zion, awake from thy sadness; Awake, for thy foes shall oppress thee no more: For bright o'er thy hills dawns the day-star of gladness; Arise, for the night of thy sorrow is o'er.

Chorus. Shout, then, your praises, ex-ult-ing-ly sing, Re-joice in the triumph of Je-sus, your King!

2 Strong were thy foes; but the arm that subdued them,
And scattered their legions, was mightier far:
They fled like the chaff from the scourge that pursued them;
And vain were their steeds and their chariots of war.—*Chorus.*

3 Daughter of Zion, the power that hath saved thee,
Extolled with the harp and the timbrel should be;
Then shout! for the foe is destroyed that enslaved thee;
Th' oppressor is vanquished, and Zion is free.—*Chorus.*
Fitzgerald's Collection. 1830.

259 LEAD ME, PRECIOUS SAVIOUR.

Mrs. J. F. Knapp.

This can be made a very impressive Infant class Hymn by observing the following motions: At commencement of each verse, hands should be together as in attitude of prayer, remaining so to words "Fold me," when arms should be folded across the breast, and then opened and slightly extended at words "I will praise," as if invoking a blessing—eyes to be turned upward during the whole exercise.

1. Lead me, lead me, Lead me, precious Sav-iour, In-to the nar-row way, In-to the nar-row way, Fold me, fold me, Fold me to thy bo-som, And may I nev-er stray, O nev-er stray; And I will praise Thee ev-ermore, yes, ev-er-more; And I will praise Thee ev-er-more, yes, ev-er-more.

2 I will love Thee,
Ever, ever love Thee,
May sinful thoughts depart,
O take them from my heart.
   Cho.—Fold me, fold me, etc.

3 Lead me, fold me,
Guide and ever keep me,
And thanks my hearts will give,
Dear Saviour, while I live.
   Cho.—Fold me, fold me, etc.

CHILDREN'S SONGS.

260 LOOKING TO JESUS.
H. R. Palmer.

1. Yield not to temp-ta-tion, For weak-ness is sin, Each vict-'ry will help us, Some oth-er to win. Fight man-ful-ly on-ward, Dark passions sub-due, Look ev-er to Je-sus, He'll car-ry you through.

Refrain.
Ask the Sav-iour to help you, Com-fort, strengthen, and keep you: He is will-ing to aid you, He will car-ry you through. *Repeat pp ad lib.*

2 Shun evil companions,
　　Bad language disdain,
　God's name hold in reverence,
　　Nor take it in vain ;
　Be thoughtful and earnest,
　　Kind-hearted and true,
　Look ever to Jesus,
　　He'll carry you through.—*Chorus.*

3 To him that o'ercometh,
　　God giveth a crown,
　Through faith we shall conquer,
　　Though often cast down ;
　He who is the Saviour
　　Our strength will renew,
　Look ever to Jesus,
　　He'll carry you through.—*Chorus.*
　　　　　　　　　　H. R. Palmer.

261 I LOVE TO HEAR THE STORY.

H. J. Gauntlett.

Joyously.

1. I love to hear the sto-ry, Which an-gel voi-ces tell, How once the King of glo-ry Came down on earth to dwell. I am both weak and sin-ful, But this I sure-ly know, The Lord came down to save me, Be-cause He loved me so.

2 I'm glad my blessed Saviour
    Was once a child like me,
  To show how pure and holy
    His little ones might be;
  And if I try to follow
    His footsteps here below,
  He never will forget me,
    Because He loves me so.
      I love to hear, etc.

3 To sing His love and mercy
    My sweetest songs I'll raise;
  And though I cannot see Him,
    I know He hears my praise;
  For He has kindly promised
    That I may surely go
  To sing among His angels,
    Because He loves me so.
      I love to hear, etc.

Emily Huntington Miller.

262 GOD WHO HATH MADE THE DAISIES.

1. God, who hath made the daisies, And ev-ery love-ly thing, He will ac-cept our prais-es, And hearken while we sing; He says, tho' we are sim-ple, Tho'

2 Though we are young and simple,
   In praise we may be bold;
   The children in the temple
   He heard in days of old.
   And if our hearts are humble,
   He says to you and me,
   "Suffer the little children,
   And let them come to me."

3 He sees the bird that wingeth
   Its way o'er earth and sky;
   He hears the lark that singeth
   Up in the heaven so high;
   He sees the heart's low breathings,
   And says (well pleased to see),
   "Suffer the little children,
   And let them come to me."

4 Therefore we will come near Him,
   And joyfully we'll sing;
   No cause to shrink or fear Him,
   We'll make our voices ring:
   For in our temple speaking,
   He says to you and me,
   "Suffer the little children,
   And let them come to me."
                               E. Paxton Hood.

263 BEAUTIFUL THE LITTLE HANDS.   *John W. Bischoff.*

2 All the little hands were made
   Jesus' precious cause to aid;
   All the little hearts to beat
   Warm in His service so sweet.—*Cho.*

3 All the little lips should pray
   To the Saviour every day;
   All the little feet should go
   Swift on His errands below.—*Cho.*

4 What your little hands can do,
   That the Lord intends for you;
   Make that thing your first delight,
   Do it to Him with your might.—*Cho.*
                               T. Corben.

264 HEAR US, HOLY JESUS.

1. Jesus, from Thy home on high,
Far above the far blue sky,
Look on us with loving eye.
Hear us, holy Jesus.

2 Little children need not fear,
When they know that Thou art near,
Thou dost love us, Saviour dear.
Hear us, Holy Jesus.

3 Little hearts may love Thee well,
Little lips Thy love may tell,
Little hymns Thy praises swell.
Hear us, Holy Jesus.

4 Be Thou with us every day,
In our work and in our play,
When we learn, and when we pray.
Hear us, Holy Jesus.

5 Make us brave without a fear,
Make us happy, full of cheer,
Sure that Thou art always near.
Hear us, Holy Jesus.

T. B. Pollock.

265 MAY WE PRIZE THE CHRISTIAN NAME. *Arthur S. Sullivan.*

1. May we prize the Christian name,
May we guard it free from blame,
Fearing all that causes shame.
Hear us, holy Jesus.

2 May we grow from day to day,
Glad to learn each holy way,
Every ready to obey.
Hear us, Holy Jesus.

3 May we ever try to be
From our sinful tempers free,
Pure and gentle, Lord, like Thee.
Hear us, Holy Jesus.

4 May our thoughts be undefiled,
May our words be true and mild,
Make us each a holy child.
Hear us, Holy Jesus.

5 Jesus, whom we hope to see,
Calling us in heaven to be,
Happy evermore with Thee.
Hear us, Holy Jesus.

T. B. Pollock.

CHILDREN'S SONGS.

266 YOUTHFUL DAYS. 8s & 7s.
German.

1. Youthful days are passing o'er us,
Childhood's years will soon be gone;
Cares and sorrows lie before us,
Hidden dangers, snares unknown.

2 O! may He, who meek and lowly
  Visited this world below,
Make us His, and make us holy,
  Guard and guide us, where we go.

3 Hark! it is the Saviour calling,
  "Come, ye children, come to me."

Jesus, keep our feet from falling,
  Teach us all to follow Thee.

4 Soon we part; it may be, never,
  Never here to meet again;
May we meet in heaven for ever,
  And the crown eternal gain.
W. Dickson.

267 GOD IS EVERYWHERE.

1. Everywhere, everywhere, God our King is everywhere; Praises sing in grateful chorus,
To our Ruler bending o'er us; Everywhere, everywhere, We may serve Him everywhere.

2 Everywhere, everywhere,
God our Judge is everywhere.
If we sin, He is beside us;
From His eye no night can hide us;
  Everywhere, everywhere,
God is with us everywhere.

3 Everywhere, everywhere,
God, our Friend, is everywhere,
Loving, Guarding, Guiding, Keeping;

He will bless us waking, sleeping;
  Everywhere, everywhere,
God can help us everywhere.

4 Everywhere, everywhere,
God our Saviour's everywhere;
When we pray, He'll ever heed us,
And to heaven at last will lead us;
  Then we'll wear crowns so fair,
He will give us glory there.

268 COME TO THE SAVIOUR.

George F. Root.

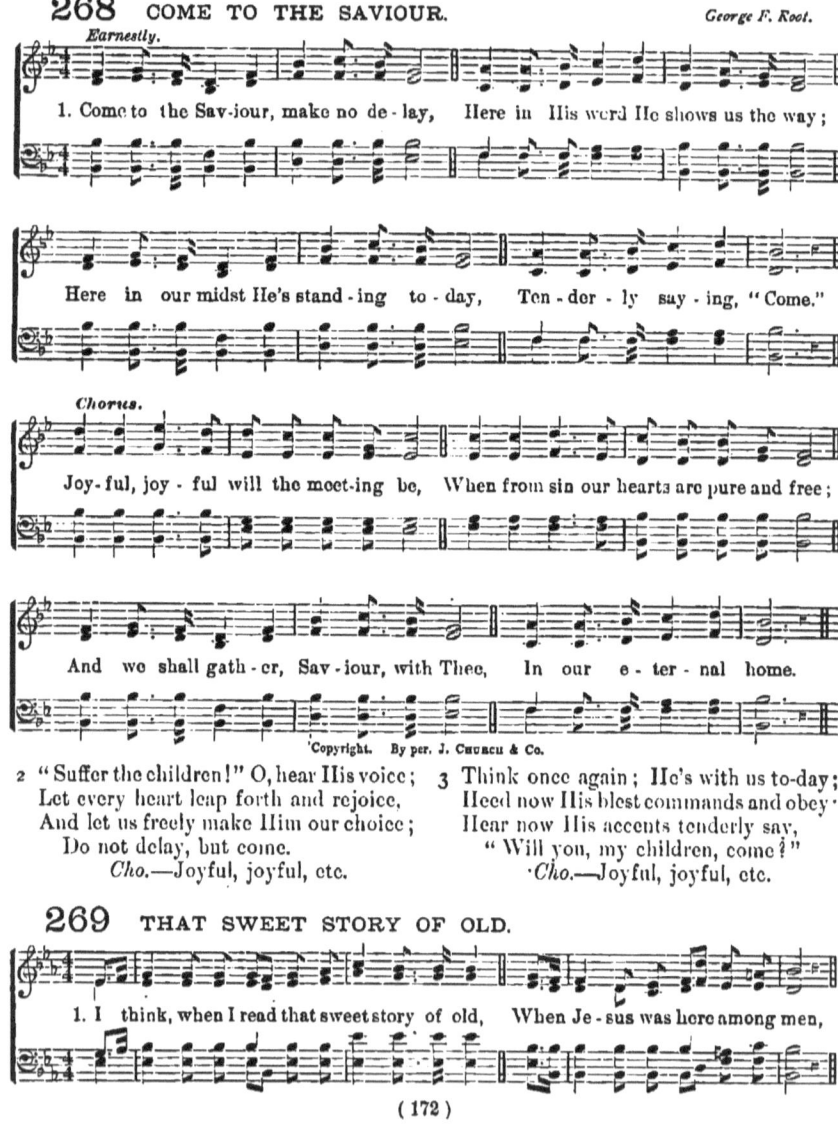

1. Come to the Saviour, make no delay, Here in His word He shows us the way; Here in our midst He's standing to-day, Tenderly saying, "Come."

Chorus.
Joyful, joyful will the meeting be, When from sin our hearts are pure and free; And we shall gather, Saviour, with Thee, In our eternal home.

2 "Suffer the children!" O, hear His voice;
Let every heart leap forth and rejoice,
And let us freely make Him our choice;
Do not delay, but come.
Cho.—Joyful, joyful, etc.

3 Think once again; He's with us to-day;
Heed now His blest commands and obey·
Hear now His accents tenderly say,
"Will you, my children, come?"
Cho.—Joyful, joyful, etc.

269 THAT SWEET STORY OF OLD.

1. I think, when I read that sweet story of old, When Jesus was here among men,

CHILDREN'S SONGS.

How He called little children as lambs to His fold, I should like to have been with them then.

 2 I wish that His hands had been placed on my head,
  That His arm had been thrown around me,
 And that I might have seen His kind look when He said,
  "Let the little ones come unto me."

 3 Yet still to His footstool in prayer I may go,
  And ask for a share in His love;
 And if I thus earnestly seek Him below,
  I shall see Him and hear Him above;

 4 In that beautiful place He has gone to prepare
  For all who are washed and forgiven;
 And many dear children are gathering there,
  "For of such is the kingdom of heaven."

270 HUSHED WAS THE EVENING HYMN. *Arthur S. Sullivan.* 1872.

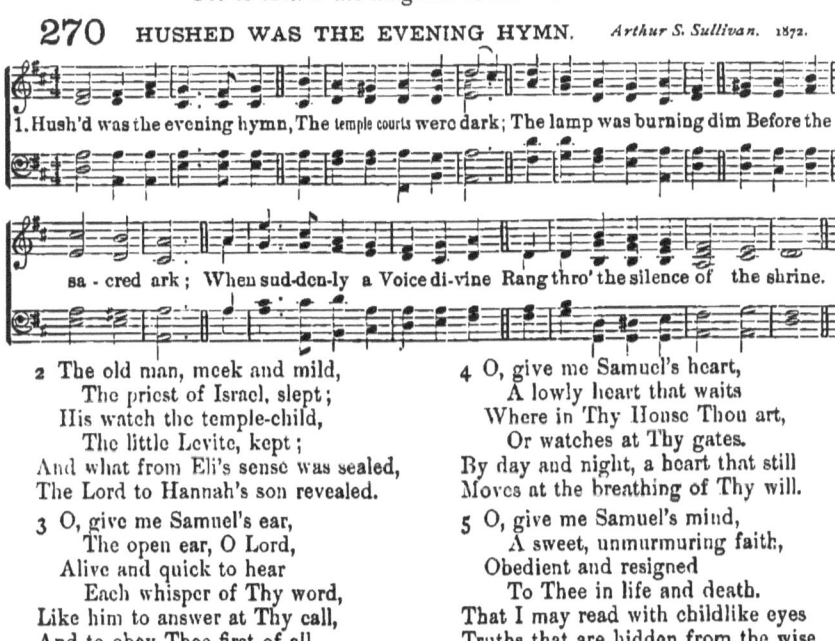

1. Hush'd was the evening hymn, The temple courts were dark; The lamp was burning dim Before the sa-cred ark; When sud-den-ly a Voice di-vine Rang thro' the silence of the shrine.

2 The old man, meek and mild,
 The priest of Israel, slept;
His watch the temple-child,
 The little Levite, kept;
And what from Eli's sense was sealed,
The Lord to Hannah's son revealed.

3 O, give me Samuel's ear,
 The open ear, O Lord,
Alive and quick to hear
 Each whisper of Thy word,
Like him to answer at Thy call,
And to obey Thee first of all.

4 O, give me Samuel's heart,
 A lowly heart that waits
Where in Thy House Thou art,
 Or watches at Thy gates.
By day and night, a heart that still
Moves at the breathing of Thy will.

5 O, give me Samuel's mind,
 A sweet, unmurmuring faith,
Obedient and resigned
 To Thee in life and death.
That I may read with childlike eyes
Truths that are hidden from the wise.
     James D. Burns. 1856.

271 THE KING'S HIGHWAY.

E. S. Lorenz. By per.

1. Wher-ev-er you may be, What-ev-er you may see, That would lead you in-to evil, say you "Nay," say you "Nay; I will not turn a-side What-ev-er may be-tide; I'll keep a-long the mid-dle of the King's high-way." The King's high-way, the King's high-way, O, turn a-side from eve-ry thing that leads a-stray; Wher-

D. S. ev-er you may be, What-ev-er you may see Just keep a-long the mid-dle of the King's high-way.

2 The meadows may be green Where by-path stile is seen;
Turn aside, the little flowers seem to say, seem to say,
Be sure you take no heed, They're trying to mislead;
Just keep along the middle of the King's highway.—*Cho.*

3 For on enchanted ground There's danger all around,
And a thousand pleasant voices bid you stay, bid you stay:
With fingers stop your ears, And never mind their jeers;
Just keep along the middle of the King's highway.—*Cho.*

4 Our God will give us light, And, walking in the night,
We shall win a crown of glory in the day, in the day
When Jesus calls His own Together round the throne,
Who kept along the middle of the King's highway.—*Cho.*

(174)

CHILDREN'S SONGS.

272 POSEN. 7s. — G. C. Strattner. 1691.

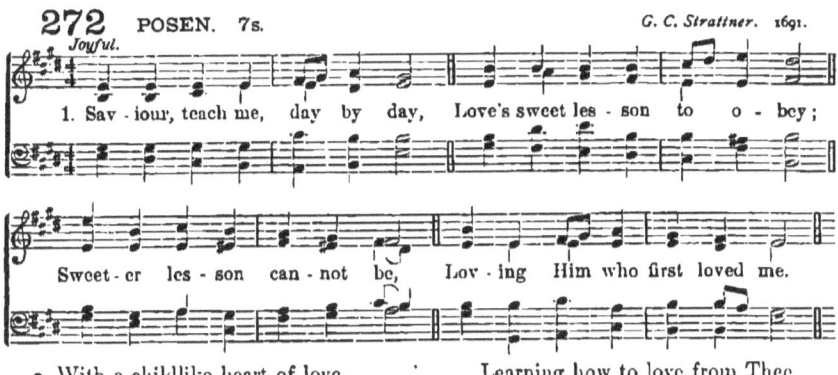

1. Saviour, teach me, day by day, Love's sweet lesson to obey; Sweeter lesson cannot be, Loving Him who first loved me.

2 With a childlike heart of love,
At Thy bidding may I move;
Prompt to serve and follow Thee,
Loving Him who first loved me.

3 Teach me all Thy steps to trace,
Strong to follow in Thy grace,
Learning how to love from Thee,
Loving Him who first loved me.

4 Thus may I rejoice to show
That I feel the love I owe;
Singing, till Thy face I see,
Of His love who first loved me.
Anon. 1854.

273 OUR LEADER. 6s & 5s. — J. Baptiste Calkin. 1871.

1. Jesus Christ our Saviour, Once for us a child, In Thy whole behavior, Meek, obedient, mild; In Thy footsteps treading We Thy lambs will be, Foe nor danger dreading While we follow Thee.

2 For all gifts and graces
While we live below,
Till in heavenly places
We Thy face shall know;
We, Thy children, raising
Unto Thee our hearts,
In Thy constant praising
Bear our duteous parts.

3 Let Thine angels guide us;
Let Thine arms enfold;
In Thy bosom hide us,
Sheltered from the cold;
As Thy love hath won us
From the world away,
Still Thy hands put on us;
Bless us day by day.
W. Whiting.

274. JESUS IS OUR SHEPHERD.

Arthur S. Sullivan.

1. Jesus is our Shepherd, Wiping ev-ery tear;.. Folded in His bosom, What have we to fear?.. Only let us follow Whither He doth lead, To the thirsty desert, Or the dewy mead.

Chorus. In Harmony.
Gladly we will follow, Guided by His hand, He at last will bring us To the heavenly land.

2 Jesus is our Shepherd,
   Well we know His voice;
How its gentlest whisper
   Makes our hearts rejoice;
Even when He chideth,
   Tender is its tone;
None but He shall guide us,
   We are His alone.—*Cho.*

3 Jesus is our Shepherd;
  With His goodness now
  And His tender mercy
  He doth us endow;

Let us sing His praises
  With a gladsome heart,
  Till in heaven we meet Him,
  Never more to part.—*Cho.*
        Tr. by John Ellerton.

275 LAMBS OF THE FOLD. *E. B. Smith.*

1. O hearken, dear Saviour, O hearken To the ten-der wee lambs of the fold;
Reach out Thy strong arm and protect us, Lest we wander a-way in the cold.

Chorus.
O shel-ter the wee lit-tle lambs of the fold, Shel-ter them warm from the biting cold.
Shel-ter the lambs, shel-ter the lambs, The lit-tle wee lambs of the fold.

2 The world is so new to our vision,
  And its pathways so many and wide,
  We never can tread them in safety,
  Blessed Saviour, unless Thou wilt guide;

3 Thy love is our only salvation,
  Give us early this lesson to learn;
  From sins and temptations of childhood,
  To its shelter, O help us to turn.

4 O, carry the lambs in Thy bosom,
  Like the tender Good Shepherd of old;
  And guard us with care all so faithful,
  That no one shall be lost from Thy fold.
        Ellen Oliver.

CHILDREN'S SONGS.

276 FERRIER. 7s.
John B. Dykes.

1. Jesus, holy, undefiled,
Listen to a little child;
Thou hast sent the glorious light,
Chasing far the silent night.

2 Thou hast sent the sun to shine
O'er this glorious world of Thine;
Warmth to give, and pleasant glow
On each tender flower below.

3 Now the little birds arise,
Chirping gayly in the skies;
Thee their tiny voices praise
In the early songs they raise.

4 Thou by whom the birds are fed,
Give to me my daily bread;
And Thy Holy Spirit give,
Without whom I cannot live.

5 Make me, Lord, obedient, mild,
As becomes a little child;
All day long, in every way,
Teach me what to do and say.

6 Make me, Lord, in work and play,
Thine more truly every day;
And when Thou at last shalt come,
Take me to Thy heavenly home.

Mrs. E. Shepcote. 1840.

277 YOUNG GLEANERS.

1. In the vineyard of our Father
Daily work we find to do;
Scattered gleanings we may gather,
Though we are but young and few;
Little clusters, Little clusters,
Help to fill the garners too.

CHILDREN'S SONGS.

2 Toiling early in the morning,
　Catching moments through the day,
　Nothing small or lowly scorning,
　　While we work, and watch, and pray;
　　Gathering gladly
　Free-will offerings by the way.

3 Not for selfish praise or glory,
　Not for things of little worth,
　But to send the blessed story
Of the gospel o'er the earth,
　Telling mortals
Of our Lord and Saviour's birth.

4 Steadfast, then, in our endeavor,
　Heavenly Father, may we be;
　And forever and forever
　　We will give the praise to Thee;
　　Hallelujah
　Singing, all eternity.

　　　　　　　　　　T. McKellar.

278   GENTLE SHEPHERD.

1. Gracious Saviour, gentle Shepherd,
　Little ones are dear to Thee;
Gathered with Thine arms, and carried
　In Thy bosom may we be;
Sweetly, fondly, safely tended,
　From all want and danger free.

2 Tender Shepherd, never leave us
　From Thy fold to go astray;
　By Thy look of love directed
　May we walk the narrow way;
　Thus direct us and protect us,
　Lest we fall an easy prey.

3 Let Thy holy word instruct us,
　Guide us daily by its light;
　Let Thy love and grace constrain us
To approve whate'er is right.
Take Thine easy yoke and wear it,
Strengthened with Thy heavenly might.

4 Taught to lisp the holy praises
　Which on earth Thy children sing,
　Both with lips and hearts unfeigned
　May we our thank-offerings bring;
　There with all the saints in glory
　Join to priase our Lord and King.
　　　　　　　　Jonathan Whittemore.

279 PASTOR BONUS.
Moderato. — *John Stainer.*

1. Christ, who once amongst us As a child did dwell, Is the children's Saviour, And He loves us well; If we keep the promise Made Him at the Font, He will be our Shepherd, And we shall not want.

2 Then it was they laid us
 In those tender arms,
 Where the lambs are carried
 Safe from all alarms;
 If we trust His promise,
 He will let us rest
 In His arms forever,
 Leaning on His breast.

3 Though we may not see Him
 For a little while,
 We shall know He holds us,
 Often feel His smile;
 Death will be to slumber
 In that sweet embrace,
 And we shall awaken
 To behold His face.

4 He will be our Shepherd
 After as before,
 By still heavenly waters
 Lead us evermore;
 Make us lie in pastures,
 Beautiful and green,
 Where none thirst or hunger,
 And no tears are seen.

5 Jesus, our good Shepherd,
 Laying down Thy life,
 Lest Thy sheep should perish
 In the cruel strife,
 Help us to remember
 All Thy love and care,
 Trust in Thee, and love Thee,
 Always, everywhere.
 W. St. Hill Bourne.

280 WE ARE BUT LITTLE CHILDREN WEAK.
C. E. Willing.

1. We are but little children weak, Nor born in any high estate; What can we do for Jesus' sake, Who is so high, and good, and great?

2 O, day by day each Christian child,
  Has much to do, without, within,
  A death to die for Jesus' sake,
  A weary war to wage with sin.

3 When deep within our swelling hearts
  The thoughts of pride and anger rise,
  When bitter words are on our tongues,
  And tears of passion in our eyes;

4 Then we may stay the angry blow,
  Then we may check the hasty word,
  Give gentle answers back again,
  And fight a battle for our Lord.

5 There's not a child so small and weak
  But has his little cross to take,
  His little work of love and praise
  That he may do for Jesus' sake.
  Cecil Frances Alexander. 1850.

281 A FRIEND FOR LITTLE CHILDREN. *John Stainer.* 1875.

1. There's a Friend for little children Above the bright blue sky, A Friend who never changes, Whose love will never die; Our earthly friends may fail us, And change with changing years, This Friend is always worthy Of that dear Name He bears.

2 There's a Home for little children
    Above the bright blue sky,
  Where Jesus reigns in glory,
    A Home of peace and joy;
  No home on earth is like it,
    Nor can with it compare,
  For every one is happy,
    Nor can be happier, there.

3 There's a Crown for little children
    Above the bright blue sky,
  And all who look to Jesus
    Shall wear it by and by;
  A crown of brightest glory,
    Which He will sure bestow
  On all who love the Saviour,
    And walk with Him below.

4 There's a Song for little children
    Above the bright blue sky,
  A harp of sweetest music,
    For hymns of victory;
  And all above is pleasure,
    And found in Christ alone;
  O come and serve Him, children,
    That all may be your own.
  Albert Midlane. 1860.

282. O COME, DEAR CHILD.

John B. Dykes. 1858.

1. O come, dear child, a-long with me, And look on yon-der clear blue sky, The moon is shin-ing bright, you see, And stars are twinkling up on high.

2. 'Tis there, my child, far, far above,
   That Heaven's eternal Kingdom lies,
  There Holy Angels dwell in love,
   And tears are wiped from off all eyes.

3. It is a happy, happy place,
   Without a sorrow, pain, or care,
   here you can see the Saviour's face,
   Who loves to take good children there.

4. O pray each night that God may bless,
   And keep you while on earth you stay,
   And give you endless happiness,
   When from the earth you pass away.

Cecil Frances Alexander. 1848.

283. INVITATION. C. M. D.

Arr. from Ludwig Spohr. (1784-1859.)

1. There is a mother's voice of love, To hush her lit-tle child; There is a father's voice of praise, So ear-nest and so mild; But there is yet an-oth-er voice That speaks in gen-tlest tone; I think that we can hear it best When we are quite a-lone.

HOME.

2 It is a still, small, holy voice,
　　The voice of God most high,
　That whispers always in our heart,
　　And says that He is by. [wrong,
　The voice will blame us when we're
　　And praise us when we're right;
　We hear it in the light of day,
　　And in the quiet night.

3 And even they whose ears are deaf
　　To every other sound,
　When they have listened in their hearts
　　The still small voice have found,
　And they have felt that God is good,
　　And thanked Him for the voice
　That told them what was right and true,
　　And made their hearts rejoice.

284　GOD BLESS THE HOME.　　　　　German.

1. God bless the home, tho' humble, So full of love's sweet light:
God bless the little children, With their sweet faces bright;
God bless the mother tender, God bless the father, too;
God make us fond and faithful, God keep us kind and true.

2 God bless the home, where daily
　　The songs of praise arise;
　Where all kneel round the altar,
　　And offer sacrifice.
　Alas! for homes where never
　　Is heard the voice of prayer;
　Alas! for homes, when Jesus
　　Is never mentioned there!

3 Alas! for homes, where sorrow
　　Like night must ever brood;
　Where children lack for clothing,
　　And for their daily food.
　God bless the home He gives us,
　　The home that gave us birth;
　God keep us fond and faithful,
　　And make it heaven on earth.
　　　　　　　　　　　　T. Corben.

285 HOME. 11s.

Henry R. Bishop. 1829.

1. 'Mid pleasures and palaces though we may roam, Be it ever so humble, there's no place like home; A charm from the skies seems to hallow us here, Which, seek thro' the world is not met with elsewhere. Home! home! sweet, sweet home! Be it ever so humble there's no place like home.

2 An exile from home, splendor dazzles in vain;
O give me my lowly, thatched cottage again!
The birds singing gayly, that came at my call,—
Give me them! and the peace of mind dearer than all.
  Home! home! sweet, sweet home!
Be it ever so humble, there's no place like home.

John Howard Payne.

286 'MID SCENES OF CONFUSION. 11s.

1 'Mid scenes of confusion and creature complaints,
How sweet to my soul is communion with saints;
To find at the banquet of mercy there's room,
And feel in the presence of Jesus at home.
  Home! home! sweet, sweet home!
Prepare me, dear Saviour, for glory, my home.

2 Sweet bonds that unite all the children of peace!
And thrice precious Jesus, whose love cannot cease!
Though oft from Thy presence in sadness I roam,
I long to behold Thee in glory, at home.—*Refrain.*

3 While here in the valley of conflict I stay,
O give me submission, and strength as my day;
In all my afflictions to Thee would I come,
Rejoicing in hope of my glorious home.—*Refrain.*

David Denham. 1837.

287. BRIGHTLY GLEAMS OUR BANNER.

Joseph Barnby. 1866.

1. Brightly gleams our banner, Pointing to the sky, Waving wand'rers onward To their home on high; Journ'ying o'er a desert, Gladly thus we pray, And with hearts united, Take our heaven-ward way.... Brightly beams our banner, Pointing to the sky, Waving wand'rers onward To their home on high.

2 Jesus, Lord and Master,
At Thy sacred feet,
Here with hearts rejoicing,
See Thy children meet;
Often have we left Thee,
Often gone astray,
Keep us, mighty Saviour,
In the narrow way.—*Cho.*

3 All our days direct us
In the way we go,
Lead us on victorious,
Over ev'ry foe:
Bid Thine angels shield us
When the storm-clouds lower,
Pardon Thou and save us
In the last dread hour.—*Cho.*

4 Then with saints and angels
May we join above,
Offering prayers and praises
At Thy throne of love;
When the toil is over,
Then comes rest and peace,
Jesus in His beauty,
Songs that never cease.—*Cho.*

T. J. Potter.

THE CHRISTIAN PILGRIMAGE.

288 ST. HILDA. 7s & 6s. D. *E. Husband.*

1. O happy band of pilgrims, If onward ye will tread, With Jesus as your Fellow, To Jesus as your Head! O happy if ye labor As Jesus did for men: O happy if ye hunger As Jesus hungered then!

2 The trials that beset you,
  The sorrows ye endure,
  The manifold temptations
   That death alone can cure:
  What are they, but His jewels
   Of right celestial worth?
  What are they but the ladder,
   Set up to heaven on earth?

3 The Cross that Jesus carried
   He carried as your due:
  The Crown that Jesus weareth
   He weareth it for you.
  O happy band of pilgrims,
   Look upward to the skies;
  Where such a light affliction
   Shall win you such a prize.
  Tr., John Mason Neale. 1862.

289 WESTON. 8s & 7s. D. *J. P. Roe.*

1. Thro' the night of doubt and sorrow, Onward goes the pilgrim band, Singing songs of expectation, Marching to the promised land. Clear before us, thro' the darkness, Gleams and

(186)

THE CHRISTIAN PILGRIMAGE.

burns the guid-ing Light; Brother clasps the hand of brother, Stepping fearless thro' the night.

2 One the light of God's own presence,
  O'er His ransom'd people shed,
Chasing far the gloom and terror,
  Brightening all the path we tread;
One the object of our journey,
  One the faith which never tires,
One the earnest looking forward,
  One the hope our God inspires.

3 One the strain the lips of thousands
  Lift as from the heart of one;
One the conflict, one the peril,
  One the march in God begun;
One the gladness of rejoicing
  On the far eternal shore,
Where the one Almighty Father
  Reigns in love for evermore.

4 Onward, therefore, pilgrim brothers,
  Onward, with the Cross our aid!
Bear its shame, and fight its battle,
  Till we rest beneath its shade!
Soon shall come the great awaking;
  Soon the rending of the tomb;
Then, the scattering of all shadows,
  And the end of toil and gloom!

Bernhard S. Ingeman. 1825.   Tr., S. Baring-Gould. 1867.

290 CHALVEY. S. M. D.
L. G. Haynes.

1. A few more years shall roll, A few more sea-sons come, And we shall be with those that rest, A-sleep with-in the tomb.

Refrain.

Then, O my Lord pre-pare My soul for that great day; O wash me in Thy precious blood, And take my sins a-way.

2 A few more storms shall beat
  On this wild, rocky shore;
And we shall be where tempests cease,
  And surges swell no more.—*Ref.*

3 A few more struggles here,
  A few more partings o'er,
A few more toils, a few more tears,
  And we shall weep no more.—*Ref.*

4 'Tis but a little while
  And He shall come again,
Who died that we might live, who lives
  That we with Him may reign.—*Ref.*

Horatius Bonar. 1844.

THE CHRISTIAN PILGRIMAGE.

291. GATHERING HOME.

W. O. Perkins.

2 Before they rest, they pass | through the strife,
  One by one, one by one;
Through the waters of death they | enter life,
  Yes, one by one.
To some are the floods of the | river still,
  As they | ford on their way to the | heavenly hill,
To | others the waves run | fiercely and wild,
  Yet they | reach the home of the | undefiled.—*Ref.*

3 We, too, shall come to the | river side,
  One by one, one by one;
  We are nearer its waters each | eventide,
  Yes, one by one.
  We can hear the noise and the | dash of the stream
    Now and again through our | life's deep dream;
  Some- | times the floods all the | banks overflow,
    And | sometimes in ripples and | small waves go.—*Ref.*

4 Jesus, Redeemer, we | look to Thee,
  One by one, one by one;
  We lift up our voices | tremblingly,
  Yes, one by one.
  The waves of the river are | dark and cold,
    We | know not the place where our | feet may hold;
  May | Thou who didst pass through in | deep midnight,
    Stand | by us, and guide us,—our | staff and light.—*Ref.*

292 THERE IS A HAPPY LAND.   S. S. *Wesley.* 1864.

1. There is a happy land, Far, far away, Where saints in glory stand, Bright, bright as day. O how they sweetly sing, "Worthy is our Saviour King!" Loud let His praises ring, Praise, praise for aye!

2 Come to this happy land,
  Come, come away:
Why will ye doubting stand,
  Why still delay?
O, we shall happy be,
When from sin and sorrow free;
Lord, we shall live with Thee,
  Blest, blest for aye.

3 Bright in that happy land
  Beams every eye;
Kept by a Father's hand,
  Love cannot die.
O, then to glory run,
Be a crown and kingdom won;
And bright above the sun
  Reign, reign for aye.
    Andrew Young. 1838.

THE CHRISTIAN PILGRIMAGE.

293 ST. BONIFACE. *Henry Gadsby.*

1. Forward! be our watchward, Steps and voi-ces joined; Seek the things be-fore us, Not a look be-hind: Burns the fie-ry pil-lar At our arm-y's head; Who shall dream of shrinking, By our Cap-tain led? *Chorus.* For-ward thro' the des-ert, Thro' the toil and fight: Jor-dan flows be-fore us, Zi-on beams with light!

2 Forward, when in childhood
  Buds the infant mind;
All through youth and manhood,
  Not a thought behind;
Speed through realms of nature,
  Climb the steps of grace;
Faint not, till in glory
  Gleams our Father's face.
    Forward all the life-time,
      Climb from height to height:
    Till the head be hoary,
      Till the eve be light.

3 Forward, flock of Jesus,
  Salt of all the earth;
Till each yearning purpose
  Spring to glorious birth;
Sick, they ask for healing,
  Blind, they grope for day;
Pour upon the nations
  Wisdom's loving ray.
Forward, out of error,
  Leave behind the night;
Forward through the darkness,
  Forward into Light!

4 Glories upon glories
  Hath our God prepared,
By the souls that love Him
  One day to be shared;
Eye hath not beheld them,
  Ear hath never heard;
Nor of these hath uttered
  Thought or speech a word:
    Forward, marching eastward
      Where the heaven is bright,
    Till the veil be lifted,
      Till our faith be sight!

Henry Alford. 1865.

294 FORWARD INTO LIGHT.

1. Far o'er yon ho-ri-zon Rise the cit-y towers, Where our God a-bid-eth; That fair home is ours; Flash the streets with jas-per, Shine the gates with gold, Flows the gladd'ning riv-er, Shed-ding joys un-told.

Chorus.
Thither, onward, thith-er, In the Spir-it's might; Pil-grims, to your coun-try, For-ward in-to light.

2 Into God's high temple
Onward as we press,
Beauty spreads around us,
Born of holiness;
Arch, and vault, and carving,
Lights of varied tone,
Softened words and holy,
Prayer and praise alone:
Every thought upraising
To our city bright,
Where the tribes assemble
Round the throne of light.

3 Nought that city needeth
Of these aisles of stone;
Where the Godhead dwelleth,
Temple there is none;
All the saints, that ever
In these courts have stood,
Are but babes, and feeding
On the children's food.
On through sign and token,
Stars amid the night,
Forward through the darkness,
Forward into light.

4 To the eternal Father
Loudest anthems raise;
To the Son and Spirit
Echo songs of praise;
To the Lord of glory,
Blessed Three in One,
Be by men and Angels
Endless honors done;
Weak are earthly praises;
Dull the songs of night;
Forward into triumph,
Forward into light!

Henry Alford. 1865.

THE CHRISTIAN PILGRIMAGE.

295 GOSHEN. 11s. *German.*

1. Though faint, yet pur-su-ing, we go on our way; The Lord is our Lead-er, His word is our stay; Tho' suf-fering, and sor-row, and tri-al be near, The Lord is our ref-uge, and whom can we fear?

2 And to His green pastures our footsteps He leads;
His flock in the desert how kindly He feeds!
The lambs in His bosom He tenderly bears,
And brings back the wand'rers all safe from the snares.

3 Though clouds may surround us, our God is our light;
Though storms rage around us, our God is our might;
So faint, yet pursuing, still onward we come;
The Lord is our Leader, and heaven is our home!

296 STAR OF MORN AND EVEN. *Edwin Pond Parker.*

1. Star of morn and e-ven, Sun of heav-en's heav-en, Sav-iour, high and dear, To us turn Thine ear; Thro' whate'er may come, Thou canst lead us home.

2 Saviour, pure and holy,
Lover of the lowly,
Sign us with Thy sign,
Take our hands in Thine,
Take our hands, and come,
Lead Thy children home.

3 Star of morn and even,
Shine on us from heaven;
From Thy glory throne
Hear Thy very own;
Lord and Saviour, come,
Lead us to our home.
Francis Turner Palgrave.

THE CHRISTIAN PILGRIMAGE.

297 HARK! HARK! MY SOUL.
John B. Dykes.

1. Hark! hark! my soul! Angelic songs are swelling O'er earth's green fields, and ocean's wave-beat shore; How sweet the truth those blessed strains are telling Of that new life when sin shall be no more. An-gels of Je-sus, An-gels of light, Sing-ing to welcome the pilgrims of the night; Sing-ing to wel-come the pilgrims, the pilgrims of the night.

2 Onward we go, for still we hear them singing,
  "Come, weary souls, for Jesus bids you come!"
And through the dark its echoes sweetly ringing,
  The music of the Gospel leads us home.—*Ref.*

3 Far, far away, like bells at evening pealing,
  The voice of Jesus sounds o'er land and sea,
And laden souls by thousands meekly stealing,
  Kind Shepherd, turn their weary steps to Thee.—*Ref.*

4 Rest comes at length, though life be long and dreary,
  The day must dawn, and darksome night be past;
Faith's journey ends in welcome to the weary,
  And heaven, the heart's true home, will come at last.—*Ref.*

5 Angels, sing on! your faithful watches keeping,
  Sing us sweet fragments of the songs above;
Till morning's joy shall end the night of weeping,
  And life's long shadows break in cloudless love.—*Ref.*

Frederick W. Faber. 1849.

298 LUX BENIGNA. 10s & 4s.
John B. Dykes. 1861.

1. Lead, kindly Light! amid th'encircling gloom, Lead Thou me on; The night is dark, and I am far from home, Lead Thou me on; Keep Thou my feet; I do not ask to see The distant scene; one step enough for me.

2 I was not ever thus, nor prayed that Thou
    Shouldst lead me on;
  I loved to choose and see my path; but
    Lead Thou me on:
  I loved the garish day, and spite of fears, [now
  Pride ruled my will. Remember not past
    years.

3 So long Thy power has blest me, sure it
    Will lead me on [still
  O'er moor and fen, o'er crag and torrent,
    The night is gone; [till
  And with the morn those angel faces smile
  Which I have loved long since, and lost
    awhile!
John Henry Newman. 1833.

299 I'M A PILGRIM. P. M.
German.

1. I'm a pilgrim, and I'm a stranger; I can tar-ry, I can tar-ry but a night!
D.C. I'm a pil-grim, etc.

Do not de-tain me, for I am go-ing To where the fountains are ever flow-ing;

2 There the glory is ever shining!
  O, my longing heart, my longing heart
    is there!
  Here in this country so dark and dreary,
  I long have wandered forlorn and weary:
    I'm a pilgrim, etc.

3 There's the city to which I journey;
  My Redeemer, my Redeemer, is its
    light!
  There is no sorrow, nor any sighing,
  Nor any tears there, nor any dying!
    I'm a pilgrim, etc.
Mary S. B. Dana. 1840.

THE BLESSED SLEEP

300 "HE GIVETH HIS BELOVED SLEEP." — Rossini.

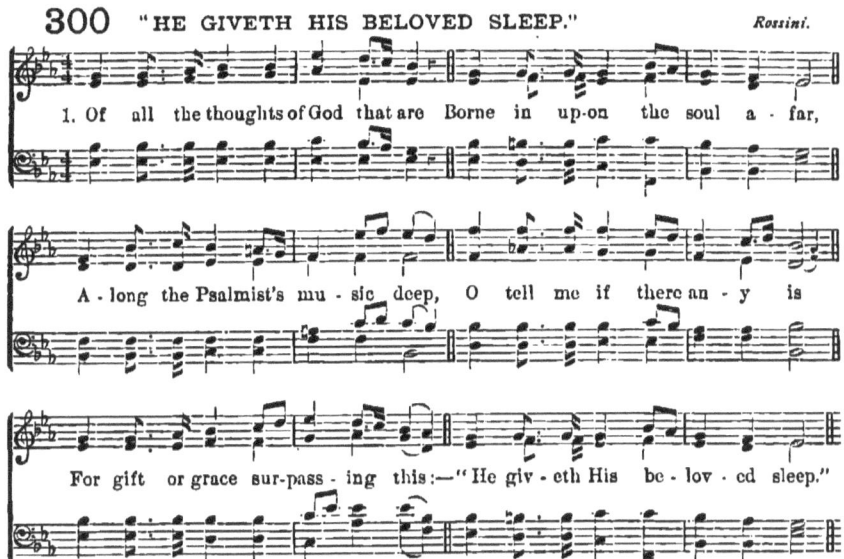

1. Of all the thoughts of God that are Borne in up-on the soul a-far,
A-long the Psalmist's mu-sic deep, O tell me if there an-y is
For gift or grace sur-pass-ing this:—"He giv-eth His be-lov-ed sleep."

2 "Sleep soft, beloved," we sometimes say,
But have no power to charm away
   Sad dreams that thro' the eyelids creep;
But never doleful dream again
Shall break their happy slumber, when
   "He giveth His beloved sleep."

3 And, friends, dear friends, when it shall be
That this low breath is gone from me,
   When round my bier ye come to weep,
Let one, most loving of you all,
Say, "Not a tear must o'er her fall,
   "He giveth His beloved sleep."
   Elizabeth Barrett Browning.

---

301 HE LEADETH ME.

1 HE leadeth me; O, blessed thought,
O, words with heavenly comfort fraught,
Whate'er I do, where'er I be,
Still 'tis God's hand that leadeth me.

Cho.—He leadeth me; He leadeth me!
By His own hand He leadeth me;
His faithful follower I would be,
For by His hand He leadeth me.

2 Sometimes 'mid scenes of deepest gloom,
Sometimes where Eden's bowers bloom,
By waters still, o'er troubled sea,
Still 'tis His hand that leadeth me.—*Cho.*

3 Lord, I would clasp Thy hand in mine,
Nor ever murmur nor repine;
Content, whatever lot I see,
Since 'tis my God that leadeth me.—*Cho.*

4 And when my task on earth is done,
When, by Thy grace, the victory's won,
E'en death's cold wave I will not flee,
Since God thro' Jordan leadeth me.—*Cho.*
   J. H. Gilmore.

THE HEAVENLY CITY.

302 HEAVENLY CITY. 8s & 7s.

1. Dai - ly, dai - ly sing the prais - es
Of the Cit - y God hath made;
In the beau-teous fields of E - den
Its foun - da - tion stones are laid.

Chorus. A little slower.

O that I had wings of an - gels,
Here to spread and heavenward fly,
I would seek the gates of Zi - on
Far be - yond the star - ry sky.

2 All the walls of that dear City
   Are of bright and burnished gold;
It is matchless in its beauty
   And its treasures are untold.—*Cho.*

3 In the midst of that dear City
   Christ is reigning on His seat,
And the angels swing their censers
   In a ring about His feet.—*Cho.*

4 From the throne a river issues
   Clear as crystal, passing bright,
And it traverses the City
   Like a sudden beam of light.—*Cho.*

5 Where it waters leafy Eden,
   Rolling over silver sands,
Sit the angels, softly chiming
   On the harps between their hands.—*Cho.*

6 There the wind is sweetly fragrant,
   And is laden with the song
Of the seraphs and the elders,
   And the great redeeméd throng.—*Cho.*

7 O I would my ears were open
   Here to catch that happy strain!
O I would my eyes some vision
   Of that Eden could attain!—*Cho.*

S. Baring-Gould.

FOREGLEAMS OF HEAVEN.

303. RUTHERFORD. P. M.
Charles d'Urhan.

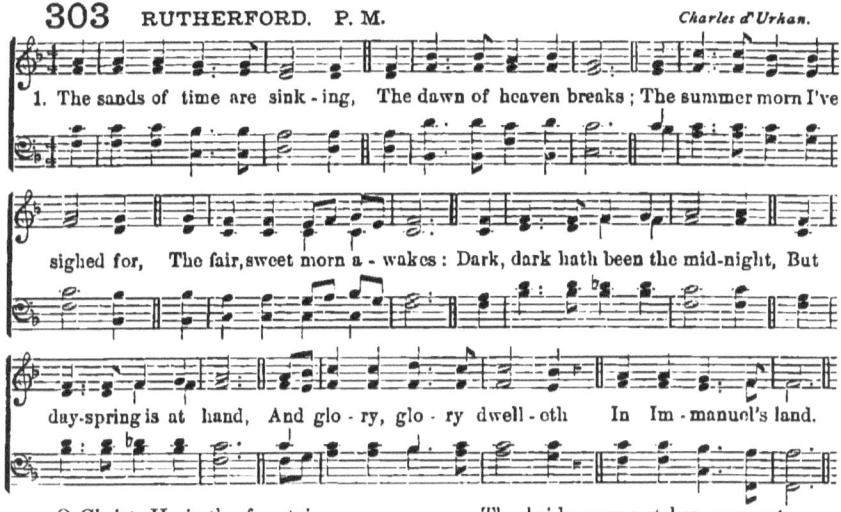

1. The sands of time are sink-ing, The dawn of heaven breaks; The summer morn I've sighed for, The fair, sweet morn a-wakes: Dark, dark hath been the mid-night, But day-spring is at hand, And glo-ry, glo-ry dwell-eth In Im-manuel's land.

2 O Christ, He is the fountain,
    The deep, sweet well of love;
  The streams of earth I've tasted,
    More deep I'll drink above.
  There to an ocean fullness
    His mercy doth expand,
  And glory, glory dwelleth
    In Immanuel's land.

3 The bride eyes not her garment,
    But her dear bridegroom's face;
  I will not gaze at glory,
    But on my King of grace:
  Not at the crown He giveth,
    But on His pierced hand;
  The Lamb is all the glory
    Of Immanuel's land.
                    A. R. Cousin.

304. LYTE. S. M.
John P. Wilkes.

1. Far from my heavenly home,
   Far from my Father's breast,
   Fainting I cry, "Blest Spirit, come,
   And speed me to my rest."

2 My spirit homeward turns,
    And faith would thither flee;
  My heart, O Zion, droops and yearns,
    When I remember Thee.

3 To Thee, to Thee, I press,
    A dark and toilsome road;

  When shall I pass the wilderness,
    And reach the saints' abode?

4 God of my life, be near,
    On Thee my hopes I cast,
  O guide me through the desert here,
    And bring me home at last.
                    Henry Francis Lyte. 1834.

(197)

FOREGLEAMS OF HEAVEN.

305 THE ROSEATE HUES. C. M. D. *Frederick A. J. Hervey.*

1. The roseate hues of early dawn, The brightness of the day, The crimson of the sunset sky, How fast they fade away! O for the pearly gates of heaven, O for the golden floor, O for the Sun of Righteousness, That setteth nevermore!

2 The highest hopes we cherish here,
   How soon they tire and faint;
   How many a spot defiles the robe
   That wraps an earthly saint!
   O for a heart that never sins,
   O for a soul washed white,
   O for a voice to praise our King,
   Nor weary day or night!

3 Here faith is ours, and heavenly hope,
   And grace to lead us higher;
   But there are perfectness and peace,
   Beyond our best desire.
   O by Thy love and anguish, Lord,
   And by Thy life laid down,
   Grant that we fall not from Thy grace,
   Nor fail to reach our crown!
   Mrs. Cecil F. Alexander. 1853.

306 HEAVEN IS OUR HOME. 6s & 4s. *Arthur S. Sullivan.*

1. We are but strangers here, Heaven is our home; Earth is a desert drear, Heaven is our home. Danger and sorrow stand Round us on every hand, Heaven is our fatherland, Heaven is our home.

FOREGLEAMS OF HEAVEN.

2 What though the tempests rage?
　Heaven is our home;
Short is our pilgrimage,
　Heaven is our home.
And Time's wild wintry blast
Soon shall be overpast,
We shall reach home at last:
　Heaven is our home.

3 There at our Saviour's side,
　Heaven is our home;
May we be glorified;
　Heaven is our home:

There are the good and blest,
　Those we love most and best,
Grant us with them to rest;
　Heaven is our home.

4 Grant us to murmur not,
　Heaven is our home;
Whate'er our earthly lot,
　Heaven is our home.
Grant us at last to stand
There at Thine own right hand,
Jesus, in fatherland:
　Heaven is our home!

T. R. Taylor.

307 THE HOMELAND. 7s & 6s. D.

1. The Homeland! O the Homeland! The land of the free-born! No gloomy night is known there, But aye the fade-less morn; I'm sigh-ing for that coun-try, My heart is ach-ing here, There is no pain in the Homeland, To which I'm drawing near.

2 My Lord is in the Homeland,
　With angels bright and fair;
No sinful thing nor evil
　Can ever enter there;
The music of the ransomed
　Is ringing in my ears,
And when I think of the Homeland,
　My eyes are wet with tears.

3 For loved ones in the Homeland
　Are waiting me to come
Where neither death nor sorrow
　Invade their holy home:
O dear, dear native country!
　O rest and peace above!
Christ brings us all to the Homeland
　Of His eternal love.

H. R. Haweis.

HEAVEN.

308 THE WHITE-ROBED ANGELS. J. W. Bischoff.

1. Will the white-robed angels meet us, When we part with friends most dear? Will their voice of welcome greet us, Will their guardian wings be near? White-robed angels, they await us, They will bear us on their breast, Where the wicked cease from troubling, And the weary are at rest.

2 Will they come from Christ to take us
To His father's mansions fair?
When amid new scenes we wake us,
Shall we find our escort there?—*Cho.*

3 Will they bear us on swift pinions,
As we mount from star to star,

Till we reach the glad dominions
Where life's streams of pleasure are?
—*Cho.*

4 White-robed angels will Christ send us,
Taken from His royal state?
Will they come? will they attend us,
Till we reach the golden gate?—*Cho.*
J. E. Rankin.

309 ALLELUIA, SONG OF SWEETNESS. 8s & 7s. E. J. Hopkins.

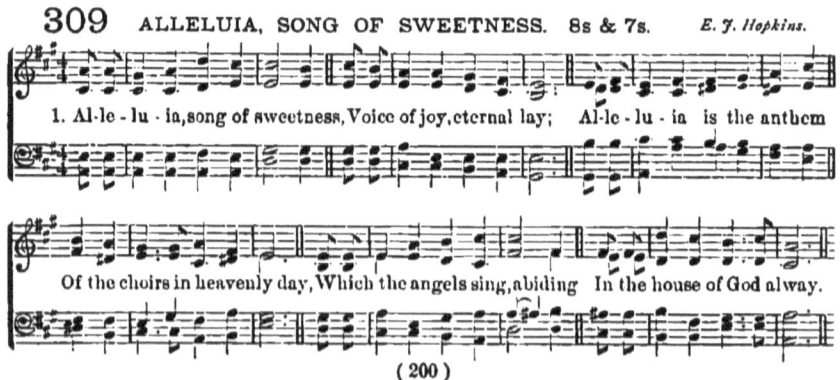

1. Al-le-lu-ia, song of sweetness, Voice of joy, eternal lay; Al-le-lu-ia is the anthem Of the choirs in heavenly day, Which the angels sing, abiding In the house of God alway.

HEAVEN.

2 Alleluia thou resoundest,
  Salem, mother of the blest;
 Alleluias without ending
  Fit you place of gladsome rest;
 Exiles we by Babel's waters
  Sit in bondage, sore distressed.

3 Alleluia we deserve not
  Here to chant for evermore;
 Alleluia our transgressions
  Make us for awhile give o'er;
 And within a voice is sounding,
  Bidding us our sins deplore.

4 O Thou King of endless glory,
  Hear Thy people as they cry;
 Grant us all our heart's deep longing
  In our home beyond the sky;
 There to Thee our Alleluia
  Singing everlastingly.

  Tr., John Mason Neale. 1851.

310 O PARADISE!
J. Barnby.

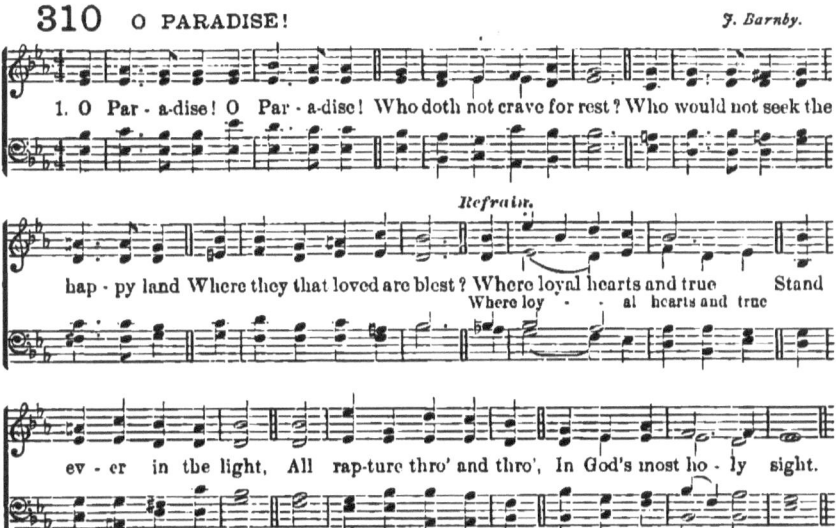

1. O Par-a-dise! O Par-a-dise! Who doth not crave for rest? Who would not seek the hap-py land Where they that loved are blest? *Refrain.* Where loyal hearts and true Stand ev-er in the light, All rap-ture thro' and thro', In God's most ho-ly sight.

2 O Paradise! O Paradise!
  The world is growing old;
 Who would not be at rest and free
  Where love is never cold?—*Ref.*

3 O Paradise! O Paradise!
  'Tis weary waiting here;
 I long to be where Jesus is,
  To feel, to see Him near.—*Ref.*

4 O Paradise! O Paradise!
  I want to sin no more,
 I want to be as pure on earth
  As on thy spotless shore.—*Ref.*

5 O Paradise! O Paradise!
  I greatly long to see
 The special place my dearest Lord
  In love prepares for me.—*Ref.*

6 Lord Jesus, King of Paradise,
  O keep me in Thy love,
 And guide me to that happy land
  Of perfect rest above.—*Ref.*

  Frederick W. Faber. 1854.

HEAVEN.

311 EWING. 7s & 6s. D. — *Alexander Ewing.* 1860.

1. Je-ru-sa-lem the gold-en! With milk and hon-ey blest, Be-neath thy con-tem-pla-tion Sink heart and voice opprest. I know not, O I know not What joys a-wait me there; What ra-dian-cy of glo-ry, What bliss be-yond compare.

2 They stand, those halls of Zion,
  All jubilant with song,
And bright with many an angel,
  And all the martyr throng.
There is the throne of David,
  And there, from toil released,
The shout of them that triumph,
  The song of them that feast.

3 And they who, with their leader,
  Have conquered in the fight,
Forever, and forever,
  Are clad in robes of white.

O land that seest no sorrow!
  O state that fear'st no strife!
O royal land of flowers!
  O realm and home of life!

4 O sweet and blessèd country!
  The home of God's elect!
O sweet and blessèd country,
  That eager hearts expect!
Jesus, in mercy bring us
  To that dear land of rest;
Who art, with God the Father,
  And Spirit, ever blest.

Bernard of Cluny. 1145. Tr., *John M. Neale.* 1851.

312 THERE IS A LAND IMMORTAL. — *Arthur S. Sullivan.*

1. There is a land im-mor-tal, The beau-ti-ful of lands; Be-side its an-cient por-tal A si-lent sen-try stands. He on-ly can un-do it, And

(202)

HEAVEN.

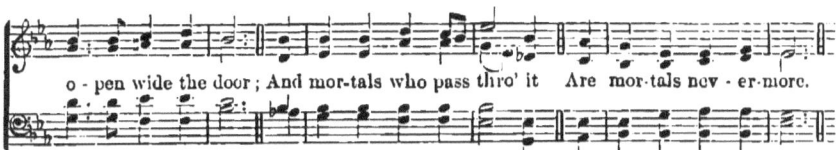

o - pen wide the door; And mor-tals who pass thro' it Are mor-tals nev - er-more.

2 Though dark and drear the passage
 That leadeth to the gate,
Yet grace comes with the message
 To those that watch and wait;
And at the time appointed
 A messenger comes down,
And leads the Lord's anointed
 From cross to glory's crown.

3 Their sighs are lost in singing,
 They're blessèd in their tears;
Their journey heavenward winging,
 They leave on earth their fears;
Death like an angel seemeth;
 "We welcome thee!" they cry;
The face with glory beameth,—
 'Tis life for them to die.

Thomas MacKellar. 1846.

313 THE BLESSED HOME.

John Stainer.

1. There is a bless-ed home, Be-yond this land of woe, Where tri-als nev - er come, Nor tears of sor - row flow; When faith is lost in sight, And pa-tient hope is crowned, And ev - er - last-ing light Its glo - ry throws a - round.

2 There is a land of peace,
 The angels know it well;
Glad songs that never cease
 Within its portals swell;
Around its glorious throne
 Ten thousand saints adore
Christ, with the Father One,
 And Spirit, evermore.

3 O joy all joys beyond,
 To see the Lamb who died,
And count each sacred wound
 In hands and feet and side;
To give to Him the praise
 Of every triumph won,
And sing through endless days
 The great things He hath done.

Henry W. Baker.

HEAVEN.

314. CHILDREN IN HEAVEN.

H. R. Palmer, 1883.

1. I see them in that world of light, Those crowds of chil-dren fair;
Their fac-es glow with ra-diance bright As God smiles on them there.
He folds them to His breast, and says, "My King-dom is of such;"
Then bursts the cher-ub-song of praise, Waked by that bless-ed touch;....
Then bursts the cher-ub-song of praise, Waked by that bless-ed touch.

2 A living rainbow o'er the throne
 Their clustered beauty forms;
How safe from sin are these, Christ's own!
 How safe from sorrow's storms!
Sweet shelter, where the Saviour feeds
 These lambs with tender care,
And up the grades of glory leads,
 His richest life to share.

3 They love us still: their rapture waits
 For us, ere 'tis complete;
And when fly back heaven's jeweled gates
 Our glad approach to greet,
Our radiant children we may see
 Upon the threshold stand,
And our first welcome theirs shall be
 Into Immanuel's land.

Charles H. Richards.

HEAVEN.

315. BEAUTIFUL HOME.

H. R. Palmer.

1. There is a home eternal, Beautiful and bright,.... Where sweet joys supernal Never are dimmed by night; White-robed angels are singing Ever around the bright throne, When, O when shall I see thee, Beautiful, beautiful home?

Refrain.
Home, beautiful home,...... Bright, beautiful home,...... Home, home of our Saviour, Bright, beautiful home.

2 Flowers forever are springing
   In that home so fair;
Thousands of children are singing
   Praises to Jesus there;
How they swell the glad anthems
   Ever around the bright throne,
   When, O when, etc.

3 Soon shall I join that anthem
   Far beyond the sky;
Jesus became my ransom,
   Why should I fear to die?
Soon my eyes will behold Him
   Seated upon the bright throne,
   When, O when, etc.

Frank Forrest.

316 THE WORD OF GOD. 7s & 6s. D.

T. R. Matthews.

1. O Word of God in-car-nate, O Wis-dom from on high, O Truth unchanged, un-chang-ing, O Light of our dark sky! We praise Thee for the ra-diance That from the hallowed page, A lan-tern to our footsteps, Shines on from age to age.

2 The Church from her dear Master
  Received the gift divine,
And still the light she lifteth
  O'er all the earth to shine.
It is the golden casket
  Where gems of truth are stored,
It is the heaven-drawn picture
  Of Christ the living Word.

3 O, make Thy Church, dear Saviour,
  A lamp of burnished gold,
To bear before the nations
  Thy true light as of old;
O teach Thy wandering pilgrims
  By this their path to trace,
Till, clouds and darkness ended,
  They see Thee face to face.
   William Walsham How. 1867.

317 BREAD OF LIFE. 6s & 4s.

Wm. F. Sherwin. 1877.

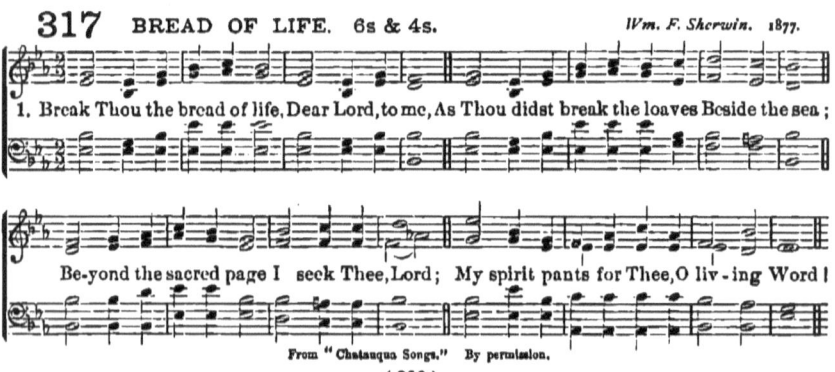

1. Break Thou the bread of life, Dear Lord, to me, As Thou didst break the loaves Beside the sea; Be-yond the sacred page I seek Thee, Lord; My spirit pants for Thee, O liv-ing Word!

From "Chatauqua Songs." By permission.

THE BIBLE.

2 Bless Thou the truth, dear Lord,
  To me—to me—
  As Thou didst bless the bread
  By Galilee;

Then shall all bondage cease,
  All fetters fall;
And I shall find my peace,
  My All-in-All!

Mary A. Lathbury. 1877.

318 HOLY BIBLE, BOOK DIVINE. 7s.

1. Holy, Bible! book divine! Precious treasure! thou art mine!
Mine, to tell them whence I came; Mine, to teach me what I am;

2 Mine, to chide me when I rove;
  Mine, to show a Saviour's love;
  Mine art thou to guide my feet;
  Mine, to judge, condemn, acquit;
3 Mine, to comfort in distress,
  If the Holy Spirit bless;

Mine, to show by living faith
Man can triumph over death;
4 Mine, to tell of joys to come,
  And the rebel sinner's doom;
  O, thou precious book divine!
  Precious treasure! thou art mine!

John Burton. 1805.

319 LAMP OF OUR FEET.

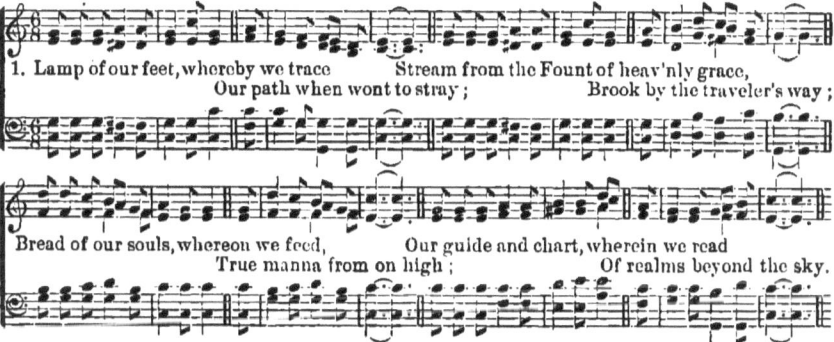

1. Lamp of our feet, whereby we trace   Stream from the Fount of heav'nly grace,
     Our path when wont to stray;   Brook by the traveler's way;
Bread of our souls, whereon we feed,   Our guide and chart, wherein we read
     True manna from on high;   Of realms beyond the sky.

2 Word of the everlasting God,
  Will of His glorious Son;
  Without thee how could earth be trod,
  Or heaven itself be won?

Lord, grant us all aright to learn
  The wisdom it imparts;
And to its heavenly teaching turn,
  With simple, child-like hearts.

Bernard Barton. 1827.

THANKSGIVING.

320 WITTEMBERG. 6s, 7s & 6s. *Johann Crüger.* 1653.

1. Now thank we all our God, With heart, and hands, and voices,
Who wondrous things hath done, In whom this world rejoices; Who from our mother's arms Hath blessed us on our way With countless gifts of love, And still is ours to-day.

2 O may this bounteous God
  Through all our life be near us,
  With ever joyful hearts
  And blessèd peace to cheer us;
And keep us in this grace,
  And guide us when perplext,
  And free us from all ills
  In this world and the next.
Martin Rinkart. 1644. Tr., *Miss Catherine Winkworth.* 1858.

321 ITALIAN HYMN. 6s & 4s. *Felice Giardini.* 1760.

1. The God of harvest praise: In loud thanksgiving raise Hand, heart, and voice; The valleys laugh and sing, Forests and mountains ring, The plains their tribute bring, The streams rejoice.

2 Yea, bless His holy name,
  And joyous thanks proclaim
    Through all the earth;
  To glory in your lot
  Is comely, but be not
  God's benefits forgot
    Amidst your mirth.

3 The God of harvest praise;
  Hands, hearts, and voices raise
    With one accord;
  From field to garner throng,
  Bearing your sheaves along,
  And in your harvest song
    Bless ye the Lord.
James Montgomery. 1822.

THANKSGIVING.

322 WILMOT. 8s & 7s. *C. M. Von Weber.*

1. Praise to Thee, Thou great Cre-a-tor! Praise to Thee from ev-ery tongue: Join, my soul, with ev-ery crea-ture, Join the u-ni-ver-sal song.

2 For ten thousand blessings given,
 For the hope of future joy,
Sound His praise thro' earth and heaven,
 Sound Jehovah's praise on high.

3 Joyfully on earth adore Him,
 Till in Heaven our song we raise;
There, enraptured, fall before Him,
 Lost in wonder, love, and praise.
 Fawcett.

323 MONKLAND. 7s. *John B. Wilkes.*

1. Praise to God, im-mor-tal praise, For the love that crowns our days! Boun-teous source of ev-ery joy, Let Thy praise our tongues em-ploy.

2 For the blessings of the field,
 For the stores the gardens yield;
 For the fruits in full supply,
 Ripened 'neath the summer sky;

3 Flocks that whiten all the plain;
 Yellow sheaves of ripened grain;
 Clouds that drop their fattening dews;
 Suns that temperate warmth diffuse;

4 All that spring with bounteous hand
 Scatter o'er the smiling land;
 All that liberal autumn pours
 From her rich, o'erflowing stores:

5 These to Thee, my God, we owe,
 Source whence all our blessings flow;
 And for these my soul shall raise
 Grateful vows and solemn praise.
 Anna L. Barbauld. 1773.

THANKSGIVING.

324 HARVEST HOME. 7s. D.
Dr. G. J. Elvey. 1860.

1. Come, ye thankful people, come, Raise the song of Harvest-home! All is safely gathered in, Ere the winter storms begin; God, our Maker, doth provide For our wants to be supplied; Come to God's own Temple, come; Raise the song of Harvest-home!

2 All the world is God's own field,
Fruit unto His praise to yield;
Wheat and tares together sown,
Unto joy or sorrow grown;
First the blade, and then the ear,
Then the full corn shall appear:
Lord of harvest, grant that we
Wholesome grain and pure may be.

3 For the Lord our God shall come,
And shall take His harvest home;
From His field shall in that day
All offences purge away;
Give His angels charge at last
In the fire the tares to cast,
But the fruitful ears to store
In His garner evermore.

4 Even so, Lord, quickly come
To Thy final Harvest-home;
Gather Thou Thy people in,
Free from sorrow, free from sin,
There forever purified,
In Thy presence to abide:
Come, with all Thine angels, come,
Raise the glorious Harvest-home.
Henry Alford. 1844.

325 SHINING SHORE.

Copyright. By per. OLIVER DITSON & Co.

1 My days are gliding swiftly by,
And I, a pilgrim stranger,
Would not detain them as they fly,
These hours of toil and danger.

Cho.—For, O, we stand on Jordan's strand,
Our friends are passing over,
And just before the shining shore
We may almost discover.

2 We'll gird our loins, my brethren dear,
Our distant home discerning;
Our absent Lord has left us word,
Let every lamp be burning.—*Cho.*

3 Should coming days be cold and dark,
We need not cease our singing;
That perfect rest naught can molest
Where golden hearts are ringing.—*Cho.*

4 Let sorrow's rudest tempest blow,
Each chord on earth to sever;
Our King says, "Come," and there's our home
Forever, O, forever!—*Cho.*
David Nelson. 1835.

(210)

THE YEAR.

326   ONWARD, THEN, AND FEAR NOT.   Henry Smart.

1. Stand-ing at the por - tal Of the opening year, Words of comfort meet us, Hush-ing ev - ery fear; Spok - en thro' the si - lence By our Fa-ther's voice, Ten-der, strong, and faithful, Bid-ding us re - joice. On-ward, then, and fear not, Children of the day, For His word shall nev - er, Nev - er pass a - way.

2 I the Lord am with thee,
　Be not thou afraid!
I will help and strengthen,
　Be not thou dismayed!
Yes, I will uphold thee,
　With my own right hand;
Thou art called and chosen
　In my sight to stand.—*Chorus.*

3 He will never fail thee,
　He will not forsake;
His eternal covenant
　He will never break.
Resting on His promise,
　What have we to fear?
God is all-sufficient
　For the coming year.—*Chorus.*
　　　　Frances Ridley Havergal.

(211)

327 GLORIFY THY NAME. 7s & 5s.

1. Fa-ther, here we ded-i-cate This new year to Thee, In what-ev-er world-ly state Thou wilt have us be. Not from sor-row, pain, or care, Freedom dare we claim; This a-lone shall be our prayer, Glor-i-fy Thy name.

2 Can a child presume to choose
Where or how to live?
Can a father's love refuse
All the best to give?
More Thou givest every day
Than the best can claim;
Nor withholdest aught that may
Glorify Thy name.

3 If in mercy Thou wilt spare
Joys we yet partake;
If on life, serene and fair,
Brighter rays may break:
Thee our hearts, while glad they sing,
Shall in all proclaim;
And, whate'er the year shall bring,
Glorify Thy name. *L. Tuttiett.*

328 O BEAUTIFUL REALM OF THE WEST. *A. J. Abbey.*

Joyously.

1. O beau-ti-ful, beau-ti-ful realm of the West! En-cir-cled by oceans, while lakes gem thy breast; Thy prai-ries are wav-ing with har-vests of gold, Thy

OUR COUNTRY.

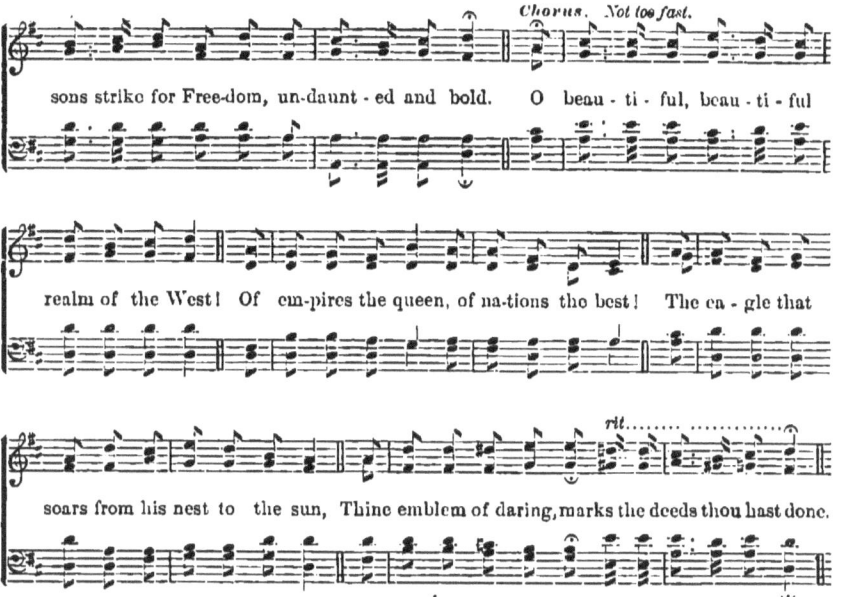

sons strike for Free-dom, un-daunt-ed and bold. O beau-ti-ful, beau-ti-ful realm of the West! Of em-pires the queen, of na-tions the best! The ea-gle that soars from his nest to the sun, Thine emblem of daring, marks the deeds thou hast done.

2 The hand of the tyrant afflicts us no more;
The heart of the freeman can swell and can soar;
For many a martyr has crimsoned earth's sod
For Freedom in state, and to worship his God.—*Cho.*

3 The shackles a tyrant once forged o'er the main,
Her flag to the breeze, she has burst them in twain;
Three millions of bondmen she freed at a fling,
And taught them the chorus of Freedom to sing.—*Cho.*

4 The nations have heard it, the hymn of the free,
The nations distressed from afar o'er the sea;
They flock to her standard, fair realm of the West,
Of empires the queen, and of nations the best.—*Cho.*

5 O beautiful, beautiful realm of the West,
The empire of Freedom, her eyrie and rest;
With mountains cloud-capped, and with rivers that leap,
With banners snow-flashing adown the rough steep.—*Cho.*

J. E. Rankin.

OUR COUNTRY.

329 RHINE. C. M. *From Friedrich Burgmüller.*

1. Lord, while for all mankind we pray, Of every clime and coast, O hear us for our native land, The land we love the most, The land we love the most.

2 O guard our shores from every foe,
With peace our borders bless,
With prosperous times our cities crown,
Our fields with plenteousness.

3 Unite us in the sacred love
Of knowledge, truth, and Thee;
And let our hills and valleys shout
The songs of liberty.

4 Here may religion, pure and mild,
Smile on our Sabbath hours;
And piety and virtue bless
The home of us and ours.

5 Lord of the nations, thus to Thee
Our country we commend;
Be Thou her refuge and her trust,
Her everlasting friend.
J. R. Wreford.

330 GLADSTONE. L. M. *W. H. Gladstone.*

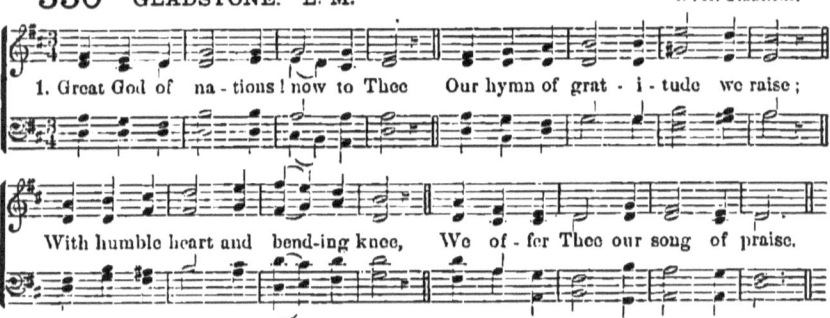

1. Great God of nations! now to Thee Our hymn of gratitude we raise; With humble heart and bending knee, We offer Thee our song of praise.

2 Thy name we bless, almighty God!
For all the kindness Thou hast shown
To this fair land the pilgrims trod—
This land we fondly call our own.

3 Here Freedom spreads her banner wide,
And casts her soft and hallowed ray;
Here Thou our fathers' steps did guide
In safety through their dangerous way.

4 We praise Thee that the gospel's light
Thro' all our land its radiance sheds,
Dispels the shades of error's night,
And heavenly blessings round us spreads.

5 Great God! preserve us in Thy fear;
In dangers still our guardian be;
O spread Thy truth's bright precepts here,
Let all the people worship Thee.
Alfred Alexander Woodhull. 1829.

OUR COUNTRY.

331   FAIR FREEDOM'S LAND.   *Carl Wilhelm.*

1. O land, of all earth's lands the best, Fair Freedom's em-pire in the West; From ris-ing to the set-ting sun, All na-tions here u-nite in one.

Chorus.
Fair Freedom's land! fair Freedom's land! Be-girt with might, long may she stand! And may her realm Christ's kingdom be From lake to gulf, from sea to sea.

2 Our fathers came as exiles here,
They saw our day with vision clear,
Despised at home, the corner-stones
Which God, the nation's Builder, owns.
   Cho.—Fair Freedom's land, etc.

3 Shall we, the sons of Pilgrim sires,
Neglect to kindle fresh the fires
They lighted on Atlantic's coast,
Which makes our land of lands the boast?
   Cho.—Fair Freedom's land, etc.

4 Ah, no! By faith Christ's standard goes
Beyond Sierra's distant snows,
To where Pacific's waters lie
Beneath the golden sunset sky.
   Cho.—Fair Freedom's land, etc.

5 By faith this goodly land I see
In Christ's own freedom doubly free;
From north to south, from east to west,
Beneath His gentle sceptre blest.
   Cho.—Fair Freedom's land, etc.
               J. E. Rankin.

332 AMERICA.

Adapted by Henry Carey.

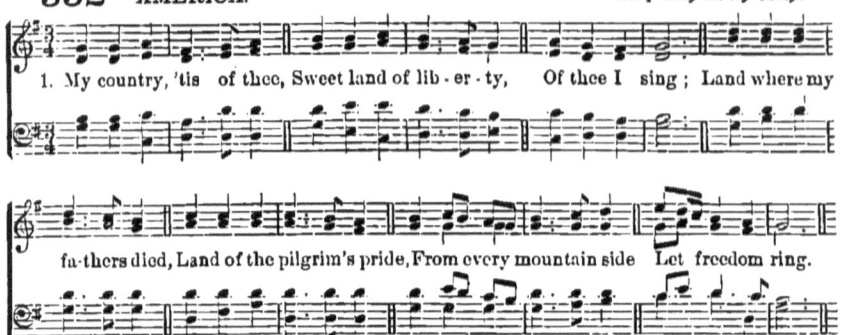

1. My country, 'tis of thee, Sweet land of liberty, Of thee I sing; Land where my fathers died, Land of the pilgrim's pride, From every mountain side Let freedom ring.

2 My native country, thee,
Land of the noble free,
  Thy name I love;
I love thy rocks and rills,
Thy woods and templed hills,
My heart with rapture thrills
  Like that above.

3 Let music swell the breeze,
And ring from all the trees
  Sweet freedom's song;
Let mortal tongues awake,
Let all that breathe partake,
Let rocks their silence break,
  The sound prolong.

4 Our fathers' God, to Thee,
Author of liberty,
  To Thee we sing:
Long may our land be bright
With freedom's holy light;
Protect us by Thy might,
  Great God, our King.
      S. F. Smith. 1832.

333 GOD SAVE THE STATE.

1 God bless our native land:
Firm may she ever stand,
  Through storm and night;
When the wild tempests rave,
Ruler of wind and wave,
Do Thou our country save
  By Thy great might.

2 For her our prayer shall rise
To God, above the skies;
  On Him we wait;
Thou who art ever nigh,
Guarding with watchful eye,
To Thee aloud we cry,
  God save the State.
      John S. Dwight.

INDEX OF FIRST LINES AND TITLES.

[Titles are printed in *Italics* ; First Lines in Roman Letters.]

	NO.
A few more years shall roll	290
A friend for little children	281
Abide with me, fast falls the eventide	108
Above the clear blue sky	22
Adoration	1
Alas, and did my Saviour bleed	149
All hail the power of Jesus' name	35
All glory, laud and honor	141
All good gifts around us	46
All praise to Him who built the hills	56
All things beautiful and fair	54
All praise to Thee, my God, this night	96
All's well	212
Alleluia, song of sweetness	309
Am I a soldier of the cross	243
America	332
Angels at the Tomb	157
Angels Holy, High and Lowly	53
Angel Voices ever singing	17
Antioch	34
Approach, all ye Faithful	132
Approach, my soul, the mercy seat	61
Arise! For Christ arise	232
Arlington	103
Arm these thy soldiers, mighty Lord	247
Art thou weary, art thou languid	183
As thy day thy strength shall be	219
As with gladness men of old	129
Ascension Hymn	160
At the Name of Jesus	38
Aurelia	165
Autumn	5
Avon	149
Awake, my soul, and with the sun	95
Awake, my soul, to grateful lays	186
Bavaria	161
Be joyful in God, all ye lands of the earth	8
Beautiful the Little Hands	263

	NO.
Beautiful Home	315
Before Jehovah's awful throne	24
Behold the throne of grace	78
Belmont	216
Bentley	203
Blakesley	80
Blessed Saviour, Thee I love	190
Blest be the tie that binds	85
Blumenthal	176
Bread of Life	317
Break Thou the Bread of Life	317
Brethren, while we sojourn here	241
Brightly gleams our banner	287
Caritas	229
Carol	127
Cast thy bread upon the waters	253
Chalvey	290
Children in Heaven	314
Children of the heavenly king	218
Children's Hosanna	139
Children's Voices	22
Christ for the world we sing	244
Christ is risen, Christ is risen	153
Christ, who once amongst us	279
Christian, dost thou see them	231
Christian, seek not yet repose	235
Christian sister, o'er the sea	256
Christians, up! the day is breaking	225
Christus Rex	29
Christmas	243
Christmas Carol	126
Christmas Hymn	128
Come at the morning hour	67
Come, Holy Ghost, in love	111
Come, Holy Spirit, come	118
Come, Holy Spirit, heavenly dove	102
Come, let us all with one accord	1
Come, let us gladly sing	29

(217)

INDEX OF FIRST LINES AND TITLES.

	NO.		NO.
Come, let us join our cheerful songs	40	Forward be our watchword	293
Come, my Redeemer, come	192	*Forward into Light*	294
Come, my soul, thy suit prepare	69	*Fountain*	150
Come praise your Lord and Saviour	33	Friends of the tempted, Christ is calling	232
Come, Thou Almighty King	9	From all that dwell below the skies	104
Come, thou Fount of every blessing	60	From every stormy wind that blows	86
Come to the Manger in Bethlehem	134	From Greenland's icy mountains	250
Come to the Saviour, make no delay	268		
Come to me for Rest	143	*Gathering Home*	291
Come unto Me and Rest	170	*Gentle Shepherd*, grant Thy blessing	201
Come unto Me, ye Weary	169	*Gladstone*	164, 330
Come ye, come ye, hear the Saviour	170	*Gloria in Excelsis*	12
Come ye faithful ; raise the strain	155	*Gloria Patri*	11
Come, ye thankful people, come	324	Glorious things of Thee are spoken	163
Come, we that love the Lord	43	*Glorify Thy Name*	327
Coronation	35	Glory be to God on high	12
Creation	48	Glory be to the Father	11
Crown Him with many crowns	26	"Glory to God," hear the angels sing	124
Crucifix	167	Go when the morning shineth	63
		God bless our native land	333
Daily, daily, sing the praises	302	God bless the Home, tho' humble	284
Daughter of Zion, awake from thy sadness	258	God has made the birds that sing	50
Dawn	82	*God is everywhere*	267
Day by Day we magnify Thee	20	God is Love, ye nations hear him	18
Dedham	36	God of heaven, hear our singing	23
Delight	30	God rest ye, merry gentlemen	130
Diademata	26	*God's Love to Me*	15
Dix	129	God that madest earth and heaven	109
Duke Street	24	*God who hath Made the Daisies*	262
		Golden harps are sounding	160
Easter Morning	152	*Goshen*	295
Ecclesia	163	Gracious Saviour, gentle Shepherd	278
Elliott	76	Gracious Spirit, Love divine	113
Elyria	113	Grander than ocean's story	15
Eoan	222	Great God of nations! now to Thee	330
Evening	101	*Greatheart*	239
Evening Hymn	96	*Greenville*	4
Evening Sacrifice	110		
Eventide	108	*Hail the Day of Praise*	2
Ever would I fain be reading	144	Hail the day that sees Him rise	159
Every morning mercies new	98	Hail, Thou God of grace and glory	162
Every Morning, the Red Sun	55	*Hallo*	219
Everywhere, everywhere	267	*Happy Day*	177
Ewing	311	*Hark, hark, my soul*, angelic songs	297
		Hark, how the angels sweetly sing!	37
Fair Freedom's Land	331	Hark, the herald angels sing	125
Far from my heavenly home	304	*Hark, the Macedonian cry*	257
Far o'er yon horizon	294	*Hark, the voice of Jesus calling*	237
Father, here we dedicate	327	Hark, what mean those holy voices	122
Father of love, our Guide and Friend	74	*Harvest Home*	324
Father, whate'er of earthly bliss	91	He giveth His Beloved sleep	300
Ferrier	276	He leadeth me, O blessed thought	301
Fierce raged the tempest o'er the deep	138	Heal me, O my Saviour, heal	172
For the beauty of the earth	52	*Hear us, Holy Jesus*	204

(218)

INDEX OF FIRST LINES AND TITLES.

	NO.		NO.
Heaven is our Home	306	Jesus lives, no longer now	158
Heavenly City	302	Jesus, my strength, my hope	71
Heavenly Father, send thy blessing	5	Jesus shall reign where'er the sun	164
Heavenly Guest	168	Jesus spreads His banner o'er us	161
Herald Angels	125	Jesus, tender Shepherd, hear me	107
Holy Bible, Book Divine	316	Jesus, the very tho't of Thee	194
Holy Night! Peaceful Night!	131	Jesus, Thy love shall we forget	185
Holy Offerings, rich and rare	84	Jesus, who knows full well	90
Holley	106	Joy to the world, the Lord is come	34
Home	285	Jubilee	122
Hopkins	114	Just as I am, without one plea	182
Horton	69		
Howard	189	Kegonsa	8
Hosanna we Sing, like the children dear	147	Kücken	68
How firm a foundation, ye saints of the Lord	214		
Hursley	81, 105	La Crosse	242
Hushed was the Evening Hymn	270	Lambeth	64, 148
		Lambs of the Fold	275
I and my Burden, my Master	175	Lamp of our Feet, whereby we trace	319
I heard the voice of Jesus say	173	Langran	171
I love Thy kingdom, Lord	166	Langton	71
I love to hear the story	261	Launch thy bark! launch thy bark	238
I love to tell the story	208	Lead kindly light, amid th' encircling gloom	298
I love to steal awhile away	66	Lead me, Precious Saviour	259
I'm a Pilgrim, and I'm a stranger	299	Let our choir new anthems raise	243
I need Thee, Precious Jesus	65	Let us gladly raise our song of praise	49
I see them in that world of light	314	Light of the World, we hail Thee	25
I think when I read that sweet story of old	269	Longwood	59
I want to be more like Jesus	224	Looking to Jesus	260
I would live like Jesus	226	Lord, dismiss us with Thy blessing	92
If thro' unruffled seas	82	Lord of my life, whose tender care	72
In heavenly love abiding	213	Lord, Thou hast taught our hearts to glow	223
In some way or other	221	Lord, while for all mankind we pray	329
In the cross of Christ I glory	93	Love Divine, all love excelling	204
In the shadow of the Rock	217	Loving-Kindness	186
In the silent midnight watches	108	Ludwig	236
In the vineyard of our Father	277	Lux Benigna	298
In Thy name, O Lord, assembling	4	Lyte	304
Incense from dews of the morning	152		
Inspirer and hearer of prayer	70	Macdonald	213
Invitation	173, 283	Maitland	174
Invocation	111	Majestic sweetness sits enthroned	42
Is thy cruse of comfort failing	229	Man's Wrongs, we will right them	233
It came upon the midnight clear	127	Marie	70
Italian Hymn	9, 244, 321	Master, the tempest is raging	137
		May Jesus Christ be praised	27
Jerusalem the golden	311	May we prize the Christian name	263
Jesus calls us, o'er the tumult	119	Merry Christmas, merry Christmas	135
Jesus Christ our Saviour	273	Messiah	7
Jesus, from Thy home on high	264	'Mid pleasures and palaces	285
Jesus, holy, undefiled	276	'Mid scenes of confusion	286
Jesus, I love Thy charming name	189	Middleton	162, 191
Jesus, I my cross have taken	191	Missionary Chant	248
Jesus is our Shepherd	274	Monkland	323

INDEX OF FIRST LINES AND TITLES.

	NO.
More like Jesus	224
More love to Thee, O Christ	188
Morning Hymn	95
Morning Praise	97
My country, 'tis of thee	332
My days are gliding swiftly by	325
My faith looks up to Thee	211
My God, how wonderful Thou art	62
My God, is any hour so sweet	76
My God, my Father, while I stray	220
My soul, be on thy guard	195
Must Jesus bear the cross alone	174
Nearer, my God, to Thee	89
Nettleton	60
Nightfall	99
Now is the accepted time	117
Now thank we all our God	320
Now when the dusky shades	97
O Beautiful Realm of the West	328
O cease, my wandering soul	116
O come, dear child, along with me	282
O could I find from day to day	73
O could I speak the matchless worth	197
O for a faith that will not shrink	216
O for a heart to praise my God	222
O for a thousand tongues to sing	36
O Gracious Redeemer, O Jesus our Lord	39
O happy band of pilgrims	288
O happy day, that fixed my choice	177
O hearken, dear Saviour, O hearken	275
O Jesus, I have promised	180
O Jesus, Thou art standing	181
O Jesus, Thou the beauty art	30
O Land of all earth's lands the best	331
O Paradise! O Paradise!	310
O Saviour, Precious Saviour	31
O sometimes the shadows are deep	207
O the sweet wonders of that cross	94
O word of God incarnate	318
Oak	188
O'er the gloomy hills of darkness	252
Of all the thoughts of God that are	300
Old Hundred	104
On our way rejoicing	3
Once Again, O Blessed Time	123
Once in royal David's city	136
One there is above all others	184
Onward, Christian soldiers	240
Onward, then, and fear not	326
Our blest Redeemer, ere He breathed	112
Our Father, who art in heaven	13

	NO.
Our Leader	278
Our Song of Praise	49
Paraclete	235
Park Street	57
Pascal	182
Pastor Bonus	279
Pilgrim, burdened with thy sin	176
Pleasant are Thy courts above	7
Pleyel's Hymn	219
Posen	272
Praise God, from whom all blessings flow	104
Praise, my soul, the King of heaven	19
Praise to God, immortal praise	323
Praise to Thee, Thou great Creator	322
Prayer is the soul's sincere desire	64
Providence	221
Psalm of Praise	52
Reapers! O Reapers! the harvest is white	228
Redhead	151
Remembrance	185
Resting from his work to-day	151
Revive Thy work, O Lord	115
Rhine	320
Richards	6
Ride on, ride on in majesty	145
Ring out the merry, merry bells	120
Rock of Ages, cleft for me	215
Room in my heart for Thee	193
Rosefield	98
Round the throne in glory seated	16
Rutherford	303
Sanctuary	16
Saviour, blessed Saviour	227
Saviour, happy should I be	200
Saviour, teach me day by day	272
Saviour, Thy dying love	187
Saviour, visit Thy plantation	87
See amid the winter's snow	121
Shirland	78
Separation	100
Serenity	73
Sicily	193
Since Jesus is my friend	199
Since thy Father's arm sustains thee	218
Sing of Jesus, sing forever	32
Singing for Jesus, our Saviour and King	28
Smyrna	225
So let our lips and lives express	41
Softly now the light of day	100
Sojourners' Song	181
Soldiers of the cross, arise	236

(220)

INDEX OF FIRST LINES AND TITLES.

Title	No.
Sometimes a light surprises	203
Song	32
Song of Mercy	50
Soon may the last glad song arise	255
Spanish Hymn	190
Spirit Divine, attend my prayer	103
Spirit of God, descend upon my heart	114
St. Aelred	138
St. Agnes	74, 102
St. Albinus	158
St. Andrew	234
St. Boniface	293
St. Gertrude	240
St. Hilda	288
St. Leonard	223
St. Sylvester	107
St. Theodulph	141
St. Thomas	166
Stand up, stand up for Jesus	246
Standing at the portal	326
Star of morn and even	206
Stephanos	183
Sullivan	172
Summer suns are glowing	51
Summer Sunshine	51
Sun of my soul, Thou Saviour dear	105
Sweet hour of prayer	88
Sweet is Thy mercy, Lord	75
Sweet the moments, rich in blessing	198
Taintor	227
Tarry with me, O my Saviour	100
Tell me the old, old story	209
Temple	109
Tempted and Tried, there is One at thy side	230
That Sweet Story of Old	260
The angels sat at the garden tomb	157
The Blessed Home	313
The Church's one foundation	165
The day is past and gone	101
The Giver of all	58
The God of harvest praise	321
The harvest dawn is near	254
The Harvest is White	228
The Homeland, O the Homeland	307
The joyful morn is breaking	133
The King's Highway	271
The Lord's Prayer	13
The Lord is my Shepherd, no want shall	59
The Love of Jesus	206
The Master has come over Jordan	142
The Mercy Seat	61
The morning light is breaking	251
The morning purples all the sky	156
The Ninety and Nine	140
The Rock that is Higher than I	207
The Roseate Hues of early dawn	305
The sands of time are sinking	303
The Shadow of the Rock	217
The Soul's Desire	226
The spacious firmament on high	48
The Springtide Hour brings leaf and flower	47
The sun is sinking fast	110
The twilight falls, the night is near	80
The Valleys and the Mountains	45
The Voyage of Life	238
The White Dove	83
The White-Robed Angels	308
The Word of God	318
There is a blessed Home	313
There is a fountain filled with blood	150
There is a green hill far away	148
There is a Happy Land	292
There is a home eternal	315
There is a land of pure delight	210
There is a land immortal	312
There is a mother's voice of love	283
There is a name I love to hear	205
There is no love like the love of Jesus	206
There sitteth a Dove, so white and fair	83
There were ninety and nine that safely	140
There's a Friend for little children	281
They are gathering homeward from every	291
They who seek the throne of grace	68
Thine forever, God of Love	79
Tho' faint, yet pursuing, we go on our way	295
Thou didst leave Thy throne and Thy	193
Thro' the day Thy love hath spared us	99
Thro' the love of God our Saviour	212
Thro' the night of doubt and sorrow	289
Thy name, O Lord, in sweet accord	6
'Tis the Saviour's tender word	143
To the Rescue	231
To Thee, my God and Saviour	10
Triumph	155
Troyte	108
Trust	200
Trust Him Still	218
Uplift the banner, let it float	245
Upward where the stars are burning	21
Unto God lift the jubilant chorus	58
Vanhall's Hymn	56
Venice	67
Victoria	247
Vigil	199

INDEX OF FIRST LINES AND TITLES.

	NO
Waiting	221
Wait, my soul, upon the Lord	221
Wake, O wake, ye weary	126
Walk in the light, so shalt thou know	196
Was there ever Kindest Shepherd	202
We are but little children weak	280
We are but strangers here	306
We are coming to our King	14
We come to Thee, dear Saviour	179
We march, we march to victory	230
We plough the fields and scatter	46
We praise Thee, O God, for the Son of Thy.	44
We stand in deep repentance	167
We will not faint nor falter now	233
Weary of earth, and laden with my sin	171
Webb	246
Welcome, *Happy Morning*, age to age	154
Weston	289
What a Friend we have in Jesus	77
What various hindrances we meet	81

	NO.
When His salvation bringing	189
When I survey the wondrous cross	146
When morning gilds the skies	27
Wherever you may be	271
Whosoever Will	178
Whosoever, O word divine	178
Will the white-robed angels meet us	308
Williams	146
Wilmot	322
With angel voices blending	128
Wittemberg	320
Woodstock	66
Work, for the night is coming	249
Ye Christian heralds, go proclaim	248
Yes, God is good, in earth and sky	57
Yield not to temptation	260
Young Gleaners	277
Youthful Days are passing o'er us	266

(222)

www.ingramcontent.com/pod-product-compliance
Lightning Source LLC
Chambersburg PA
CBHW031817230426
43669CB00009B/1173